An Introduction to Diverse Literacies in Primary Classrooms

How can teachers be prepared to support all children in becoming literate? How can teachers best mediate the technical aspects of literacy and make these meaningful and relevant to their children? What kinds of pedagogical practices can enable children to become creative and critical users and producers of digital and non-digital texts?

An Introduction to Diverse Literacies in Primary Classrooms brings together the voices of academics, classroom teachers, student teachers and children to answer these questions.

Research into children's literate lives illustrates that literacy is very much integrated into children's ongoing home, community and school experiences, and these rich and diverse literate lives are very often digitally mediated. This essential and practical book explores key themes in literacy education such as diversity, drama, literacy and play, reader response, grammar and children's authorship to understand the interrelationship between children's diverse literacy practices and ways that these can be mediated within the English school curriculum.

Written by a team of outstanding ITE English tutors and esteemed literacy researchers, this book is an essential reference for all student and practising teachers, and a must read for literacy coordinators and those interested in literacy research.

Karen Daniels is Associate Professor of Early Literacies at Sheffield Hallam University. Karen began her career as a primary and early years teacher and moved into higher education in 2010. Her current research involves exploring the relationships between embodied meaning making and children's early literacy practices.

Marie Helks is an Associate Head at Sheffield Institute of Education (SIoE). Before joining Sheffield Hallam University in 2012, Marie taught in a number of primary schools and universities, holding responsibility for English subject development work. Her main research interest is grammar teaching and learning in primary education.

"This book demonstrates how literacy education can flourish when togetherness, community and diversity are at the core of the literacy pedagogy, when teachers work with children to generate safe spaces where it is possible for children to experiment with meaning making and, through doing so, to play with possibilities for who they might be and what they might do."

Cathy Burnett, *Professor Emerita, Sheffield Hallam University, UK*

An Introduction to Diverse Literacies in Primary Classrooms

Perspectives on Pedagogy and Practice

Edited by Karen Daniels
and Marie Helks

Routledge
Taylor & Francis Group
LONDON AND NEW YORK

Designed cover image: © Getty Images

First published 2025
by Routledge
4 Park Square, Milton Park, Abingdon, Oxon, OX14 4RN

and by Routledge
605 Third Avenue, New York, NY 10158

Routledge is an imprint of the Taylor & Francis Group, an informa business

British Library Cataloguing-in-Publication Data
A catalogue record for this book is available from the British Library

ISBN: 978-1-032-46298-1 (hbk)
ISBN: 978-1-032-46297-4 (pbk)
ISBN: 978-1-003-38101-3 (ebk)

DOI: 10.4324/9781003381013

Typeset in Bembo and Helvetica Neue
by KnowledgeWorks Global Ltd.

Contents

List of contributors

Mark Avis, Sheffield Hallam University, UK

Chris Bailey, Sheffield Hallam University, UK

Susan Borland, Sheffield Hallam University, UK

Cathy Burnett, Sheffield Halla University, UK

Karen Daniels, Sheffield Hallam University, UK

Cara Doxey, Sheffield Hallam University, UK

Ginny Doxey, Primary School Teacher

Marie Helks, Sheffield Hallam University, UK

Lisa Hesmondhalgh, Aspire Educational Trust, UK

Siobhan Hunt, Primary School Teacher

Jamila Hussain, Bishop Grosseteste University, UK

Guy Merchant, Sheffield Hallam University, UK

Jemma Monkhouse, Sheffield Hallam University, UK

Julia Myers, formerly Sheffield Hallam University, UK

Deb Sanders, Education Consultant and formerly Executive Primary Head

Sheila Sharpe, Sheffield Hallam University, UK

Laurel Smith, Sheffield Hallam University, UK

Moira Taplin, Primary and Early Years Teacher

Lynsey Wigfull, James Montgomery Academy Trust, formerly Sheffield Hallam University, UK

Foreword

If we refer only to international league tables, then we might see literacy as relatively straightforward – simply a case of acquiring a set of predetermined and measurable skills. If we continue with this logic then improving literacy education (whether as a teacher, a school leader, a policy maker or whoever) is simply about doing this better than it has been done before – of finding out 'what works' and sticking with it. This book presents a rather different view of literacy and of literacy education which chimes more closely with the ways in which we experience literacy in everyday life. It is a book which has meaning making at its core, a book which recognises that literacy is always felt as well as thought and which attends to the creative, communicative, collaborative and critical dimensions of literacy which are so central to children's current and future lives.

Many readers will be pleased to find that this is a deeply practical book. It provides plenty of guidance on what you might *do* as a literacy teacher. It is packed with inspiring examples of work by teachers to develop literacy classrooms full of creativity, playfulness, reflection and personal growth (Chapter 11), practices that foster digital repertoires (Chapter 10), value and nurture children's meaning making as communicators (Chapters 2) and recognise children as critical consumers and producers of multimodal texts (Chapter 8). Importantly it approaches the teaching of literacy as much more than a technical activity. The reader is invited to reflect, to critique and to imagine what might be possible in literacy classrooms building on a set of shared principles designed to ensure that literacy education is not just effective but empowering, energising and ethical (Chapter 1).

The chapters are studded with compelling summaries of research findings generated through a wide range of different kinds of research. Much has been written about the role of evidence in informing teachers' work. The chapters of this book demonstrate the importance of drawing on a range of evidence types as the starting point for teachers' decision-making, reflection, creativity and critique. We see, for example, what can be learned from seeking out evidence of children's views (Chapter 3), visual mapping (Chapter 4), careful noticing (Chapter 11) and photographs (Chapter 6).

There are some warning flags, too: the risk of perpetuating deficit perspectives on children's language and literacy that help to sustain inequalities with disastrous effects on many children's experience of literacy at school (Chapter 9); of creating classrooms in which writing is experienced as a 'battle' or a 'struggle' (Chapter 6); of focusing so relentlessly on skills and knowledge that the urge to read and write dissipates (Chapter 7); and of engaging in the type of teacher talk that squeezes out space and time for children to explore their own ideas (Chapter 5). Very few schools or teachers would set out to do any of these things. But they can happen as teachers juggle with the competing pressures and priorities associated with curriculum, accountability and performance. Classrooms can be strange places in which language and literacy are made in strange ways with meaning making somehow lost along the way.

But, as we see in so many of the chapters of this book, the 'strangeness' of classrooms can also be a marvellous thing. While there is something strange – and often challenging – about 30 or so children and one or more adults spending quite so much time together in one space, this gathering together also offers huge potential for nurturing children's communicative repertoires. This book demonstrates how literacy education can flourish when togetherness, community and diversity are at the core of the literacy pedagogy, when teachers work with children to generate safe spaces where it is possible for children to experiment with meaning making and, through doing so, to play with possibilities for who they might be and what they might do.

At the time of writing, there is much discussion about the role of generative AI for what literacy and literacy education might become. The literacy teachers of the next few decades will need to engage with profound questions about authorship, readership, authenticity and multimodality. Literacy does not stand still and we do children a disservice if we try and pretend that it does. Much better is to do as the chapters in this book do: to lay down principles on which to build and to approach literacy education with the flexibility, criticality and imagination needed to foster a literacy education that is fit for literacy in life.

Cathy Burnett **July 2024**

CHAPTER

1

Principles for literacy education in a world of diverse literacy practices

Karen Daniels and Marie Helks

Introduction

Young and school-aged children's journey towards confident and creative engagement with ways of being and doing literacy is a fascinating one. It is one of ongoing interest and concern to teachers, parents, researchers, policy makers and essentially, to children themselves. The chapters in this volume offer detailed reflective accounts of what diverse literacy practices in classrooms can be, and how these can be understood. Rather than providing a 'guide' on 'how to' teach English, we present a series of perspectives on literacy that are illustrative of the rich and complex (and often surprising) relationships between teachers and children that play out as children encounter literacies in classrooms.

Doing literacy and being a teacher of literacy is a complex endeavour that calls for an understanding of what literacy is, how it is constantly changing and how it is shaped by our own and others' home, community and life experiences. Advances in digital technology have changed the way we understand and do literacy and these changes have important implications for understanding the kinds of literacy practices children bring to the classroom. In addition, experiences of literacies outside the classroom will shape the ways in which children access literacy in school. We see this as inevitable change and embrace it by inviting the reader to reflect on those literacy practices commonly associated with schooling and education (for example, see Helks and Myers on teaching grammar, Chapter 7, and Wigfull on teaching writing, Chapter 6), but also to consider a bigger picture and engage with those literacy practices children experience outside school and the ways in which these intersect with literacies in classrooms (for example, see Monkhouse and Bailey on digital play, Chapter 10). Although literacies in school look very different to some of the literacy practices that children encounter in their homes and communities, we see the distinction between those practices as one that is 'porous'. For this reason, we refer to young people in this book, that is those that we work with as educators and researchers, as 'children' throughout, rather than pupils. While children can be seen as 'in role' as pupils in classroom contexts, our decision to use the term children is motivated by our aim of avoiding distinctions between children's literate lives in schools and the literate lives of their home and community contexts.

Throughout the chapters authors share various ways in which they have personally investigated children's literacy practices in community and classroom settings, and the ways that these have shaped the authors' thinking about literacy. Some of the chapters are sole authored, while

DOI: 10.4324/9781003381013-1

others are co-authored. Across the chapters you will read about the combined perspectives of children, practising teachers, academics and researchers. We uphold that this is a good way to proceed as children, families, teachers and academics do literacy 'together'. It may be unhelpful, therefore, to see too strong a distinction between children's literacy practices, and the kind of practices and pedagogical approaches that adults use around children. Instead, we think about literacy as a phenomenon that takes place across people and within communities as we make meaning and share thinking and ideas together.

Our accounts are underpinned by theoretical perspectives about literacy, and you will see some names recurring – Brian Street, Shirley Brice Heath, Ann Dyson and Gunther Kress's theorisation of literacy as a set of multimodal practices, where reading, writing and oral language takes place alongside other modes of multimodal communication. These are the theorists and pioneers that have inspired and guided us and who have shaped ways of thinking about literacy that are often very different to the standard understandings of 'schooled literacies' where writing, reading and technical accuracy more readily spring to mind. This is not to say these things are not important – but they are only part of the story of the human phenomenon of literacy.

The chapters include extracts of empirical data, from the authors' own research projects and from those who are studying similar topics. Our research is predominately qualitative in nature, as this allows us to look in depth at what is taking place in classrooms. We include the voices of children, teachers and researchers and this is central to our approach in this book. Ultimately, we invite you to examine the relationship between research, theory and pedagogical practice by presenting the following features: *Prompts for Critical Reflection, Spotlight on Research* and *Ideas for Classroom Practice*. We also include the feature *Case Study Focus* where chapter authors provide reflective examples of their classroom practice.

This introductory chapter introduces a view of literacy that is expansive – that is, it recognises the broad, all-encompassing and ever-changing nature of literacy. Furthermore, it acknowledges how literacy impacts on our own lives and experiences and those of the children we teach. Individually, each chapter in this volume presents the authors' unique perspectives on literacy. We believe that this is an important stance to take, as it is our view that although we have some shared understandings of what counts as literacy, we experience and understand literacies differently. To begin examining shared understandings, we reflect on the question 'What is English' and why do we teach it?

What is English?

Very often when we think of English and English teaching, we think first of reading and writing – or literacy. We might also think about how oral language supports the reading and writing process. These are the most likely things to spring to mind when we think about literacy. We might also think about various 'components' of reading and writing, such as handwriting, spelling, comprehension, decoding or more specific activities such as writing stories or news reports, reading poetry or drama activities. These things are commonly associated with 'doing' English. But we might also ask the question about *why* we teach English, and which models we might follow. At first, this may seem obvious to answer, but it is worth reflecting on this question more deeply.

In a landmark report, Cox (1991) presented five views of English Teaching which he claimed reflected what was then 'current' thinking about why we teach English as a subject. These include:

1. A 'personal growth' view focuses on the child: it emphasises the relationship between language and learning in the individual child, and the role of literature in developing children's imaginative and aesthetic lives.

2. A 'cross curricular' view focuses on the school: it emphasises that all teachers have a responsibility to help children with the language demands of different subjects on the school curriculum.
3. An 'adult needs' view focuses on communication outside the school: it emphasises the responsibility of English teachers to prepare children for the language demands of adult life, including the workplace, in a fast-changing world.
4. A 'cultural heritage' view emphasises the responsibility of schools to lead children to an appreciation of those works of literature that have been widely regarded as amongst the finest in language.
5. A 'cultural analysis' view emphasises the role of English in helping children towards a critical understanding of the world and cultural environment in which they live. Children should know about the processes by which meanings are conveyed, and about the ways in which print and other media carry values.

Goodwyn (2008) suggested that these views can be seen as distinct but overlapping, and raised the point that not all of them are compatible. This critique arguably will shift focus as general understandings of the nature of language and literacy shift over time. Certainly, an issue that seems pertinent in recent years is the question of who decides what is the 'finest' literature? This certainly seems at odds with a 'cultural analysis' view, where print can implicitly or explicitly convey the values of the author. In addition, thinking of English as preparation for later life of work seems instrumental, and perhaps synonymous with views of English that foreground the teaching of a set of discrete skills, which some see as contrasting starkly with ideas of expanding children's imaginative and aesthetic lives. Despite four decades having passed since the previous five views were written by Cox, you might want to ask where these views are reflected in current thinking about teaching English, and what has changed. The recent focus on heritage texts in some English programmes, for example, reflects a policy re-focus (point 4 of Cox's views). The debate over literacy standards that has raged over the past three decades often seems to be spurred by the need to ensure the adult workforce has adequate literacy skills to contribute to wider society (point 3). English and its links across the Primary curriculum (point 2) is reflected in Monkhouse and Smith (Chapter 11) and Wigfull (Chapter 6).

In fact, what English is and why and how we should teach it has been hotly debated for decades and this is almost certain to continue. A very brief delve into Cox's five views brings to the fore some of the tensions that teachers, policy makers, academics and researchers experience when trying to make decisions about how best to research and teach English. These tensions can be challenging, however, when teaching English; we need to be aware of them and think critically about what we are teaching, why we are teaching it and what will be its impact on children's literate lives.

Within the chapters in this book, you will see some of these models reflected in the kinds of practices that chapter authors recommend. Doxey and Doxey (Chapter 3), for example, reflect reading aloud as a strategy to nurture personal growth (point 1). Borland, Daniels and Hunt (Chapter 8) define a 'cultural analysis' (point 5) view of literacy, foregrounding the need for critical literacy, stressing its importance more than ever in a world where texts are multimodal and predominantly digitally mediated. Monkhouse and Smith's (Chapter 11) approaches to drama suggest amongst other things a commitment to personal growth (point 1) and the use of highly regarded literary texts.

As you read through each chapter of this book, you might reflect on the five views, and ask if there are other links with the chapters and the five views of English presented by Cox. You might also ask yourself – what else? What is missing from the list? If you were to define 'five views of English', what would they look like?

Principles for English teaching

As an introduction to the book, and in response to the provocation on Cox's five views of English, we offer a set of principles about literacies that we have used to guide our own thinking as we have assembled the book chapters. Despite the chapters being authored by people with different views, experiences and areas of expertise, there are some clear commonalities in our thinking. We have termed these 'principles' as they act as a guide, not only our thinking about an inclusive perspective on literacy pedagogy for contemporary classrooms, but importantly, they guide how we enact our roles as teachers, academics and researchers of literacy. Central to this is that children's diverse home, community, linguistic and cultural experiences and differences are recognised and respected. These principles are illustrated and explored in the chapters in this book:

- Literacies are multiple, diverse, ideological and changing.
- The kinds of literacies children encounter in school and home and community settings shape what they think literacy is, who it is for and what literacy is for.
- Literacies are powerful – being literate has many benefits and literacy can exert power on individuals and groups.
- Literacies are social and cultural practices; they are material and affective.

Principle 1: Literacies are multiple, diverse, ideological and changing

The first principle recognises that there is not one, fixed version of literacy, but instead there are *literacies*. In this book we will be thinking of literacy as a *social practice*, that is, that literacy happens across people and groups of people as they communicate meaningfully together. The kinds of practices, and ways of understanding and doing literacy, will vary significantly across time and place (Gutierrez et al., 2011) as it is shaped by cultural, linguistic, social and economic factors (Street, 1995). Literacy practices are also shaped by the kinds of materials that people engage with; for example, you might compare how communication by letters amongst friends and relatives, popular at the beginning of the 20th Century, differs from the ways in which we might now communicate and experience relationships as a member of a WhatsApp group, now and again dropping in on a Facetime call. This is a very straightforward comparison when in fact, the ways in which technologies and other materials around us have shaped the ways in which we communicate is much more complex. This necessitates a focus on critical literacy of both print and digitally mediated, multimodal texts (see Borland, Daniels and Hunt, Chapter 8). You will notice throughout the chapters, the ways in which this complexity is seen through our interactions with children in classrooms and the ways in which the authors come to understand and make sense of children's participation in literacies.

A second point to note is that literacies are connected to communication and any act of communication is *ideological*, that is, it conveys either explicitly or implicitly the values and beliefs of the text producer. For these reasons, literacy practices are entrenched with power relationships about how and why literacy should be 'performed'. Furthermore, some ways of being and doing literacy are more valued or privileged and therefore 'more powerful' than others. The literacy practices associated with schools, such as those of teaching grammar, phonics and reading of print-based texts, have a much higher status and power than, for example, the playground rhymes and chants that children enjoy, or the gaming activities children readily chat about and socialise around with friends. The status and power of schooled literacies arise not because these practices are inherently superior in any way, but because they are enshrined in policy and particular ways of thinking about literacy, how it can be taught and how it is to be learned by children.

Due to the need to have a shared view on how to teach literacy, it is often presented in policy as a sequence of incremental skills for the individual child to learn. Brian Street (2003) referred to this as an 'autonomous' view of literacy, in that it fails to acknowledge the ideological nature of literacy, presenting it instead as a neutral set of skills to acquire. It is important to say here that mastering literacy skills is beneficial to children on their journey to becoming print literate. But as teachers, it is crucial to remember that what are often termed literacy skills are only a partial picture of what it takes and means to be literate in contemporary society. The purpose of this book is to share perspectives on an inclusive understanding of literacy in classrooms. This necessitates acknowledging that literacy is never neutral, but that any act of literacy is always ideologically driven and received.

Principle 2: The kinds of literacies children encounter in school shape what they think literacy is, what it is for and who it is for

For over four decades, cultural and linguistic differences between home and school environments have been cited as influential in children's success in the education system. Shirley Brice Heath (1983), for example, noted that certain types of language socialisation impacted positively or negatively on children's reading development on entry to school. Brice Heath's suggestion was that teachers should strive to understand and accommodate children's ways of being and doing literacy in the classroom, and to help them bridge their home and community experiences with the expectations and practices of school. Recent policy directions in England, however, often see diversity as an education crisis or problem, focusing attention on language deficit models of young children's communicative practices, and seeking 'remedies' to fill 'gaps'. In this book, we hope to share with you the richness of young children and pupils' repertoires for language and literacy, and encourage a respectful approach, taking the time to know and understand what children know and can do. In addition, we offer suggestions for practice and encourage critical reflection on pedagogical practice and its underpinning research and theory.

Principle 2 is central when thinking about an inclusive approach to literacy. Children enter school settings with a range of home and community experiences of literacy, and this difference no doubt continues throughout their school life. This in itself is not an issue, but is rather a reflection of the nature of literacy, that is, literacy practices; the ways in which we do and understand literacy will always vary across people and places. The kind of literacy children encounter in schools is a specialised form of 'schooled literacy', deemed as the official version of literacy, often defined in curriculum documents and statutory orders. Where difficulties can arise, however, is where the 'official' version of literacy is seen as superior, and any other expression of being literate is seen as unimportant, inferior or sadly, even deficient. This issue is raised in several of the chapters in this book. Smith and Sanders (Chapter 4) discuss how too rigid a policy on standard English can disenfranchise children from minority ethnic backgrounds or certain socio-economic backgrounds, as well as create tensions for teachers. Avis and Hesmondhalgh (Chapter 5) remind us that supporting children's linguistic repertoires can be empowering by equipping children with the skills to express and develop their ideas and thinking. Daniels and Hussain (Chapter 2) present the case for a supportive and responsive approach when working with very young children that looks at what they can do through a variety of 'lenses' that gives us a view that lies beyond simplified developmental literacy 'milestones'.

Our language and literacy experiences are deeply interconnected with our understanding of ourselves and our world, and they shape how we make sense of our experiences. As Smith and Sanders explore (Chapter 4) our unique language experiences are closely related to our identities, sense of self and agency. Smith provides a framework for reflecting on our own language identity, charting this and reflecting on those key experiences that have shaped us: it is by understanding our own histories and language experiences that we can better understand those of the children we teach. In many ways, this chapter epitomises a key tenet of this volume: how the social construction of literacy practices means that these are never static, but always changing and enacted by us each time we take part in language and literacy. Indeed, this constant change through the social construction of literacy practices is what gives rise to diversity of practice.

This book is about diverse literacies, and diversity takes many forms in this volume. The chapter authors offer their own insights into literacy from their work with children over time, with student teachers and as researchers in their field. What is offered is a rich array of perspectives that show ways of looking at and thinking about literacy in ways that consider children's own unique experiences. Furthermore, these insights veer from the more typical constructions of literacy more commonly understood and reflected in national policy. For example, Doxey and Doxey (Chapter 3) remind us that when selecting texts in the classroom, we should consider the ethnic, linguistic and social diversity of children, including neurodiversity (Monkhouse and Bailey, Chapter 10). The authors draw our attention to the neurodiversity of our childrenand ask us to consider with care the children's literature that reflects diversity positively. In many ways, the authors of these chapters bring their own perspectives on literacy to the fore – and these in themselves are diverse.

Principle 3: Literacies are powerful – being literate has many benefits and literacy can exert power on individuals and groups

Possessing good skills in language and literacy is often viewed as synonymous with success in education and more broadly linked to positive overall life chances. In many ways literacy has been seen as a panacea to the inequalities that exist in society and indeed, by some, 'poor' literacy skills are seen as synonymous with a lifetime of poverty, poor lifestyle and even an increased likelihood to commit legal offences. Such possible devastating implications have provided impetus to decades of policy interventions with the aim of 'raising literacy standards' facilitating 'social justice' and 'solving' the perceived problems of low standards in literacy. Perhaps ironically, policy initiatives aimed at raising literacy standards have increasingly shaped what literacy is and how it might best be taught in schools. In some cases, this has led to a narrowing of the literacy curriculum in some areas of English teaching where the focus has become one of addressing children's technical skills in literacy. Where literacy is framed as an incremental set of technical skills to be acquired by the individual child or pupil, the value and purpose, and what we understand about literacy as a socio-cultural practice, can be reduced and undervalued. Literacy can never be 'given' neutrally to a passive class of children. It is always saturated with power relationships (see the work of Brian Street) and thinking about literacy as a set of skills presents a kind of 'neutrality' that does not reflect or acknowledge the power relationships that exist in literacies, but instead glosses over them. Helks and Myers (Chapter 7) propose a structured approach to working with real texts to support children's understandings of how grammar works in texts to create meaning, and how to integrate grammar in meaningful ways, thus empowering children as language users. In this volume, Sharpe and Taplin (Chapter 9) chart policy moves over four decades that mark shifts in English policy over time. Sharpe and Taplin are clear to point out that notions of 'inclusivity' in literacy need to go further than simply providing access to literacy in classrooms, and instead need to consider *belonging* and *participation*. Within the chapters in this volume, these two concepts are taken-up and explored as we ask the question – How can we facilitate children's participation in literacy activity and how can we nurture their sense of belonging?

Principle 4: Literacies are social and cultural practices; they are material and affective

At the time of writing of this book, the dominant education policy from the English government presents literacy in a way that Street (1995) would likely identify as autonomous. In the light of this, defining an inclusive literacy pedagogy that recognises diversity may seem like a 'closed chapter', where there is little room for manoeuvre. However, it is important to acknowledge that curriculum documentation and policy are only part of the story of what happens in literacy classrooms when teachers enact literacy pedagogy. As teachers, we are tasked with working with the statutory curriculum in ways that translate programmes of study into experiences that mean something to children, and that are relevant to their lives and experiences. An example of this is Wigfull's chapter (Chapter 6) on writing which places the child-author at the centre of the writing endeavour.

Our authors aim to expand on the definition of literacy presented in dominant policy and call for open-ended opportunities for children to critically examine what literacy is and how they can be critical and active participants in text creation and consumption. The idea of *playfulness* is key to such a pedagogy – and an antidote to what may be lost when teaching emphasises technical accuracy over expression of meaning, where reading is defined as accurate decoding and writing defined as grammatical correctness. You will see many episodes of playfulness reflected across the chapters, for example, Monkhouse and Bailey (Chapter 10) present the ways in which children's playfulness leads to creative expression when exploring digital worlds. This playfulness and creativity lead to the production of imaginative texts that are meaningful to children's lives and interests and sees them as agentic.

More recent theorisations of literacy take account of the materials that surround us, and that we may use, during literacy activity. The pens, pencils, crayons, screens, tables, books, chairs and all other materials around us are not merely 'tools' that we use to do literacies. In fact, they shape *how* we do literacy, and what might be seen as possible – that is, tools of literacy have affordances. Socio-material thinking about literacy considers the ways in which the objects and things around us shape literacy in particular ways. A clear example of this is Monkhouse and Smith's chapter (Chapter 11) that explores how the props, costumes and children's bodies shape particular kinds of 'texts' of expression and meaning.

Earlier thinking about literacy often overlooked the bodily sensations of the experience in taking part in literacy activity. Leander and Boldt (2012) drew attention to the ways in which whenever we take part in any literacy activity, it is accompanied by feelings and sensations that are significant. Prior to this, dominant thinking about literacy is that it was an act that takes place in your 'head' or purely as a 'cognitive' activity. However, more recent research has been examining embodied theorisations about literacy, about the sensations of changes in the body that we experience as we take part in literacy activity. Social and cultural practices from this perspective are therefore far from purely linguistic. They are material and interrelated with bodily experiences of literacy. While this work is in its infancy (in contrast to more traditional thinking about literacy) it is raising debates about the nature of inclusion, participation and what gives rise to social inequalities, and importantly, how these can be addressed.

The overarching messages arising from these principles are clear:

- There are many ways of thinking about literacy. No way of thinking is inherently superior to the other, but each offers a lens for understanding literacy differently, in a more expansive way.
- Some ways of thinking about literacy offer a deficit view of children and families. They focus on what children *cannot* do. The tendency is to view literacy practices that are different to schooled literacies as *deficient* in some way. In this volume we take an asset perspective, focusing on what children *can do* and consider how teachers can build on and support children's repertoires.
- Literacy is about participation and classrooms are communities where teachers need to look for opportunities to nurture belonging through literacy.
- Taking time to think about children's literacy practices, including those that are digitally mediated and incorporate these into our teaching, can foster belonging in a literate community and provide children with confidence and agency to become creative and critical consumers and producers of print and multimodal texts.

Chapter summary

In this chapter we have shared a number of perspectives on what literacy can be and some of the underlying principles for literacy education that are consistent with those perspectives. As you read on, you will see that our authors – literacy researchers, teachers, children– each present a unique view of their experiences of 'doing' literacy. Literacy means different things to different people, but the principles we shared early in the chapter are common across all voices: literacies are multiple, diverse, often digitally mediated and powerful.

Becoming literate is a long journey, and one could argue it never ends because language and literacy practices evolve and change. In the final chapter of this book, Merchant looks back at how literacy 'used to be' and what it might be in future. Importantly, in his final paragraph, Merchant stresses the need to approach literacy 'with a sense of appreciation … [of] the vibrancy of childhood culture … a culture that does not distinguish between digital and non-digital worlds, but it is one in which communication is part and parcel of everyday life', where technology plays an important part. Engaging children in this process – equipping them to take part in literacy in all its manifestations in a critical, positive and responsible way – is the task we face as literacy educators, researchers and academics. The role of the teacher in this endeavour is crucial.

References

Brice Heath, S. (1983). *Ways With Words: Language, Life and Work in Communities and Classrooms.* Cambridge: Cambridge University Press.

Cox, B. (1991). *Cox on Cox: An English Curriculum for the 1990's.* Hodder and Stoughton: London.

Goodwyn, A. (2008). English teachers and the Cox models. *English in Education*, 26(3), 4–10.

Gutierrez, K., Bien, A., Selland, M. & Pierce, D. (2011). Polylingual and polycultural learning ecologies: Mediating emergent academic literacies for dual language learners. *Journal of Early Childhood Literacy*, 11(2), 232–261.

Leander, K. & Boldt, G. (2012). Rereading 'A Pedagogy of Multiliteracies': Bodies, text, emergence. *Journal of Literacy Research*, 45(1), 22–46.

Street, B. (1995). *Social Literacies: Critical Approaches to Literacy in Development, Ethnography and Education.* London: Routledge.

Street, B. (2003). What's 'new' in New Literacy Studies? Critical approaches to literacy in theory and practice. *Current Issues on Comparative Education*, 5(2), 77–87.

CHAPTER

2

Encountering literacies in early years classrooms

Karen Daniels and Jamila Hussain

Introduction

This chapter provides the reader with perspectives on young children's literacy practices in early years settings. On entering school, children bring understandings of literacy from their home and community experiences and this chapter foregrounds the practitioner's/teacher's role of building on what children know and can do. The chapter considers the ways in which early literacy can be understood as a social practice; as involving multiple semiotic modes and materials; as increasing confidence with literacy skills; and as an embodied and affective experience. Drawing from the United Kingdom Literacy Association's 'Holistic View of Early Literacies' framework, this chapter will describe how these ways of understanding literacy each provide valuable insights into the kinds of teaching strategies that can support young children's early literacy practices.

Multiple perspectives on early literacies

The aim of this chapter is to take a broad look at what literacy is and how it can be understood in early years classrooms. In England, early literacy is very often thought of as gaining mastery of the alphabetic code through activities such as book sharing, phonics, name writing and letter formation. As discussed in Chapter 1, current education policy often shapes the kinds of teaching strategies that are taken up in classrooms. In the light of this, in this chapter we offer the framework 'Holistic Approaches to Early Literacy Education: Theory, Beliefs and Values, and Classroom Practices'. The framework was developed by Karen Daniels and Lucy Rodriquez-Leon as part of their work as convenors of the Early Literacy in Education Special Interest Group in 2021, on behalf of the United Kingdom Literacy Association (UKLA). The document was produced as a way of presenting some of the ways in which literacy can be theorised and understood. Our position was that each way of understanding early literacy shows us something different about literacy, and that these insights are important in developing a pedagogy for early literacy that is supportive of all children. This position also underpins this chapter and highlights the fundamental way in which language and literacy are understood in this book: any literate act is embedded within a range of meaning making practices, and therefore it should be understood as such.

The framework presents five distinct but overlapping ways that literacy can be theorised: as a social and cultural practice; as an embodied and affective experience; as a set of multimodal practices; as connected with play, including narrative play; and in written English, as mastery of the alphabetic code. This final theoretical perspective is consistent with the account of early literacy

DOI: 10.4324/9781003381013-2

in current education policy in that it foregrounds the importance of individual skills that children may need to acquire to decode (read) and encode (write), such as phonic decoding, handwriting/letter formation. Within the framework presented in this chapter, early literacy and children's pathways to this are seen as including but also involving far more than mastery of the alphabetic code.

The framework itself (see Table 2.1) is set out so that it presents each theoretical 'category' in turn. Reading across from left to right, the document presents each theoretical perspective, then the beliefs and values about early literacy that we see as consistent with the theoretical perspective. In the final column, suggestions for pedagogical practices that align with the theoretical perspective are provided. The pedagogy and classroom practice column also acknowledges the ways in which early literacy pedagogy can radically shape children's understanding of what literacy is and what it can do. Indeed, young children need to see themselves as literate beings, who can create meanings through digital and non-digital texts and present these to the world in a meaningful way. A suitable pedagogy for early literacy, therefore, requires a sensitive approach that recognises who children are and what they bring to their early literacy experiences.

Table 2.1 Holistic approaches to early literacy education: theory, beliefs and values, and classroom practices (Literacy in Education Special Interest Group, UKLA, 2020)

Theoretical Principles Literacy and early literacy learning can be theorised in multiple ways	**Belief and Values** The ways in which we theorise literacy underpins our beliefs and values about literacy pedagogy.	**Pedagogy and Classroom Practice** Early literacy pedagogy and classroom practice radically shapes children's understandings of what literacy is, who it is for and their literate identities.
Literacy (alongside language) can be thought of as a social and cultural practice that varies across time and place (Barton and Hamilton, 2000; Street, 1984)	This theoretical viewpoint underpins the notion that there are multiple emerging and evolving literacies in use in society and that cultural and linguistic diversity is a feature of contemporary society. On entering educational settings, young children bring knowledge and lived experience of a diverse range of texts and literacy practices, shaped by their home and community experiences. It is important to recognise that the languages and literacies that children encounter in one context may not occur in another. These include commercial and environmental print and digitally mediated literacies.	Broad, rich and contextualised classroom practices enable children to make meaning, relationships and identities through creating and consuming meaningful text. This approach to pedagogy: • Acknowledges, celebrates and builds upon children's existing linguistic repertories and literacies, such as knowledge of commercial logos, picture books, digital technology and apps, cultural texts (e.g. greetings cards), comics, catalogues, popular culture texts or instant messaging. • Values and provides texts in children's home languages and represents diverse ethnic and cultural backgrounds. • Enables children to draw upon their 'funds of knowledge' by providing time, space and a wide range of resources and diverse texts, such as books and other media (including digital technology) that have personal significance and resonate with their wider home and community experiences. • Celebrates and legitimises children's early attempts at graphic representation and writing on paper or screen, acknowledging that children's text in non-conventional form can 'say' and 'mean' what the author intended. • Includes practitioner modelling of a broad range of authentic literacy practices, such as reading aloud, writing notes/lists and thinking out loud when using a search engine or composing a text.

(Continued)

Table 2.1 Holistic approaches to early literacy education: theory, beliefs and values, and classroom practices (Literacy in Education Special Interest Group, UKLA, 2020) *(Continued)*

Literacy can be conceptualised as an embodied and affective experience (Hackett, 2014; González Rey, 2008; Olsson, 2009)	This theoretical proposition further underscores that literacy is far more than simply a set of skills to be learnt. Young children's early encounters with literacies and texts can be experienced through movement, feeling and sensation. The nature of children's early experiences with text shapes their understanding of literacy, and of themselves and others as users of literacy.	Sensitive classroom practices recognise the inseparability of cognition and emotion and of mind and body. This approach to pedagogy: • Includes practices, texts, symbols and stories which resonate personally with children to enhance active engagement. • Recognises and capitalises on children's interests and preferences when introducing new ideas, knowledge and skills. • Provides open-ended resources and opportunities for a diverse range of play, giving children time and space to explore, express and develop their thoughts and ideas. • Involves careful observation of children's activity with literacy, noticing their responses (e.g. intrigue, surprise, anxiety, excitement) and sensitively building on their lines of inquiry. • Recognises that fostering children's need, desire or will to read influences their skill to read – and vice versa. • Develops children's positive dispositions towards learning (for example, creativity, curiosity, cooperation, concentration, playfulness and wanting to communicate).
Language and literacies can be understood as multimodal practices (Kress, 2010)	Early communication combines words, facial expression, intonation, movement, gesture and posture. These are all resources that children draw on to communicate meaning. Young children's contemporary literacy practices often involve multimodal texts, comprising alphabetic script, still or moving image, distinctive fonts, and increasingly, emoticons. Under Article 12, UNCRC, children have a right to be heard. Recognising their emerging multimodal language and literacy repertoires constitutes their right.	Print and media rich classroom environments include a wide range of accessible, multimodal texts and resources that encourage children to share their thinking and ideas in diverse ways. This approach to pedagogy: • Blends signs, symbols and images with alphabetic script in the environment. • Encourages children to use illustration in picture books to tell, adapt and reimagine narratives. • Includes relevant real-world texts such as cookbooks, maps, comics, alongside apps and websites based on popular culture or TV programmes that enable children to draw upon, express and share their detailed knowledge. • Encourages children to create multimodal texts to express their ideas and thoughts and to connect with others. These include story making apps, collage, models, role play and enactments, in addition to more conventional drawing and early writing.

(Continued)

Table 2.1 Holistic approaches to early literacy education: theory, beliefs and values, and classroom practices (Literacy in Education Special Interest Group, UKLA, 2020) *(Continued)*

Early literacy practices emerge in children's play. Narrative is a driver of children's meaning making, which in turn supports symbolic representation needed for reading and writing (Wohlwend, 2008; Engel, 2005)	Opportunity for collaborative, imaginary play enables children to co-construct and represent narrative based on their experiences of lived events, experiences of TV, film and books, their cultural interests and concerns, and their imaginations.	Opportunity for free flow peer play using open-ended resources provides and promotes opportunity for narrative play to spontaneously evolve. This approach to pedagogy:
		• Incorporates open-ended resources that promote collaborative play and imagination, including:
		  • Upcycled materials such as cardboard boxes and fabric.
		  • Role-play props including dressing up clothes and hats.
		  • Resources that represent ethnic and cultural diversity.
		  • Small world play resources such as figures, model farm animals or dinosaurs.
		  • Superhero play props.
		• Values resources and rich opportunity for children to record and retell their narratives, either on paper, through re-enactments or digitally.

In English, Welsh and other European languages, the relationship between spoken language and the conventional alphabetic script in which it is represented is mostly phonographic (speech sounds are represented by letters and letter combinations) (Goswami and Bryant, 2016) **It is important to note that this is not the case for all languages; many bilingual and multilingual children may be experiencing different systems**	In English (and other phonographic systems), learning the letter/sound correspondence of commonly used single-letter graphemes, digraphs and trigraphs enables children to decode and encode unfamiliar words. This is a highly useful strategy when used in combination with language knowledge, contextual knowledge and whole word recognition.	Prior to phonics teaching, many children benefit from developing phonological awareness, that is, an ability to discriminate between the speech sounds that are used in their language. Rather than explicit teaching, phonological awareness should be encouraged through an approach to pedagogy that includes: • A language-rich environment. • Nursery rhymes, songs and poetry with rhythmic patterns that break down the flow of speech. • Listening games. • Music and percussion instruments. • Contextual, playful activities that encourage children to identify and produce rhyming words and alliterative phrases and to blend and segment individual phonemes in words. Through these activities, young children come to understand that speech is made up of combinations of individual sounds. When appropriate, some explicit phonics instruction may be beneficial for the majority of children. Research evidence shows that this enables children to make better progress than unsystematic or no phonics instruction (Torgerson et al., 2019). It is crucial that systematic phonics teaching is both phonetically and phonically accurate, and also pedagogically sound (Brooks et al., 2019).

What are 'schooled' literacies and why do we need to look more broadly?

Literacy can be thought of as a social and cultural practice that varies across time and place (see Barton and Hamilton, 2000; Street, 1984). When we think of early literacy in school settings, we often think of those kinds of materials and practices commonly associated with schooling and the classroom, such as pens, pencils, paper, decodable books, reading and sharing stories with children, teaching the alphabet and the sound symbol correspondences of the English alphabetic code. We may think about digital technologies and the use of computers, the interactive whiteboard, or iPads, and children's use of these in classroom settings. In other words, our own experiences of being a child in school, or as a teacher or researcher, will shape what we 'see' when we think of literacy. It is very likely that what comes to mind as we think about literacy will be guided by education policy. Currently, dominant policy is very often presented in a way that aims to address 'low standards' in literacy attainment (see also Sharpe and Taplin, this volume). Due to early literacy – and in particular, early reading – being under the spotlight of policy makers in recent years, there has been a focus and increasing emphasis of teaching early literacy skills, often from an early age. For many children, early phonics activities start at age 3. Current policy often places emphasis on a narrow and limited set of literacy skills, and this can divert attention to any other ways that children can be seen as literate (see Daniels, 2019). This narrow focus can inadvertently lead to pedagogical practices that undervalue the home and community literacy experiences that children bring to the classroom.

In this and other chapters you will notice reference to the Rose Review of Early Reading (Rose, 2006) and the Simple View of Reading (SVoR), which has become the dominant model in framing understandings of how children learn to read. The SVoR suggests that reading comprehension is facilitated by two dimensions: word reading and language comprehension. The SVoR is a conceptual framework first presented by Gough and Tunmer (1986) suggesting that reading comprehension is facilitated by two dimensions: word reading and language comprehension. Increasingly, schooled literacies, and the way in which literacy policy is delivered, has been defined by this conceptual framework.

As Street (1995) points out, language and literacy are always a matter of power relationships and there are always significant power relations between children's home literacy practices and those associated with school which have greater influence and power. Looking more broadly at literacy involves reflecting on children's home experiences of language and literacy and the ways that these are shaped by cultural, linguistic, social and economic factors (Street, 2003). From an early age, children are far from passive recipients of literacies and children's broader literate lives often mean that they experience a range of literacy practices and therefore encounter 'varied and multiple literacies' as they move across settings (Pahl and Burnett, 2013, p3). These varied and multiple literacies may work very differently to the ways of being literate in school. Given that literacy practices across homes and communities and schools are diverse, we need to think carefully about the ways in which we support young children's journey into literacy. As Heath (1983) explained, practitioners should take time to understand a child's home and community experiences and language and literacy practices, to support school-based literacy learning.

It is important to acknowledge that young children experience literacy practices as part of their everyday life. On entering schools, they already know much about the world of literacy and how it operates – they are immersed in literacies. They will already have favourite books, TV shows, media characters, video games. They will see adults reading and writing in their daily lives, both digitally and using more traditional tools, such as pens and paper. Literacy is not something separate from their overall experience, and as children's understandings of literacy grow, they will also be building ideas about what literacy is, what it is for, who it is for and what it can do. As early years teachers, therefore, we are tasked with the job of understanding and building sensitively on what children bring from their home and community settings and supporting them into the literacies associated with schools and education.

The following *Spotlight on research* from Deborah Wells Rowe and Carin Neitzel illustrates how children's early encounters with literacy are shaped by their play interests.

SPOTLIGHT ON RESEARCH

Deborah Wells Rowe & Carin Neitzel (2010) Interest and Agency in 2-and 3-Year-Old's Participation in Emergent Writing. *Reading Research Quarterly*, 45(2) 169–195

The role of agency and motivation in text creation has been observed in children as young as 2 years old. Wells Rowe and Neitzel (2010) collected mark making profiles of 2- and 3-year-old children and noted how they chose interactions, materials and activities and that these were guided by their play interests and play behaviours (conceptual, creative, social and procedural). The authors noticed that children's approaches to writing appeared to be related to broader play interests. The authors summarised how personal interest is a facet of children's socially situated identities, which are shaped by their personal histories of participation in literacy practices.

Studies such as Wells Rowe and Neitzel's remind us that even the youngest children are guided by their cultural experiences and experiences of texts, and that this is expressed through their play, and the sorts of things they choose to do. By closely observing young children's activity in classrooms, we are better equipped to provide literacy experiences that build on their interests and experiences. Importantly, Wells Rowe and Neitzel's perspective positions young children as active agents in literacy and acknowledges what they bring to early literacy activities in classrooms. Sensitive adult scaffolding of early literacy is paramount, and this includes providing children with the right stimulus and materials to talk and make marks and representations about the things that matter to them.

Young children's multimodal communication

Children's activity is often stimulated by their play interests, their interactions with other children or the materials and resources in the classroom. When observing young children in classrooms, we may be drawn to those moments and activities where children are acting in ways that 'look' like literacy. Looking more closely it becomes apparent that these literacy events are in fact multimodal experiences (Daniels and Taylor, 2018). As children make meaning they may use movement such as eye contact, gesture or larger bodily movements, and they may talk or make sounds as they manipulate materials and objects.

Social semiotic theory had done much to draw early years educators' attention to children's play and meaning making as a series of complex multimodal orchestrations. Bomer (2003) and Rowe (2008) examined how young children's repertoires are shaped by the materials and resources that surround them in classroom contexts. Wohlwend's (2011) investigations into young children's multimodal play explored how young children draw on visual, audio, gestural and spatial modes, and how children readily integrate resources in their environment into their shared and imagined meanings. In this way, bodily movements with and around the material resources of classrooms are seen as significant in young children's emerging communicative repertoires.

In *Before Writing*, Kress (1997) explained how young children are primarily guided by synaesthetic activity; he describes the young child drawing a car, and how the child traces the movement of the wheels of the car. The child may talk about the picture they are drawing, in effect, they are combining multiple modes to communicate meaning such as gesture, hand movements, gaze, sounds, marks on the page, smiles, words. Very often, we focus on the text, or the words and sentences children produce, but when we look closely at what is taking place and marks that are produced, what we see is a complex orchestration between the child's movements, gestures and words, the materials available to them and other children in the setting, which are in turn all influenced by children's ideas, preferences and practices.

Literacy as play, including narrative play

There is a significant body of literature that examines the role of play in early learning and education and the field of literacy is no exception to this. Researchers have examined the role of multimodal play in providing a stimulus for early reading and writing and this has generated insights into the ways in which children innovatively weave literacies into their early play. Adults working alongside children in playful contexts, following children's lead, can support early literacy in a way that builds on children's interests and scaffolds their journey into early literacy.

Collaborative narrative play is a common feature of children's play, which is expressed through multiple modes (actions, gestures, use of materials, words). Nicolopoulou (1996, p204) suggested that children's narrative play supports narrative 'competence', or their storying practices. This takes place particularly when the narrative play occurs in the context of children's social relationships and reflects their concerns, interests and life experiences. Nicolopoulou suggests that such play not only enables children to shape meaning when taking part in collaborative play, but it also facilitates their ability to shift meanings across different sign systems as they manipulate and order materials and spaces. Sawyer and DeZutter (2007) propose that narrative competence supports children in accessing the symbolic written code of writing. Symbolic transformation, metaplay and narrative competence support children's representational skills, which are a prerequisite of engaging in the symbolic representation involved in early literacy.

SPOTLIGHT ON RESEARCH

Anne Haas Dyson (2002) *The Brothers and Sisters Learn to Write: Popular Literacies in Childhood and School Cultures*. Teachers' College Press

Anne Dyson carried out a series of ethnographic studies in the USA, working with children from diverse cultural and socio-economic backgrounds. She carried out close examinations of children's literacy practices in classrooms and described what children did in their day-to-day activities. Her work is pioneering in that it looked broadly at a range of meaning making practices that took place around literacies (playing, singing, action, drawing, talking, making), rather than only focusing on the written texts that children read and produced. Dyson proposed that children rely on their own cultural and social experiences to find a way into schooled literacies, and often draw on their unofficial worlds of football, popular music, video gaming and media characters, constructing identities for themselves. Children's interests became interwoven with play and written texts in what Dyson terms a 'symbolic mixing'. This 'symbolic mixing' provided the children with the potential for communicative flexibility and adaptability. For Dyson, this flexibility and adaptability in manipulating the affordances of the meaning making resources is paramount to literacy development.

Dyson made a number of points about how literacy might be understood: firstly, becoming literate is an active process of making sense, and therefore children are not passive recipients in the process; secondly, children's participation in literacy is facilitated when they are invited to bring their own interests and concerns into the classroom; thirdly, literacy is not static, but it is constantly being produced, re-produced, re-imagined and re-purposed by the children themselves. Pedagogical approaches that acknowledge these three things are more likely to be inclusive and supportive of young children's participation in literacy activity.

So far in this chapter, we have seen children as active participants in the early literacy classroom, who may respond in many ways to the opportunities that are offered to them. We have also seen how the practitioner is crucial in facilitating children's participation. Our suggestion here is that children should be offered supportive and flexible pedagogical approaches to support them towards becoming literate. Ongoing classroom activity gives rise to child produced meanings, and by observing these closely we can learn about children's interests and recognise what they can do. This puts us in a good position to be able to build on these interests to support early literacy. Popular culture characters, experienced through books, films and other digital media, are important to children's early literacy experiences. For many children, narrative play, or storying, is also significant in bridging more informal play literacies with the stable and structured literacies associated with early reading and writing (see Daniels, 2014).

Early literacy education needs to be guided by its learners, their unique backgrounds and needs. Children have rich and varied interests, and these are often shaped by cultural influences. The careful planning and delivery of books and stories, the types of genres experienced as a learner of English, can have considerable impact on the experience on children, and for many children, they may be learning English as an additional language (Kennedy et al., 2012).

PROMPTS FOR CRITICAL REFLECTION
Jamila's experience as a child new to English

Next, Jamila talks about her own experience of being a child in school in England, whose first language was Punjabi, and how she made sense of early literacy in the classroom.

As a young child, new to English, I remember my first experiences of literacy in the classroom. It was the teacher reading a story book out aloud at the end of every day. The teacher read from a hand-sized book and shared some of the pages with illustrations with the children. As a bilingual learner, I found the traditional tales that were read by the teacher fascinating. I had not come across anything so magical before, and the stories entranced me with their unexpectedness and distance from real life. After a while, I realised that there were repeated phrases in the story and as the children joined and chanted, I too learned these phrases and said them out aloud. I recall saying the phrases from The Three Little Pigs tale. I was unsure of what they meant, until one day the teacher decided to bring the story to life in the classroom – she picked a few children to enact the story. Suddenly, the story became alive for me. I could see what was meant by the 'Big Bad Wolf, huffing and puffing' and I could see the three little pigs teasing the wolf and not letting him into their houses, 'not by the hair of my chinny chin chin!'. Being new to the English language, there were some aspects of traditional tales that I could not grasp. I understood talking wolves and giants living in castles in the clouds. But I could not understand, e.g., how a harp could sing. How can an object sing? I remember thinking this for a long time, even in nursery rhymes, such as 'Hey diddle diddle', how can the dish run away with a spoon?

The ways in which children respond to early literacy experiences is a fascinating area of exploration, and Jamila's reflection illustrates how children often strive to make sense and participate in what is offered to them.

After reading Jamila's story, consider the following questions:

- What does Jamila's story tell you about her experience of learning English as an additional language in a literacy lesson?
- What are the key messages about the ways in which the teacher worked to facilitate participation and belonging? What other strategies could you suggest?
- Think about your own practice or your own research study. What teaching strategies do you use/have you observed, that ensure that all children can take part and make sense of literacy?

In the following *Case study focus*, early years teacher Emma describes how she supports children in drawing on their funds of knowledge, recognising children's early attempts at graphic representation.

CASE STUDY FOCUS

Emma teaching early writing

I remember one lesson in particular... my class of four and five-year-olds were very much enjoying our topic on 'pets' and I planned a shared writing activity. I explained to them that one pet in particular, a hamster, had been in the pet shop a while, and I asked the class if we might put up a poster that would encourage someone to buy him. After all, he had been in the shop for a while and was hoping someone might buy him soon. One child asked if the hamster was sad, and I asked why they thought that might be the case.

'He is hungry'

'He is missing his mummy'

'One of the other animals has bitten him!'

I asked them for ideas to write on the poster, that might make someone want to buy him.

'He has soft ears', said one child;

'He doesn't bite', said a second.

'He is very friendly', added another.

I broke the sentences into words, then the words into sounds, and we wrote the sentences together, re-reading them to make sure they made sense and we had spaces between words. From the carpeted area where we were seated, I stood up and took the shared writing to the pet shop and attached it to the classroom wall that formed a corner of the pet shop.

Throughout the morning, I sat in the pet shop area. Many of the children came to me and asked to make a poster. Some making random marks for which I supplied the written words to match their articulation. Others wrote phonetically plausible words to express their ideas. We attached each one of the posters to the wall once these were finished, and the authors went off to play elsewhere within the free flow of the classroom.

The next morning it wasn't long before one child noticed that the hamster had gone from the shop. The news quickly spread across the class, and I explained to them that someone had come and bought him and taken him home!

I often reflect on why this kind of session went well, and why it encouraged so many children to join in. For me, I think it is that it built on that group of children's interests and involved them as a group who could do something about something that mattered to them. They clearly cared about the hamster and what happened to it. But it also does something else – it shows children what writing is and what it can do, and that they can take part in this. They could all have a go. No child could fail, and they could all create their own messages at whatever stage they were at. They were learning about authorship and what it can do. On reflection, if we give children the right things to do, then they really can do them. We just need to give them the right kinds of literacy activities that will help them see themselves and find ways into literacy'.

This case study example reflects the need to structure and support children's literacy experiences, while always being open to their own interpretations and responses. Essentially, these reflections illustrate how children respond differently to classroom literacy activities, based on their cultural experiences, and the ways in which participation is an orchestration between the children and the teacher/practitioner, guiding them towards literacy.

Literacy as mastery of the alphabetic script

Written English draws on an alphabetic code, that is, it works from a system of 26 letters, combined in ways to produce approximately 44 phonemes, which make up the sounds of the English language, with some regional variations in pronunciation. Phonics is an abstract complex code, as the symbols (letters) themselves do not denote meaning but represent sounds in language. Many schools have adopted phonics schemes to teach children sound-symbol relationships, and these involve a structured programme and teaching sequence. What is important is that as well as learning sound-symbol correspondences, young children are given the opportunity to draw on their phonic learning in meaningful reading and writing activities. In the following extract, Jamila recalls her early experiences of learning phonics as a child new to English, and how she was encouraged to segment sounds in words, but then lost the sense of meaning. Jamila explains how stories provided meaningful contexts for learning a second language.

PROMPTS FOR CRITICAL REFLECTION
Jamila's experience of learning phonics

I remember my very early childhood literacy experience at a nursery in Bradford. I remember the adults saying short words such as cat and tap and looking at the printed letters and repeating the words – wholly. But then, the teachers took away the concrete print of the letters and started to say single sounds, t-a-p and then expected me to repeat the sounds. They would say, tap, t-a-p, I would say tap. They would say, t-a-p. I struggled as the sounds they said floated away from me, I could only recall the final sound, I remember holding and hanging onto it, repeating it, p – but it was not what they wanted to hear. It would have been better to have the individual letters in front of me, making the abstract concept of the phoneme more concrete, enabling me to see the mapping between the temporal sequence of the phonemes in the spoken word and the spatial sequence of letters in the printed word (Johnston and Watson, 2004). I could not retain all of the sounds in order, the individual sounds made no sense to me. I had not heard the individual sounds before, ever. So, I could say whole words, as they were spoken in everyday language. People said tap, wash your hands under the tap, open the tap, close the tap, get some water from the tap. That word made complete sense. They did not say, wash your hands under the t-a-p!

Although phonological awareness was a critical aspect of early literacy development for Jamila, having stories read to her for meaning helped her to make sense of the words

(Shanahan and Lonigan, 2010). On reflection, synthetic phonics developed the phonological awareness skills needed by children who start school with little knowledge of the sounds in English spoken words (Johnston and Watson, 2004). For learners like Jamilla, the spoken sounds in the new language were very different from the sounds spoken at home.

Read about Jamila's experience and consider the following questions:

- Jamila makes several comments about the challenges she experienced in learning to read as a child new to English. What are these challenges and why do they arise?
- What kinds of experiences enhanced Jamila's experience of early literacy?
- Consider the cultural experiences and languages of the children you are working with as a researcher or teacher. How can you work to support them in making sense of learning a new language in literacy activity? (See also Smith and Sanders, this volume.)
- How might your own linguistic experiences shape the kinds of practices that you engage in during literacy lessons?

Table 2.1 stresses the importance of a language-rich environment including nursery rhymes, songs and poetry with rhythmic patterns, listening games and contextualised playful activities, to support early literacy learning. Indeed, Jamila's account in the *Prompts for critical reflection* box reminds us that while phonics-based learning supports early literacy (encoding and decoding) ultimately, language and literacy is about making meaning and that it is essential that the teaching of literacy skills is only a small part of a meaningful literacy experience for all children, particularly those whose language and cultural experiences vary from those associated with schooled literacies.

Young children's digital literacy practices

The previous sections highlight the significance of young children's home and community experiences, how these shape their early literacy practices, and why considering these can support young children in taking-up schooled literacies. In this next section we consider how digital technologies have become part of young children's everyday lives and therefore become part of their repertoire of meaning making and literacy practices. Young children are very often comfortable in using digital devices, such as smartphones and iPads to make meaning, and access these playfully and creatively in the home. Touch screen devices seem to hold appeal to pre-school children (Merchant, 2014) and many confidently engage in activities such as scanning family photographs, clicking on links to their favourite YouTube videos and selecting iPad icons to access favourite games (see Burnett and Daniels, 2016). Children's engagement with digital technologies illustrates how young children fluidly integrate the ways of being and doing literacy from their experiences into their own repertoires. However, despite this, young children's engagement with digital devices is often positioned as being 'at odds' with the need to acquire schooled literacies.

SPOTLIGHT ON RESEARCH

Karen Daniels (2017) Children's Engagement with iPads in Early Years Classrooms: Exploring Peer Cultures and Transforming Practices. In. C. Burnett, G. Merchant, A. Simpson & M. Walsh (Eds), *The Case of the iPad: Mobile Literacies in Education* (pp. 195–210). Singapore: Springer Nature

Daniels presents data collected from observations of 4- and 5-year-old children in an early years setting. Data collection involved filming children while they were taking part in continuous provision. Conducting a multimodal analysis of the children's activity with iPads drew close attention to children's communicative repertoires as they engaged with apps such as Hairy Letters © by Nessy Learning Limited, Toca Robot Lab by Toca Boca © and Lego Story Maker © by Lego.

Through close observation and analysis of film footage, Daniels noted how collaborative interaction around apps offered opportunities for creative engagement as children explored the possibilities of the apps. This engagement was often driven by their life experiences and cultural interests. The apps children accessed were very often designed to support existing print literacy goals, such as letter formation or knowledge of phoneme grapheme correspondences. However, these goals were only part of what was realised as children collaboratively and creatively engaged with apps. Apps became a site for collaborative participation and friendships where new meaning making practices and peer cultures emerged. This iPad itself shaped the kinds of activity that took place, through its multimodal animations, its presence and shape, and the haptic skills needed to operate the device. Haptics were integrated into children's communicative repertoires and gestures, and these seemed to influence what was taking place and the kinds of meanings that emerged.

Literacy as embodied and affective

The final section in the Holistic Framework refers to an embodied understanding of early literacy. That is, literacy is not something that is purely related to thinking or cognition. Literacy is experienced by our whole bodies, through our sensations' ongoing bodily movement and its relationship with meaning making. Although this relationship has been an area of exploration for over a decade (Wetherell, 2012), it is still a relatively new area of study. Thinking about how mind and body and bodily experience are intricately connected with meaning making is of particular significance when supporting young children (Daniels, 2019). (See also Monkhouse and Smith, this volume.)

According to Thrift (2007), our experiences are not just related to our thoughts but are felt by our bodies as moments pass. Transitions across moments can be 'felt' by the body as a change in capacity, as non-conscious visceral experiences or sensations of being able to act, move or, conversely, being not able to act. Affect, as defined by Massumi (2002), refers to the body's capacity to affect and be affected as it moves through the ever-changing material environment. The implication of this is that the physical environment (the furniture, resources, classrooms spaces and walls), the kinds of pedagogical approaches children experience, and the materials they have access to (paper, pens, scissors, glue, PCs and so on) are interrelated with our bodily experiences and all these things have a significant impact on the ways in which children experience literacies at school more broadly.

Much is written about the role of the practitioner or teacher in early literacy education. Less is written or understood about the interrelated impact of all the factors that influence children's early literacy experiences. In current policy, the adult is often seen as one who 'imparts' literacy to children. In contrast, understanding literacy as embodied and affective suggests that the role of the adult involves being attuned to affective flows of movement and symbolic expression, and being responsive to these. This topic was of interest to Olsson (2009), who traced young children's activity as practitioners followed children's movements and interests. Olsson (2009) highlighted how this heightened practitioners' understandings of children's lines of inquiry and potential for learning in the here and now.

As a relatively new field of inquiry in early years literacy research, thinking about affect focuses our attention to what is taking place 'in the moment', and how we and the children are experiencing this. As teachers of literacy, how we respond when literacy is taking place is critical. So much of our work as early literacy teachers can become focused on where we want children to be, and the list of hierarchical skills we wish them to acquire. Thinking about what literacy 'feels like', and its affective flows in our classrooms, and how young children are experiencing literacy as it takes place, can help us to navigate our work. As stated in Chapter 1, the ways in which we respond to young children's literacy practices will shape what they think literacy is, what it is for and, ultimately, whether it is for them.

Chapter summary

In this chapter, we have looked at a number of perspectives on literacy. Indeed, literacy is at once an embodied, affective, social, cultural phenomenon that is shared with children through their family, community experiences and those that take place in schools. Very often we understand literacy in simple terms of phonics teaching, letter formation and book reading. This is an important part, but not the only part of early literacy that we need to focus on.

Many young children experience digitally mediated literacies (see also Monkhouse and Bailey, this volume, and Borland, Daniels and Hunt, this volume) and participate in digitally mediated environments, often moving fluidly across digital and print forms of literacy.

Early literacy encounters should respect the diverse literacies that are in circulation in broader society and recognise children's linguistic and cultural backgrounds. Supporting children's home languages and cultures supports inclusivity and can ensure that children feel valued. Early literacy is always a negotiation between the child and the practitioner/adult and facilitating participation through this negotiation is an essential goal of the early years teacher.

Literacy is a complicated, multidimensional phenomenon that is inseparable from language, communication and other social practices. There is no single all-encompassing theory that can fully explain the complexities of early literacy learning (Kress, 2003). The ways in which literacy is understood or theorised shape educators' beliefs and values which, in turn, shape enactments of literacy curricula and classroom practices. Table 2.1 illustrates the theories, beliefs, values and classroom practices that underpin broad, balanced and inclusive approaches to literacy education in the early years.

References

Barton, D. & Hamilton, M. (2000). Literacy practices. In D. Barton, M. Hamilton & R. Ivanič (Eds), *Situated Literacies: Theorising Reading and Writing in Context* (pp. 25–32). London: Routledge.

Bomer, R. (2003). Things that make kids smart: A Vygotskian perspective on concrete tool use in primary literacy classrooms. *Journal of Early Childhood Literacy*, 3(3), 223–247.

Brooks, G., Beard, R. & Ampaw-Farr, J. (2019). 'English has 100+ phonemes': Some errors and confusions in contemporary commercial phonics programmes. *Research Paters in Education*, 36(2), 1–31.

Burnett, C. & Daniels, K. (2016). Technology and literacy in the early years. In S. Garvis & N. Lemon (Eds), *Understanding Digital Technologies and Young Children. An International Perspective* (pp. 18–28). London and New York: Routledge.

Daniels, K. (2014). Cultural agents creating texts: A collaborative space adventure. *Literacy*, 48(2), 103–111.

Daniels, K. (2017). Children's engagement with iPads in early years classrooms: Exploring peer cultures and transforming practices. In C. Burnett, G. Merchant, A. Simpson & M. Walsh (Eds), *The Case of the iPad: Mobile Literacies in Education* (pp. 195–210). Singapore: Springer Nature.

Daniels, K. (2019). Movement, meaning and affect and young children's early literacy practices. *International Journal of Early Years Education*, 29(1), 41–55. doi:10.1080/09669760.2019.1701998

Daniels, K. & Taylor, R. (2018). Children as learners: Multimodal perspectives on play and learning. In D. Fitzgerald & H. Maconochie (Eds), *Early Childhood Studies: A Students' Guide* (pp. 47–62). London: Sage. Retrieved from https://uk.sagepub.com/en-gb/eur/early-childhood-studies/book253819

Engel, S. (2005). The narrative worlds of what-is and what-if. *Cognitive Development*, 20, 514–525.

González Rey, F. (2008). Subject, subjectivity, and development in cultural-historical psychology. In B. Van Oers, W. Wardekker, E. Elbers & R. Van Der Veer (Eds), *The Transformation of Learning: Advances in Cultural-Historical Activity Theory* (pp. 137–154). Cambridge: Cambridge University Press.

Goswami, U. & Bryant, P. (2016). *Phonological Skills and Learning to Read.* Abingdon: Routledge.

Gough, P. B. & Tunmer, W. E. (1986). Decoding, reading and reading disability. *Remedial and Special Education*, 7, 6–10.

Hackett, A. (2014). Zigging and zooming all over the place: Young children moving in time, place and more-than-human worlds. *Journal of Early Childhood Literacy*, 17(3), 374–391.

Heath, S. B. (1983). *Ways With Words: Language, Life and Work in Communities and Classrooms.* Cambridge: Cambridge University Press.

Johnston, R. S. & Watson, J. E. (2004). Accelerating the development of reading, spelling and phonemic awareness skills in initial readers. *Reading & Writing*, 17(4), 327–357. https://doi-org.bishopg.idm.oclc.org/10.1023/B:READ.0000032666.66359.62

Kennedy, E., Dunphu, E., Dwyer, B.,Hayes, G., McPhillips, T., Marsh, J., O'Connor, M. & Shiel, S. (2012). Literacy in early childhood and primary education (3–8 years). The National Council for Curriculum and Assessment. https://ncca.ie/media/2137/literacy_in_early_childhood_and_primary_education_3-8_years.pdf

Kress, G. (1997). *Before Writing: Rethinking the Path to Literacy.* London: Routledge.

Kress, G. (2003). *Literacy in the New Media Age.* London: Routledge.

Kress, G. (2010). *Multimodality. A Social Semiotic Approach to Contemporary Communication.* New York: Routledge.

Massumi, B. (2002). *Parables for the Virtual: Movement, Affect, Sensation.* London: Duke University Press.

Merchant, G. (2014). Keep taking the tablets, iPads, story apps and early literacy. *Australian Journal of Language and Literacy*, 38(1), 3–11.

Nicolopoulou, A. (1996). Narrative development in social context. In D. Slobin, J. Gehrards, J. Guo & A. Kyrazis (Eds), *Social Interaction Social Context and Language. Essays in Honour of Susan Ervin-Tripp* (pp. 369–390). Mahwah, NJ: Lawrence Erlbaum.

Olsson, L. (2009). *Movement and Experimentation in Young Children's Learning. Deleuze and Guattari in Early Childhood Education.* London: Routledge.

Pahl, K. & Burnett C. (2013). Literacies in homes and communities. In. K. Hall, T. Cremon, B Comber & I. Moll (Eds), *International Handbook of Research on Children's Literacy, Learning and Culture* (pp. 3–14) West Sussex: John Wiley and Sons.

Rose, J. (2006). *Independent Review of the Teaching of Early Reading.* Department for Education and Skills.

Rowe, D. W. (2008). Social contracts for writing: Negotiating shared understandings about text in the preschool years. *Reading Research Quarterly*, 43(1), 66–95.

Sawyer, K. & DeZutter, S. (2007). Improvisation: A lens for play and literacy research. In C. Roscos & E. Christie (Eds), *Play and Literacy in Early Childhood* (2nd Ed; pp. 21–36). Oxon: Taylor & Francis Group.

Shanahan, T. & Lonigan, C. J. (2010). The National Early Literacy Panel: A summary of the process of the report. *Educational Researcher*, 39(4), 279–285.

Street, B. (1984). *Literacy in Theory and Practice*. Cambridge: Cambridge University Press.

Street, B. (1995). *Social Literacies: Critical Approaches to Literacy in Development, Ethnography and Education*. London: Routledge.

Street, B. (2003). What's 'new' in New Literacy Studies? Critical approaches to literacy in theory and practice. *Current Issues in Comparative Education*, 5(2), 77–91.

Thrift, N. (2007). *Non-Representational Theory: Space, Politics, Affect*. London: Routledge.

Torgerson, C., Brooks, G, Gascoine, L. & Higgins, S. (2019). *Phonics: Reading policy and the evidence of effectiveness from a systematic "tertiary" review. Research Papers in Education*, 34(2), 208–238.

Wetherell, M. (2012). *Affect and Emotion: A New Social Science Understanding*. Thousand Oaks, CA: Sage.

Wohlwend, K. (2008). Play as a literacy of possibilities: Expanding meanings in practices, materials, and spaces. *Language Arts*, 86(3), 127–136.

Wohlwend, K. (2011). *Playing Their Way into Literacies: Reading, Writing and Belonging in the Early Childhood Classroom*. New York: Teachers College Press.

CHAPTER

3

Reading aloud

Cara Doxey and Ginny Doxey

Introduction

This chapter provides an insight into the role of reading aloud to Key Stage 2 children and links this to reading for pleasure. Reading aloud to children has been investigated in numerous ways, with benefits often being described in terms of increased skills and increases in reading attainment: a cognitive-psychological perspective. An alternative view, the socio-cultural perspective, focuses on the importance of the social and cultural context where learning occurs rather than purely focusing on personal skills. Using research from Cara's thesis – focus group interviews with children and observations from the classroom – coupled with Ginny's experiences as a classroom practitioner, this chapter will explore the experience of reading aloud to children. Cara's doctoral study involved children in Class 5 (9- to 10-year-olds) and was conducted in England. The children were asked to take photographs to represent 'reading' in their school. These images were discussed in small groups. Data were analysed using thematic analysis (Braun and Clarke, 2006). In what follows, we will discuss the findings from the study and implications for class teachers hoping to develop reading aloud pedagogy.

Socio-cultural perspective on reading

A socio-cultural perspective on literacy focuses on the importance of the social and cultural context where learning occurs rather than on personal skills. Vygotsky (1978) viewed learning and development as a social phenomenon whereby children become encultured into ways of thinking, feeling and acting by significant others: 'Human learning presupposes a specific social nature and process by which children grow into the intellectual life of those around them' (p88). The adults use language in context and 'scaffold' the reading activity, helping the child to understand their role within it (Bruner and Watson, 1983).

This socio-cultural perspective challenges the view of literacy as a 'private mental possession' which can be 'quantified and measured in terms of discrete decontextualized skills' (Gee, 1991, p31). Instead, literacy is viewed as a social practice with practice being defined by Barton et al. (2000) as 'cultural ways of utilising literacy' (p8). The authors go on to describe 'literacy events' as activities where talk occurs around a central text or texts, pointing to the fact that this always exists within a social context. This view highlights the necessary involvement of attitudes, beliefs and practices in literacy events, recognising that those who have 'been taught empowering ways with the words they read, are far more likely to be empowered than those who have not' (Smith, 2004, p414).

DOI: 10.4324/9781003381013-3

Reading for pleasure and reading aloud

'Reading for pleasure' is a term that has been used to describe an act of reading that involves 'the reader's volition, their agency and desire to read' (Cremin et al., 2009, p5). Research suggests that engagement in reading can support academic outcomes (Brozo et al., 2007; Smith et al., 2012) illustrated by increases in vocabulary and better comprehension (Andreassen and Bråten, 2010; Krashen, 2004; Schiefele et al., 2012). The Reading Framework (DfE, 2023) outlines that reading aloud can be a 'powerful driver for improving pupils' reading and all-round education, as well as having a positive impact on their social and emotional wellbeing' (p101). Drawing on an extensive review of available research, The Reading Agency concluded that reading for pleasure leads to 'enjoyment, relaxation and escapism, increasing understanding of self and social identities, empathy, knowledge of other cultures, relatedness, community cohesion and increasing social capital' (The Reading Agency, 2015, p4).

Developing a reading for pleasure culture involves consideration of factors such as environment, social reading, independent reading and reading aloud. Reading aloud is an activity whereby the teacher shares a text with the children and has been identified as an important activity in relation to developing reading for pleasure (Cremin, 2014). Listening to someone read aloud can encourage the view of reading as a pleasurable activity and for those who have not yet developed adequate decoding skills, it provides access to texts that match children's comprehension levels (Goodwin, 1995).

The significance of reading aloud to children was reported by Wells (1986). He found that of the three frequently occurring activities that had been considered as possibly helpful preparation for the acquisition of literacy, only one was significantly associated with later test scores: listening to stories. Listening to stories, and perhaps the context in which these activities occur, appears to present children with an experience of literacy that develops not only their knowledge of words but also their understanding of how and why language is used.

There have been multiple studies carried out exploring the benefits of reading aloud across all subjects. Boyd (2009) believes that reading aloud is a powerful educational tool that has the potential to encourage empathy, creativity and focus. Cron (2012) expanded on this, highlighting that humans are hard-wired to listen to stories and make meaning; reading aloud from fictional texts can encourage children to explore ideas further.

Reading aloud can involve literature from a range of genres (Franzese, 2002) including fiction and nonfiction. It is recommended that every class should listen to a story as part of their daily routine using books, poems, articles or book chapters (Rasinski and Padak, 2004). Neuman et al. (2000) declared that reading aloud is the single most important activity for reading success.

In the United States of America, the Department of Education Commission explored over 10,000 studies and discovered that the most crucial and important activity for 'building skills and background for eventual success in reading is reading aloud to children' (Anderson, Hiebert, Scott and Wilkinson, 1985, p86). Furthermore, there is evidence to suggest that reading aloud to children allows them to process and understand 'challenging context, text features and vocabulary' (Heisey and Kucan, 2010, p665). This is applicable to subjects such as science and technology, not just subjects normally linked with reading aloud. In addition to this, reading to children aged 4–5 years old leads to higher reading, maths and cognitive skills at ages 8–9 years (Kalb and van Ours, 2014). Reading aloud provides children with the opportunity to develop 'concepts about print, story structure and other elements of text' and 'provides the child with a wealth of information about the processes and functions of written language' (Rog, 2001, p7). Reading aloud has also been found to develop children's listening ability and attention span (Dragan, 2001).

Research into reading aloud to children has often focused on the benefits of this activity in terms of improving skills. Reading to young children is viewed as beneficial in terms of 'acquiring literacy' and providing children with a 'head start' in life (Kalb and van Ours, 2014; Massaro, 2017). Studies with primary-aged children point to increases in vocabulary (Read et al., 2022; Suggate et al., 2013) and improved inference skills (Dempsey, 2020). Additionally, reading aloud appears to have a positive impact on the amount of time children spend reading silently (Pegg and Bartelheim, 2011). Research has also focused on attitude and motivation, suggesting that reading aloud has a positive effect on lifelong reading habits and reading identity (Merga, 2017); children consider adults who read with expression and emotion as role models (Merga, 2016).

Reading aloud also develops the relationship between children and reading which leads to an increase in the number of children who identify as readers (Cremin et al., 2009). The act of a teacher reading to children is an important task that can motivate and inspire children to read independently (Batini et al., 2018). Mooney (1990) also highlighted that benefits included an increase in their desire to listen and learn about books and their aspiration to become a reader.

The role of 'flow'

Csikszentmihalyi (1990) suggests that the experience of 'flow' can impact children's attitudes, describing it as *intrinsically* rewarding. Engeser (2012) links this to reading suggesting that it occurs when an individual is 'completely immersed in an activity without reflective self-consciousness' or, referring specifically to reading, as Kuijpers et al. put it, a reader becomes 'lost in a book' (2024, p3). Csikszentmihalyi considers 'flow' as the process whereby an actor and action 'become one', pointing to this as a motivating factor for children in relation to reading. Reading aloud to children has the potential to support 'flow'. The findings from Ryan and Schatt's (2014) study are perhaps relevant here in relation to developing children into lifelong readers. They considered the role of 'flow' as part of a storytelling event.

SPOTLIGHT ON RESEARCH

P. Ryan and D. Schatt (2014) Can you describe the experience? *Storytelling, Self, Society*, 10(2), 131–155

Ryan and Schatt (2014) investigated the impact of the longest running storytelling program in the US by interviewing the program's current and former students. Although storytelling is different from reading aloud (storytelling is an oral practice whereas reading aloud involves sharing a written text), Barton (1986) suggests that there are similarities in that the teacher's performance can draw the children together in a community event. The insights from Ryan and Schatt's study suggested that the impact on individuals was 'enduring' and 'lifelong'. Participants spoke of their emotional responses to listening to stories describing the experience as 'emotionally relaxing' and declaring that it was 'the best' and 'paradise' (p143). All the interviewees stated that the program had encouraged a love of stories in adulthood. Interestingly, most of the participants could not remember the stories that were told but many had strong recollections of the rituals of 'walking to the library' and 'being triggered into a calmer state when sitting on the rug' (p16). Ryan and Schatt identified these as experiences of 'flow' (Csikszentmihalyi, 1990), highlighting its importance in relation to promoting reading for pleasure long term.

Exploring children's and teachers' experiences of reading aloud

In Cara's research study, children in Class 5 described the experience of being read to as one of relaxation. During a reading aloud session one child commented:

> It's really nice because you can relax, and you don't have to do anything. You just need to listen to him read. And it's actually really nice because sometimes I don't really want to read. Sometimes I like people reading to me.

Brock et al. (2008) suggest that for children to develop a love of reading they may benefit from certain forms of encouragement. When considering the experience of listening to a story, teachers need to consider aspects such as seating positions, comfort, classroom environment and delivery of the text. Ensuring that the classroom is a happy, comfortable environment can strengthen a child's relationship with reading.

Research suggests that the aesthetics of a reading environment can aid children's growth and progression as readers (Guthrie et al., 2007) through the arousing of their senses including visual, feeling, smelling, hearing and imagination (Rushton and Juola-Rushton, 2008). Consideration of the environment should therefore be a priority for teachers as this may also develop the children's enjoyment and perceptions of reading overall (Blachowicz et al., 2006). An environment where children can relax and one that also looks enticing can help to promote the love of reading. Ensuring that displays are current and relevant and that reading areas are comfortable with a wide range of texts would seem important. Other factors may also be considered during the reading aloud event. For example, the children in Class 5 found 'comfy spots' by lying on the floor on coats and bags. Wigfield (2010) suggested that the environment can significantly impact student learning outcomes and Mashburn et al. (2008) highlighted that comfortability and happiness in a reading area can develop and reinforce a child's motivation to read.

Another aspect that teachers need to consider is the way in which they deliver the text. Acosta-Tello (2019) suggests that using different voices for characters has a positive impact on the reader, creating enthusiasm and intrigue towards the story. This is supported by the Reading Framework (DfE, 2023) which highlights the importance of teachers using 'voices' and 'pauses' when reading aloud. An enthusiastic delivery can help to develop children's relationships with the characters, enabling them to visualise the events and become 'part of the story itself' (Acosta-Tello, 2019, p4). This requires the teacher to become somewhat of a performer. As Barton (1986) suggests, reading aloud is similar to storytelling where the teacher's performance can draw the children together in a community event (Chambers, 2011).

The children in Class 5 commented positively on their teachers' use of voices:

> It's got different characters and voices, he's very good at that. Because when we were reading a book about these Scottish elves, he did an amazing Scottish accent. It was really funny.

This appeared to engage the class in the story with one child sitting at their teacher's feet like 'he is in a trance'. This would seem to link to Csikszentmihalyi's idea of 'flow' where child and teacher 'become one' in a shared event.

The teacher, therefore, is central in terms of sparking, developing and sustaining an interest in reading and how a teacher talks about a shared text can have a huge impact on the children's views. In addition, being a reader is an important aspect of a teacher's practice. Research exploring teachers as readers (Cremin et al., 2009) highlights the role a teacher can play in developing a love of reading. If teachers have read the class book already, this can allow for specific emphasis, discussion of certain relevant aspects and creation of 'inside-text talk' (Cremin, 2019). Inside-text talk is the discussion of a book leading to the understanding of characters and context. This can create exciting engagements between children who feel passionate about the book. Cremin (2019) refers to this as 'book blether' (Cremin, 2019). If teachers are also engaged with the story, it allows them to be involved, make genuine comments and develop children's thinking further. In *Prompts for critical reflection*, which follows, Ginny reflects on her experiences in the classroom relating to the importance of the reading aloud.

PROMPTS FOR CRITICAL REFLECTION

Reading aloud

Reading aloud, or story time, was a timetabled part of our everyday routine, 20 minutes after lunchtime. Ensuring story time was after lunchtime and not before another activity, allowed me to leave the story on a cliffhanger nearly every time and we would never cut the reading aloud session short which often happens at the end of the day due to tidying up, collecting belongings etc. Valuing and prioritising story time demonstrates to the children the importance of that session. The children would place a sign outside the door stating that 'Storytime was in progress'. We had a phrase that the children repeated regularly – 'story time is the most important part of the day'.

It was of paramount importance to create a classroom that would be deemed safe by the children. I also strived for the concept of 'cosy'. We had fairy lights around the room, soft furnishings in the reading area and, during story time, a fireplace on the board with the lights turned off. Students were allowed to remove their shoes, put their heads on their jumpers and close their eyes. Reading the book before delivering it to the class can be incredibly exciting. You can pinpoint where you are going to finish for that section. It also provides an opportunity to develop voices for the characters and actions throughout the story.

After every story time, the children and I would discuss some exciting sections of the text: which characters we liked and what we thought was going to happen next. I tried to make sure the children only contributed voluntarily as I did not want them to think it was a reading lesson where there was a right and wrong answer. Children shared their interesting insights into the story, often continuing their conversations at playtime.

Other ways I developed 'inside-text-talk' (or book blether) were through personal reading every morning. I provided opportunities for 'quiet' reading and 'chatty' reading, allowing children to have time alone to get into the flow of their literature or to discuss their reading with friends. After each morning reading session, I would ask the children 'Where have you all been this morning?' to which they would reply as if they were the protagonists in their stories, telling me about their wild adventures or the information they had learned. This gave the children a brief insight into the literature others were reading and highlighted texts they might enjoy as well as creating links with texts they had already read. Children also connected through shared texts, identifying other children with similar reading interests. Encouraging children to share their reading habits can create a domino effect, whereby they want to read more and share their reading adventures together.

Ginny's reflection is a reminder of how the teacher often strives to make time for areas of literacy pedagogy that are important, and which may not be reflected or prioritised within the primary curriculum and busy school day.

After reading Ginny's reflection, consider the following questions

- How is Reading for Pleasure developed in your own context? How are children encouraged to feel safe and to enjoy listening to stories?
- What other strategies could you consider?
- What are your priorities for fostering a love of reading through reading aloud to children? What are the challenges faced by teachers?
- How can you seek to understand children's experiences of being read to and how they feel about this?

Choice of books to read aloud in the classroom – some considerations

The choice of text is an important factor when reading aloud. If the curriculum is to value children's interests, it may be useful to consult children and acknowledge their views (McTavish et al., 2012; Reedy & De Carvalho, 2021). Drawing from Cara's research involving classroom observations and interviews with children, the next *Spotlight on research* provides insights into the ways in which the children expressed a desire for the teacher to 'know' them as readers and understand their preferences in reading.

SPOTLIGHT ON RESEARCH

Book choice and children's reading preferences

As part of Cara's doctoral research, the children in 'Class 5' shared their responses to three texts read aloud during the course of the academic year: *The Wee Free Men*, by Terry Pratchett (2003); *Ratburger*, by David Walliams (2012); and *Room 13*, by Robert Swindells (1989). Cara explored why the books were chosen by the teacher and how children responded to them.

The teacher, Mr Dickens, began the school year reading aloud from *The Wee Free Men* (Pratchett, 2003). He was passionate about Terry Pratchett's books and personally owned many copies. This approach to selecting texts meets the criteria that teachers should be enthused and excited about the books that they read aloud to children (Acosta-Tello, 2019). However, this enthusiasm was not replicated by the children in the class. One child, who was an avid reader, commented that:

> *I think I don't really get the book. It's a little bit hard and a little bit olden days.*

This lack of enthusiasm was supported by classroom observations.

> *He is reading Terry Pratchett. The children keep shuffling, swapping places. I think the story is too difficult for them to understand … There is a funny bit in the book – no one laughs. I don't think they are listening.*

Research suggests that teachers often rely on their favourite texts from their own childhood (Cremin & Durning, 2020). This is somewhat understandable. When we enjoy a text, we perhaps assume that others will too. However, to be able to make choices that are relevant for the children in a class, teachers should have a wide knowledge of texts (Cremin et al., 2008; Cremin, 2014).

The children's response to a text that linked to a recent school residential trip was more positive. *Room 13* (Swindells, 1989) tells the story of a class of 10- and 11-year-olds who visit Whitby, a seaside resort on the east coast of England. The children in the study had visited the town earlier in the academic year. Janine summarised the plot:

> *[It's] about a girl who goes on a school residential to near where we went in Whitby. And she goes to a hotel in Whitby, and there's a room called room 13. But it's not actually a room. It's a storage cupboard place. But at midnight, it turns into room 13.*

Such was the enthusiasm about the text, several of the children purchased copies of the book so that they could read along with the teacher or even read ahead. Claire told me that Janine had got a copy of *Room 13*:

> *She keeps it in the drawer … She follows along with him*

Claire also had a copy and field notes reported that she:

> *... rolls onto her back and holds the book up in the air as she follows the text.*

Observational notes showed how children in the class expressed disappointment when the teacher stopped reading and those with personal copies enjoyed their privileged position:

> *Mr Dickens says, 'we'll leave it there'. The children groan. Claire gives Mr Dickens a knowing look, as if to say she shares the knowledge of the book and recognises something bad is going to happen in the story.*

When texts endorse children's reading preferences or relate meaningfully to their lives, they seem enthusiastic, engaged and motivated to read. In the case of *Room 13* (Swindells, 1989) this might be due to the relevance of the story, the suspenseful plot and the links with a recent experience in their lives. However, the extent to which texts for reading aloud should be based on children's preferences might not be straightforward.

Many of the children expressed a desire to hear stories by the celebrity author, David Walliams. Walliams was a popular author in the class and many children had personal copies of his books. The experience was reflected in a conversation with Tulip:

> *I ask Tulip if she likes the story. She says yes. She says there was a really funny bit last time called 'sizzling bottoms'. I ask what happened. She can't remember but she liked it because it was funny.*

As we can see, Tulip could not really explain her ideas about the 'funniness' of the text. It would seem important, therefore, for teachers to discuss how books create effects, such as humour. It may also be an opportunity to draw attention to the way in which books and stories could reinforce stereotypes through the portrayal of their characters, thereby using this as an opportunity to develop children's critical literacy. In addition, this can highlight the difficulty teachers might experience when choosing suitable class novels and the extent to which children's preferences should be considered. Teachers have a responsibility to share texts that they believe are suitable for the children in their care. They are in a position to introduce their classes to a wide variety of authors and genres and, with a knowledge of their children's reading preferences, and make personal recommendations. For teachers to effectively support reading for pleasure and provide suitable book recommendations, they will need to read children's books (Cremin et al., 2009) as this will enable them to make judgements about their suitability for the classroom and for the children that they are teaching. It is only by reading texts themselves that teachers are in a position to make judgements about which texts are suitable for their children. Additionally, if teachers are familiar with the story, they will be better placed to support 'inside-text talk' (Cremin, 2019) and provide opportunities for exciting and genuine engagements, supporting deep thinking about a text.

Diversity in children's literature

The books introduced by teachers provide opportunities for children to learn about themselves and the wider world. It is important to ensure that children feel represented and noticed (see also Sharpe and Taplin, this volume). The Reading Framework (DfE, 2023) suggests that children should be able to consider themselves in the role of protagonist, highlighting the importance of diversity in the text we choose to share. In 2022, the Centre for Literacy in Primary Education (CLPE) reported that although the representation of characters from Black, Asian and Minority Ethnic Backgrounds has increased (4% in 2017 to 20% in 2021), this is still not representative of the 33.5% of children who are from a minority ethnic background in the UK primary school population. Teachers need to consider this when choosing and selecting books for their class. It is important to develop these understandings and social sensitivities, values and belief systems (Norton, 1990) whilst still being able to engage empathetically and emotionally, making connections to the world and developing a desire to understand (Kucirkova et al., 2017). Such an approach helps to nurture children as active participants in the community, where they feel a sense of belonging and are supported.

It is also important to ensure that the literature available to children relates to the Lesbian, Gay, Bisexual, Transgender, Queer or Questioning (LGBTQ+) community. It is clear that over the last 15 years, the inclusion of LGBT issues in the curriculum has increased with current guidance in England stating that LGBT relationships must be taught in school. However, with 45% of lesbian, gay, bisexual and transgender childrenreporting incidents of bullying (including 64% of transgender children) there is still a long way to go before we can truly say we have an inclusive education system (Bradlow et al., 2017). LGBT-friendly books in primary schools can help to increase awareness, acceptance and understanding by broadening the reader's experience of the world. The use of such texts in story time can provide space for discussion, allowing for further understanding of the self and others. During the opportunity to discuss ideas with peers, friendships can arise, especially when children feel seen, heard and represented. C. S. Lewis once said, 'Friendship is born at the moment when one person says to another "What! You too? I thought I was the only one"'.

In the *Ideas for classroom practice* that follows, Ginny and Cara provide strategies to support reading aloud in the classroom and recommendations of books to read to children.

IDEAS FOR CLASSROOM PRACTICE
Strategies for reading aloud in the classroom

Ginny's reflection:

> *I always ensure that I read a text before sharing it with the class. This is essential not only to assess the text's suitability, but also to support your delivery. I try to find texts that link with the children's experiences and backgrounds as well as their reading preferences. An example of this was when I read Morris Gleitzman's* Boy Overboard. *The children had been asking questions about events in Afghanistan and this provided some insight into what life may have been like for children who lived there. I also try to ensure that the texts I read aloud are both diverse and representative of the children in the class.*
>
> *Another consideration is how characters are represented in a text. For example,* The Last Firefox *by Lee Newbury is a story that includes a family with two dads. The dads were not central to the story, but their inclusion helped develop awareness of this family structure for the children in the class.*

Some suggestions:
Familiarity with a story can aid anticipation and help your confidence when reading aloud. Aim to leave on a cliffhanger!

Being comfortable:
On the floor | at desks | lying down | blankets | pillows | shoes off | options of having their eyes shut.

Environment:
Lights off | fireplace with a crackle on the board | general quietness | a sign on the door saying 'do not disturb' | fairy lights.

Delivery:
Voice: high – low | fast – slow | loud – quiet | exaggerate pauses | movements and gestures to support the text | read the room and respond to their feedback both verbal and non-verbal | consider pace – count 2 for a full stop and 1 for a comma | move around the room or sit still depending on the text | ask occasional questions or share your thoughts.

Book recommendations:
Here is a list of books we would recommend for reading aloud in class. You are the best person to choose which texts would suit your class. Consider children's wider background, hobbies and interests along with their experience of being a reader.

Year 3	Year 4
Saving Winslow Sharon Creech (author) Sarah Horne (illustrator) **Dragonsitter** Josh Lacey (author) Garry Parsons (illustrator) **Pugs of the Frozen North** Philip Reeve (author) Sarah McIntyre (illustrator) **Puppy Academy** Gill Lewis (author) Sarah Horne (illustrator) **Planet Omar** Zanib Mian (author) Nasaya Mafaridik (illustrator)	**The Last Firefox** Lee Newbury (author) Laura Catalán (illustrator) **The Lion Above the Door** Onjali Q. Rauf (author/illustrator) **Armistice Runner** Tom Palmer (author) Tom Clohosy Cole (illustrator) **Malamander** Thomas Taylor (author/illustrator) **Varjak Paw** S. F. Said (author) Dave McKean (illustrator)
Year 5	**Year 6**
The Boy with the Butterfly Mind Victoria Williamson (author) **All to Play For** Eve Ainsworth (author) Kirsti Beautyman (illustrator) **Highland Falcon Thief** M. G. Leonard and Sam Sedgman (author) **Front Desk** Kelly Yang (author) **How to be More Hedgehog** Anne-Marie Conway (author) Raahat Kaduji and Danielle Daye (illustrators)	**The Eleventh Trade** Alyssa Hollingsworth (author) **Boy 87** Ele Fontain **A Kind of Spark** Elle McNicoll (author) Kay Wilson (illustrator) **The Light in Everything** Katya Balen (author) Sydney Smith (illustrator) **Jamie** L.D.Lapinski (author) Harry Woodgate (illustrator)

Chapter summary

In this chapter, we have explored the role of reading aloud in primary school and reflected on its importance in supporting reading for pleasure. Adopting a socio-cultural perspective, we considered the findings from Cara's doctoral thesis along with Ginny's experiences in the classroom to highlight possible areas of interest for current classroom practitioners.

Recognising the value of 'flow', we examined the importance of the classroom environment, text choice and the teacher's role, acknowledging that in today's packed curriculum, reading aloud should be a timetabled activity to ensure that it is embedded into everyday classroom practice and does not just become an optional extra. As Ginny suggests, reading aloud is 'the most important part of the day!'

References

Acosta-Tello, E. (2019) Reading aloud: Engaging young children during a read aloud experience. *Research in Higher Education Journal*, 37.

Andreassen, R. & Bråten, I. (2010) Examining the prediction of reading comprehension on different multiple-choice tests. *Journal of Research in Reading*, 33(3), 263–283.

Anderson, R. C., Hiebert, E. H., Scott, J. A. & Wilkinson, I. A. G. (1985) *Becoming a Nation of Readers: The Report of the Commission on Reading*. The National Academy of Education, The National Institute of Education, The Center for the Study of Reading.

Barton, B. (1986) *Tell Me Another: Storytelling and Reading Aloud at Home, at School and in the Community*. Portsmouth: Heinemann Educational Books Inc.

Barton, D., Hamilton, M. & Ivanič, R. (Eds.). (2000) *Situated Literacies: Reading and Writing in Context*. London: Routledge

Batini, F., Bartolucci, M. & Timpone, A. (2018) The effects of reading aloud in the primary school. *Psychology and Education*, 55(1–2), 111–122.

Blachowicz, C. L. Z., Fisher, P. J. L., Ogle, D. & Watts-Taffe, S. (2006) Vocabulary: Questions from the classroom. *Reading Research Quarterly*, 41(4), 524–539. https://doi.org/10.1598/RRQ.41.4.5

Boyd, B. (2009) *On the Origin of Stories: Evolution, Cognition, and Fiction*. Cambridge, MA: Harvard University Press.

Bradlow, J., Bartram, F., Guasp, A. & Jadva, V. (2017) *School Report: The Experiences of Lesbian, Gay, Bi and Trans Young People in Britain's Schools in 2017*. London: Stonewall.

Braun, V. & Clarke, V. (2006) Using thematic analysis in psychology. *Qualitative Research in Psychology*, 3(2), 77–101.

Brock, L. L., Nishida, T. K., Chiong, C., Grimm, K. J. & Rimm-Kaufman, S. E. (2008) Children's perceptions of the classroom environment and social and academic performance: A longitudinal analysis of the contribution of the Responsive Classroom approach. *Journal of School Psychology*, 46(2), 129–149. https://doi.org/10.1016/j.jsp.2007.02.004

Brozo, W. G., Shiel, G. & Topping, K. (2007) Engagement in reading: Lessons learned from three PISA countries. *Journal of Adolescent & Adult Literacy*, 51(4), 304–315.

Bruner, J. S. & Watson (1983) Child's talk: Learning to use language. *Child Language Teaching and Therapy*, 1(1), 111–114.

Chambers, P. (2011) Narrative and reflective practice: Recording and understanding experience. *Educational Action Research*, 11(3), 403–414. https://doi.org/10.1080/09650790300200229

Cremin, T. (2014) Reading teachers: Teachers who read and readers who teach. In T. Cremin, M. Mottram, F. Collins, S. Powell and K. Safford (Eds), *Building Communities of Engaged Readers* (pp. 67–88). Routledge.

Cremin, T. (2019) *Reading Communities: Why, What and How?* Primary Matters.

Cremin, T. & Durning, A. (2020) Inspiring a love of reading: Professional learning to develop a culture of reading for pleasure. In E. Hargreaves & L. Rolls (Eds), *Reimagining Professional Development in Schools* (pp. 122–137). Routledge.

Cremin, T., Mottram, M., Bearne, E. & Goodwin, P. (2008) Exploring teachers' knowledge of children's literature. *Cambridge Journal of Education*, 38(4), 449–464.

Cremin, T., Mottram, M., Collins, F., Powell, S. & Safford, K. (2009) Teachers as readers: Building communities of readers. *Literacy*, 43(1), 11–19.

Cron, L. (2012) *Wired for Story: The Writer's Guide to Using Brain Science to Hook Readers From the very First Sentence*. Ten Speed Press.

Csikszentmihalyi, M. (1990) *Flow: The Psychology of Optimal Experience* (Vol. 1990, p. 1). New York: Harper & Row.

DfE (Department for Education). (2023) The Reading Framework. London: Department for Education.

Dempsey, L. (2020) Understanding story read-alouds: The influence of story goal structure and event knowledge on pre-readers' inferencing abilities. *Early Child Development and Care*, 190(5), 685–697.

Dragan, P. B. (2001) *Literacy From Day One*. Westport, CT: Heinemann.

Engeser, S. (2012) Theoretical integration and future lines of flow research. *Advances in Flow Research*, 187–199.

Franzese, R. (2002) *Reading and Writing In Kindergarten: A Practical Guide*. London: Scholastic Professional Books.

Gee, J. (1991) Socio-cultural approaches to literacy (literacies). *Annual Review of Applied Linguistics*, 12, 31–48.

Goodwin, P. (1995) *Reluctant to Read?* Reading and Language Information Centre.

Guthrie, J. T., Hoa, A. L. W., Wigfield, A., Tonks, S. M., Humenick, N. M. & Littles, E. (2007) Reading motivation and reading comprehension growth in the later elementary years. *Contemporary Educational Psychology*, 32(3), 282–313. https://doi.org/10.1016/j.cedpsych.2006.05.004

Heisey, N. & Kucan, L. (2010) Introducing science concepts to primary students through read-alouds: Interactions and multiple texts make the difference. *The Reading Teacher*, 63(8), 666–676.

Kalb, G. & van Ours, J. C. (2014) Reading to young children: A head-start in life? *Economics of Education Review*, 40, 1–24.

Krashen, S. D. (2004) *The Power of Reading: Insights from the Research*. Bloomsbury Publishing USA.

Kucirkova, N., Littleton, K. & Cremin, T. (2017) Young children's reading for pleasure with digital books: Six key facets of engagement. *Cambridge Journal of Education*, 47(1), 67–84.

Kuijpers, M. M., Lusetti, M., Lendvai, P. & Rebora, S. (2024) Validation of the story world absorption scale through annotation of online book reviews. *Journal of Cultural Analytics*, *9*(1).

Mashburn, A. J., Pianta, R. C., Hamre, B. K., Downer, J. T., Barbarin, O. A., Bryant, D., Burchinal, M., Early, D. M. & Howes, C. (2008) Measures of classroom quality in prekindergarten and children's development of academic, language, and social skills. *Child Development*, 79(3), 732–749. https://doi.org/10.1111/j.1467-8624.2008.01154.x

Massaro, D. W. (2017) Reading aloud to children: Benefits and implications for acquiring literacy before schooling begins. *The American Journal of Psychology*, 130(1), 63–72. https://doi.org/10.5406/amerjpsyc.130.1.0063

Merga, M. (2016) 'I don't know if she likes reading': Are teachers perceived to be keen readers, and how is this determined? *English in Education*, 50, 255–269. https://doi.org/10.1111/eie.12126

Merga, M. K. (2017) What would make children read for pleasure more frequently? *English in Education*, 51(2), 207–223. https://doi.org/10.1111/eie.12143

McTavish, M., Streelasky, J. & Coles, L. (2012) Listening to children's voices: Children as participants in research. *International Journal of Early Childhood*, 44, 249–267.

Mooney, M. E. (1990) *Reading To, With, and By Children*. Richard C Owen Pub.

Neuman, S. B., Copple, C. & Bredekamp, S. (2000) *Learning to Read and Write: Developmentally Appropriate Practices for Young Children*. Washington, DC: National Association for the Education of Young Children.

Norton, D. E. (1990) Teaching multicultural literature in the reading curriculum. *The Reading Teacher*, 44(1), 28–40.

Pegg, L. A. & Bartelheim, F. J. (2011) Effects of daily read-alouds on students' sustained silent reading. *Current Issues in Education*, 14(2), Article 2. https://cie.asu.edu/ojs/index.php/cieatasu/article/view/771

Pratchett, T. (2003) *The Wee Free Men* (1st Ed.) New York: HarperCollins Pub.

Rasinski, T. & Padak, N. (2004) Beyond consensus—beyond balance: Toward a comprehensive literacy curriculum. *Reading & Writing Quarterly*, 20(1), 91–102.

Read, K., Rogojina, A. & Hauer-Richard, O. (2022) Rhyme over time: Vocabulary learning through daily reading aloud at home with children. *First Language*, 42(3). https://journals.sagepub.com/doi/abs/10.1177/01427237221079475

Reedy, A. & De Carvalho, R. (2021) Children's perspectives on reading, agency and their environment: What can we learn about reading for pleasure from an East London primary school? *Education, 3*–13, 49(2), 134–147.

Rog, L. J. (2001) *Early Literacy Instruction in Kindergarten.* Newark, DE: Order Department, International Reading Association.

Rushton, S. & Juola-Rushton, A. (2008) Classroom learning environment, brain research and the No Child Left Behind initiative: 6 years later. *Early Childhood Education Journal*, 36, 87–92. https://doi.org/10.1007/s10643-008-0244-5

Ryan, P. & Schatt, D. (2014) Can you describe the experience? *Storytelling, Self, Society*, 10(2), 131–155.

Schiefele, U., Schaffner, E., Möller, J. & Wigfield, A. (2012) Dimensions of reading motivation and their relation to reading behavior and competence. *Reading Research Quarterly*, 47(4), 427–463.

Smith, V. (2004) Empowering teachers: Empowering children? How can researchers initiate and research empowerment? *Journal of Research in Reading*, 27(4), 413–424.

Smith, J. K., Smith, L. F., Gilmore, A. & Jameson, M. (2012) Students' self-perception of reading ability, enjoyment of reading and reading achievement. *Learning and Individual Differences*, 22(2), 202–206.

Suggate, S. P., Lenhard, W., Neudecker, E. & Schneider, W. (2013) Incidental vocabulary acquisition from stories: Second and fourth graders learn more from listening than reading. *First Language*, 33(6), 551–571. https://doi.org/10.1177/0142723713503144

Swindells, R. (2011) *Room 13.* New York: Double Day.

The Reading Agency (2015) *Literature Review: The Impact of Reading for Pleasure and Empowerment.* BOP Consulting.

Vygotsky, L. S. (1978) *Mind in Society: Development of Higher Psychological Processes.* Cambridge, MA: Harvard University Press.

Walliams, D. & Ross, T. (2012) *Ratburger.* London: HarperColllins Children's Books.

Wells, G. (1986) *The Meaning Makers: Children Learning Language and Using Language to Learn.* Portsmouth, OH: Heinemann Educational Books Inc.

Wigfield, A. (2010) Children's motivations for reading. In J. Malloy, B. Marinak and L. Cambrell (Eds), *Essential Readings on Motivation* (pp. 13–27). Newark, DE: International Reading Association.

CHAPTER

4

Diversity and identity in a language-rich learning environment

Laurel Smith and Deb Sanders

Introduction

Language is about communicating with others and the world around us. It is the way in which we are able to articulate and share our thoughts and meanings, and the way in which we understand others. Through our lives, we learn to be skilled manipulators of language, using and adapting language in different contexts, times and places, and for different purposes. But it is more than just simply communicating. As an inherently social practice, our language learning is also entwined with our connections and relationships with others and our identities – our sense of self. Language is imbued with feelings, emotions, beliefs, values; it both reflects and shapes who we are as an individual living and interacting within our communities and wider societies. Whilst this may seem a rather grandiose and perhaps romantic way to start to consider diversity and identity in a language-rich environment, it is important because it is this understanding of the fundamental nature of language to our sense of self and relationships with others that can help us, as teachers, become reflective practitioners.

During the 20th Century, Vygotsky's and Bruner's social constructivist view firmly established learning and cognitive development as a process mediated through language and social interaction (Alexander, 2008; Bearne and Reedy, 2018; Lyle, 2008). This has clear implications for children's experiences in school as the social and cultural setting for learning, and for teachers' central role in providing language-rich opportunities which develop children's thought, knowledge and understanding (Alexander, 2008). Spoken language and talk can be seen as not just the basis for children's development in reading and writing, but 'the bedrock of children's personal, social, cultural, cognitive, creative and imaginative development' (Bearne and Reedy 2018, p13). Effective practice within language-rich learning environments recognises the interconnectedness of language (reading, writing, speaking and listening), and provides diverse opportunities for children to first and foremost talk, but also to explore each of these language modes (Bearne and Reedy, 2018; Dyson, 2020).

This chapter begins with a focus on our teacher identity in relation to language. Drawing on Laurel's doctoral research, this first section explores why such a focus is important and offers a model through which to critically reflect on your own linguistic identity, along with extracts from one student teacher participant's story within the research study. The second section moves out from these understandings to consider how our teacher identities and histories intersect with those of the

DOI: 10.4324/9781003381013-4

children we teach. Here, children's own identities, agency and linguistic diversity are considered in the context of theory and educational policy, recognising the inherent complexities and tensions this presents. The final section explores how key principles and practices can support an aim to celebrate linguistic diversity in a language-rich learning environment. A particular focus is placed on multilingual and English as an Additional Language (EAL) learners, and as a means to establish underpinning approaches to support the linguistic development of all learners.

Understanding our teacher identity in relation to language

Increasingly, we are understanding teachers' professional identities as being shaped by past experiences and beliefs about practice (Hong et al., 2017) and that the development of this professional identity is a socially constructed process (Villegas et al., 2020). Thus, there is no more important place to start this chapter than reflecting on our own language histories and experiences, home languages and dialects, and the ways in which these may change over time and in different contexts.

As teachers, our social contexts include the classrooms in which we teach, and these are places and spaces which can both shape and be shaped by our personal and professional sense of self (Sherry et al., 2019). It is important, therefore, to reflect on and understand our own personal language histories as these include the beliefs, values and experiences that can be valuable in helping to shape the kind of teacher of language and literacy that we want to be. We can do this by examining our past experiences of language – as a child, as an adult, as a learner and in our personal and professional lives – and the ways in which we use language within the classroom, including our own language use in the context of our teaching practice and the range of language opportunities we provide in our classrooms. From this reflection, we can then identify which aspects of our own language histories might provide insight and relevance to our practice, as well as those aspects which may be more challenging or demanding for us and therefore useful areas to develop through our own professional development.

SPOTLIGHT ON RESEARCH
The importance of teachers' own stories

Harold Rosen (1919–2008) made the centrality of stories within education – both for children and teachers – a fundamental part of his life's work as an educationalist, and highlights the powerful nature of telling, writing and reading stories. He called for the creation of an authentic narrative space for teachers to construct, articulate and share their stories in the context of their professional roles: 'A special place must be given to teachers telling their own stories, including those of their lives as teachers, as a constructive point for curriculum reform' (Rosen, 2017, p195). Whilst the extent to which this has happened is a question for debate beyond the scope of this chapter, it indicates how rich and illuminating the use of stories can be as part of teachers' reflective practices: '*Thus in the art of articulating autobiography we do not simply unmask ourselves for others, we too await to know the face under the mask*' (Rosen, 2017, p442).

Supporting critical reflection

You may find the following reflective model helpful to support you in exploring your linguistic identity as a teacher. The model begins with the use of short reflective autobiographical narratives as the starting point and stimulus for this process, which are important because our stories are who we are and how we navigate and shape the world around us (Rosen, 2017). Entwined with our relationships with others and other voices within our sense of self, they can be seen as articulations of the teacher self in the past, present and future (Henry, 2019). Telling or writing some of our autobiographical stories helps us consider our own relationship with and experiences of language, and is then explored through a visual mapping approach which is a way of 'seeing' and 'navigating' the landscapes of your professional identity in relation to language.

It is worth noting that teachers' professional identity construction is a dynamic process in that teachers experience ongoing transformations in their identity construction throughout their careers, but that this is most pronounced during their early years of training and teaching (Henry, 2019; Solari and Ortega, 2022). Henry (2019) suggests that for teachers at the beginning of their careers, the future-oriented aspect of this dynamic process is particularly strong as they imagine different possible self-identities. The final step of the reflective process, then, is identifying what you want your future practice and identity in a language-rich learning environment to be:

- What language experiences do you want to provide for the children you teach and why do you believe this is important?
- What kind of language role model do you want to be, and how might this help the children you teach to develop their own linguistic identities in a diverse and engaging culture of classroom language and literacy learning?

Finally, whilst core beliefs form the basis of our teacher identity, these continue to be shaped and changed through experience (Wyk, 2011). Thus, once created, your map is a potentially useful tool to return to, reflect on and add further layers of experience as you continue to develop your practice.

PROMPTS FOR CRITICAL REFLECTION

Reflecting on your linguistic identity as a teacher: a reflective model

Reflective autobiographical writing

Choose an experience from your past or present (e.g. as a child/adult in your home or community, as a learner or as a teacher) and spend 10–30 minutes writing about this experience: How did it make you feel and why do think that was? Who else was part of this experience and how did language connect you in that moment? What sticks in your mind about that time, place, context, and how did that shape the language you used? Why do you feel it was/is significant for you then and now?

Repeat this process to reflect on at least two or three significant memories. Remember, these don't need to be long pieces of writing – you may feel more comfortable just noting down key thoughts and ideas in response to the previous questions, and you may wish to simply spend 10 minutes on this at a time and keep returning to it.

Visual mapping

Using your narratives as a starting point, start to create a visual map based on Figure 4.1. Add key words and phrases to each of your map's key areas (past and present experiences) and then consider the connections – or pathways – between these language experiences. The idea is to gain a sense of 'stepping back' and reflective 'viewpoint'. This can be as detailed or simplistic as you like, but if you want to create a more detailed map you might want to consider using a key to further reflect on your professional teacher identity in relation to language. For example, identifying different types of landscape (forests, lakes, mountains, etc.), using arrows to show connections and interactions with others, adding weather symbols to show lightning-bolt 'a-ha!' moments or aspects which perhaps created stormy feelings of tension and conflict.

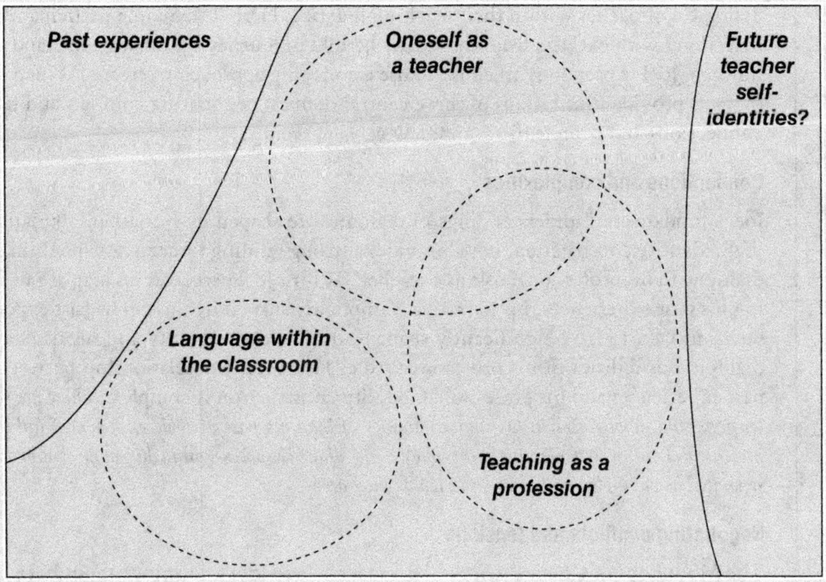

Figure 4.1 Visual map

Current and future self-identities

Finally, reflect on your map and consider what this means for your current professional identity, or the meanings you make of yourself as a teacher of language and literacy, and how you imagine your professional self in the future. Again, add key words and phrases to these areas on your map. What does this mean for you in terms or your professional development, your practice, your pedagogical and subject knowledge and the language environment within your classroom? How might you draw on the practices explored within this chapter, and the rest of this book, to realise your 'imaginings' and aspirations for yourself and the children you teach?

Teachers' professional identities: exploring dialogic experiences, spaces and possibilities

Drawing on Laurel's doctoral research, the following *Spotlight on research* presents an extract from one student teacher participant's story within the research study, as he reflects on his linguistic and professional identity.

SPOTLIGHT ON RESEARCH

Exploring linguistic identity

In this research study, I worked with two student teachers to explore and reflect on their linguistic identities using the reflective model set out earlier. Whilst the reflective model can be used to consider language more broadly, my study focused specifically on understanding how student teachers' own dialogic experiences might shape and influence dialogic approaches within their teaching practice. Here, I share one participant's visual map along with extracts from the stories he told of journeying through the landscape of his map. Joel (a pseudonym) chose to use a collaging approach to create his map and the extracts provide illustrations of three central themes: negotiating conflicts and tensions; connections and complexities; and new ways of seeing.

Connections and complexities

Joel's fundamental understandings of dialogue are shaped by his father, a key figure in Joel's identity construction, who 'provides a strong guiding force in how he thinks about dialogue in his professional role as a teacher'. Whilst Joel perceives his map as not including his past experiences, his narrative is implicitly shaped by these. His past experiences seem, in fact, to have significantly shaped both his own identity and his navigation of dialogic possibilities in his professional role. However, the relationship between these past experiences and his professional identity construction is complex: *There are conflicts, tensions and ambiguities in his understandings of how his past dialogic experiences influence his present and future self-identities; the places and dialogic spaces within his map cannot be easily separated as entangled and interconnected as they are.*

Negotiating conflicts and tensions

The Mountains of Change seem to be a space where Joel's meanings about both himself as a teacher and teaching as a profession are negotiated. It is wrought with conflict and tension between the voiced positions of institutional and political discourse – 'the restraints of policy, curriculum, time' – and the excitement, uncertainty and freedom that he wants to draw on from the voiced position of his own personal journey of growth. However, Joel is not a passive figure within this landscape; he makes choices and decisions in relation to dialogue, professional practice and identity: *Joel seems to find a strong sense of transformation, affirmation and – importantly – agency...Through this ongoing, dynamic negotiation, he moves forward purposefully to embrace his future professional self-identities.*

New ways of seeing

As he moves further into the forest, Joel reflects that although this central area of his map joins the rest of the areas together, he had left it blank until the very end of his map-making. Could this perhaps be because he wanted to leave the past behind, he wonders? To not dwell on it, to move forward? But this explanation doesn't seem to satisfy Joel either. As he leads us further down this reflective path, he tries out different words in his attempt to understand and articulate what this area means to him and his professional identity: 'Not purgatory [laughter] that is far too extreme. Limbo!' Then, as if entering a clearing filled with sunlight, he reaches a moment of realisation:

> Ah! Thinking about it actually, this is you, this is to be filled in, this is a blank canvas. This is what comes from these experiences...And perhaps that's why it was blank, yeah, that makes sense. I think that there's something personal for the individual to fill in.

Children's identity, agency and linguistic diversity

The previous section described how our own identity as a teacher is shaped by language experiences. In this section, we consider how teachers' identities and histories intersect with those of the children they teach. This has particular significance for multilingual and EAL learners who come to our classrooms with unique linguistic backgrounds and needs, and we consider this in more detail within the final section of this chapter. However, every child we teach brings their own individual language experiences and histories, and so the focus in this section is on language in relation to children's identities more broadly. As previously noted, language is not just about *communicating* with others and the world around us, it is a central part of an inherently social practice. For the children we teach, their language learning also encompasses their relationships, identities and sense of self. Thus, our classrooms are, in themselves, ongoing and dynamic sites of negotiation through language, linguistic experiences and interactions with others. Here, we explore children's identity and agency within the context of language-rich learning environments, then consider current debates around standard English and the challenges this presents for children's linguistic diversity.

Voice and agency: recognising diverse literacies within and beyond the classroom

Just as our language histories and experiences are a fundamental part of our identity as teachers, for the children we teach language is entwined with their own identities – the language they experience *inside* the classroom and the language they use, engage with, speak, listen to, read and write *outside* the classroom. Research is increasingly understanding children's linguistic development as fundamentally connected to their identities, where linguistic interactions are the way in which identity is co-constructed (García-Mateus and Palmer, 2017). This challenges the predominant focus on language development as purely concerning skills and knowledge, and on language learning as a primarily pedagogical concern for teachers. Instead, language is positioned as mediating the construction of self (Alexander, 2008) and identity is positioned as socially co-constructed (Sherry et al., 2019). Consequently, classroom language and dialogue can be understood as both shaping and being shaped by teachers' and children's conceptions of self (Sherry et al., 2019). The linguistic environments – the spoken, written and multimodal language and linguistic opportunities – we create in our classrooms, then, need to provide spaces and opportunities for children to use, explore, manipulate and play with language in ways that reflect their identities. The ethos and culture of our classrooms should reflect the diversity of the children within them and the wider communities and societies within which our children live (Dyson, 2020).

SPOTLIGHT ON RESEARCH

'Mirrors, windows, and sliding glass doors'

Through reading, children should be able to see their own identities represented as well as immerse themselves in worlds that are different from their own, supporting them to explore and experience other realities. This diversity in children's literature is a particularly powerful aspect of an inclusive classroom and highlights the importance of children encountering a range of identity markers – including race, disability, sexuality and socio-economic status – in the books they read (McNair and Edwards, 2021). In her groundbreaking article (1990), Bishop conceptualised the power of this diversity as being like 'mirrors, windows, and sliding glass doors' and this analogy continues to shape our understanding in education today:

> Books are sometimes windows, offering views of worlds that may be real or imagined, familiar or strange. These windows are also sliding glass doors,

> and readers have only to walk through in imagination to become part of whatever world has been created or recreated by the author. When lighting conditions are just right, however, a window can also be a mirror. Literature transforms human experience and reflects it back to us, and in that reflection we can see our own lives and experiences as part of the larger human experience. Reading, then, becomes a means of self-affirmation, and readers often seek their mirrors in books (Bishop, 1990, cited in McNair and Edwards, 2021, p207).

Official and unofficial literacies

Dyson (2008) refers to children's dual language experiences within and outside the classroom as 'official' and 'unofficial' literacies. This points to a potentially problematic framing of language within the English curriculum, which is limited in its recognition of the rich language many children experience within their homes and communities. This issue, combined with the centrality of language in learning and identity construction, suggests the need to challenge a deficit view of children's home languages and language practices by understanding that 'every child has some unique experience or resource to offer and deserves respect ... and, indeed, an opportunity to share themselves with others' (Dyson, 2020, p12). Recognising that children come with a wealth of linguistic experiences and understandings – albeit not necessarily those which fit the relatively narrow conceptualisations of 'official' literacies within the curriculum – opens our practice up to the possibility of a broader understanding of children's identities, agency and linguistic diversity. The diversity of children's 'unofficial' language experiences offers a rich and valuable resource within the classroom and can contribute to the development of a language-rich environment for all children.

An inclusive approach to language, then, is one that aspires to celebrate and value diversity, in all its varied cultural, racial, ethnic and social forms. Consequently, an inclusive linguistic classroom is one in which children are encouraged and given opportunities to share their home languages, vocabularies and dialects in spoken and written forms. It is a space that embraces broad understandings of literacy practices and children's 'unofficial' literacies (Dyson, 2008), and recognises language as a key part of supporting children's agency. Alexander (2008, p35) asserts that '"voice" ... is about empowerment' and equates spoken language with the ability to challenge falsehoods and hold those in power to account (see also Avis and Hesmondhalgh, this volume). He suggests that the communicative rights established within the classroom have implications far beyond its four walls, but addressing the inherently unbalanced teacher–child power dynamics within our 'inherited educational culture' (Alexander, 2008, p18) is no easy task. It is no coincidence that in considering the challenges of moving towards a more democratic and dialogic approach to talk and spoken language, researchers have highlighted the significant power shifts this requires (see for example, Alexander, 2008; Lyle, 2008): having a voice is a powerful thing. It is perhaps these issues of power and agency that make the role of language in teaching practice a complex area. Indeed, giving more power to children can sometimes feel like relinquishing control – an especially difficult idea in an education system dictated by high-stakes testing, rigid accountability and hierarchical control. However, as Larrivee (2000, p293) asserts, as teachers we must 'find ways to create authentic learning communities by adjusting the power dynamics to turn power *over* into power *with* learners'.

PROMPTS FOR CRITICAL REFLECTION

Reflecting on the power of language within society

Significant events in the world, society and communities in which we live can often draw attention to the power of language. Consider, for example, that in our recent social history events such as Covid-19, the Black Lives Matter movement, #MeToo and the Climate Crisis have brought into sharp relief both the benefits of rich linguistic experiences and the huge challenges we still face as a society to ensure everyone has a voice. As teachers, reflecting on significant events within the world around us and the children we teach and what these particular events draw attention to, in relation to the power of language, can deepen our understanding of language within our classroom.

Questions for discussion and reflection:

1 How did Covid-19, or other significant events, affect your experiences of language and communication with others? What about the children and families you know, or teach?

2 What does this suggest to you about the role of language within 'official' literacies within school, and how these connect or disconnect from the 'unofficial' literacy realm (Dyson, 2008)? What does this suggest about the power of language within schools and communities?

3 What other significant events have resonated with you in some way and how was language a part of this? How might these events have shaped your perceptions around language?

Standard English and the policy discourse

The political and ideological questions Alexander (2008) raises – about the power of language to challenge falsehoods and hold those in power to account – have particular resonance when considering the status of standard English within our classrooms. Policy discourse has long resisted more democratic conceptualisations of language in favour of a social class model giving prominence to standard English (Coultas, 2015). Historically, policy and the narrow definitions of standard English favoured by politicians has been at odds with broader sociolinguistic conceptualisations which frame language as a democratic notion within progressive ideologies (Coultas, 2015; Jones, 2017). Cox's (1992, cited in Coultas, 2015, p78) assertion that Margaret Thatcher chose 'to delete the words "where appropriate" at the end of a sentence that stated that children should be taught to use standard English' particularly seems to highlight the policy agendas of reducing language to matters of correctness, elocution and the 'superiority of standard English'.

Within educational reform, language is a tool to enact change and/or maintain existing educational ideas and agendas, communicating philosophical ideas and political ideologies (Nordin and Sundberg, 2018). Thus, policy reflects the power of language to shape social constructs (Hyatt, 2013) and establish truth and value which privileges some ideas and speakers over others (Ball, 2013). Since the mid-1990s, policy reform has been driven by fundamentally conservative philosophies and ideas, and global capitalism and the knowledge economy has shaped what can be understood as a neoliberal marketisation of education (Ball, 2013; Bates et al., 2011). These ideological drivers and the language of policy reform appear to be in conflict with social justice agendas and advance narratives of economic usefulness and accountability through measurable standards (Hyatt, 2013). Comparisons of educational performance data through the

OECD's Programme for International Student Assessment (PISA) and national Standardised Attainment Tests (SATs) have helped to drive a narrow focus on measurable standards in reading and writing. This, alongside policy discourse which reflects seemingly narrow views of what is valued within education, has arguably left us with an English curriculum which broadly lacks recognition of wider views of literacy, language or linguistic diversity.

Cushing (2020, p443) argues that the issues around policy discourse and language in UK classrooms, highlighted earlier, reflect in essence a 'policing' of children's language usage. He suggests that whilst the standardisation of language within education has received much vocal criticism from linguists, less attention has been paid to the socio-political discourse surrounding conceptualisations and stigmatisations of language within schools. Linguistic diversity is not just the multiple home languages that children in our class may identify with, but also the range of accents, dialects and 'unofficial' (Dyson, 2008) languages that they bring to the linguistic environment of the classroom. Curricula that focus on standardised languages can lead to a linguistic ideology which views language as being fixed and easily delineated (Cushing, 2021). As the recognised and approved linguistic form of academia, law and professional spaces, standard English is promoted as a correct form of language usage and carries with it a sense of prestige. Thus, it perpetuates the ideologies and power of social groups that represent white, western, male and middle-upper class perspectives, whilst at the same time excluding, subordinating and disparaging non-standardised forms (Cushing, 2021).

The ideological perspectives embedded within this idea of 'standard English' can also be seen in the current focus on closing the 'word gap'. Here, the reduction of 'language' to simply 'words' is interlinked with a deficit view of marginalised children's language and literacy practices (Cushing, 2022). As Cushing notes, these ideologies within the UK are about race, socioeconomic status and social class, where 'low-income and racialized speakers' language practices are perceived as deficient, incomplete, and indeed, full of gaps when compared against the language practices of the idealized white middle-classes' (2022, p2). Thus, he argues, interventions to 'address' such a word gap are actually about changing behaviour, language and culture which is firmly positioned as both a deficiency and the primary cause of social inequity. Understanding this broader policy context is important, then, if we wish to embrace linguistic diversity within our classrooms and resist policy drivers which seek to 'suppress, control, and regulate stigmatised forms of English in the classroom through oral or written "corrections"'(Cushing, 2020, p426).

PROMPTS FOR CRITICAL REFLECTION

Questions for discussion and reflection:

1. How might you, as a teacher, challenge a deficit view of children's 'unofficial' languages (Dyson, 2008) and instead embrace and celebrate these as a positive place to build from in the classroom?
2. What communicative rights do you think children have within primary classrooms, and why do you think this might be? How might you *move towards* more equal communicative rights and what challenges might this present – for you and for children themselves?
3. What are your perspectives on Cushing's (2020) view that focusing on standard English within the classroom actually results in something akin to the policing of language and language use? How might you balance the use of standard English with valuing linguistic diversity within the classroom, and what might this mean for your practice?

Celebrating linguistic diversity in language-rich learning environments

In the previous sections we have considered how language learning is fundamentally a social practice, reflected on language within teachers' professional identities and how this might shape the kinds of linguistic environments we create in our classrooms, and explored language in relation to children's identities, sense of voice and agency. In this final section, we focus on what celebrating linguistic diversity in language-rich learning environments might look like in practice. We begin by considering the specific principles and practices which underpin the effective teaching and support of multilingual and EAL learners. A case study, drawn from the experiences of a Primary PGCE student, invites you to reflect on how these principles shaped her developing practice in relation to supporting two EAL children within her placement class. Finally, Deb draws from her experiences as an Education Consultant and retired Executive Primary Head to provide practical ideas for developing your own teaching practice within a language-rich learning environment.

Principles and practice for teaching multilingual and English as an Additional Language (EAL) learners

Multilingual and EAL learners come to our classrooms with unique linguistic backgrounds and needs, and, as we have already acknowledged, this linguistic diversity is also a fundamental part of their identities as learners. Consequently, it is important that we recognise and develop our understanding of how we can support this positively within our classrooms. Lucas et al. (2008) assert that for EAL learners, their linguistic development in English is inextricably linked with the content and language of the school curriculum, and the multiple modes of language – speaking, listening, reading and writing – through which learning takes places in the classroom. For this reason, it is a complex process but one that does not often form a significant part of Initial Teacher Education (ITE) for mainstream teachers. We highlight the following six key principles for developing practice which celebrate diversity and support multilingual children (Lucas et al., 2008):

1. There is a fundamental difference between proficiency in conversational and academic language, the latter of which takes significantly more time to become fluent in.
2. To support the development of English language learners (ELLs), teachers need to provide opportunities for learning which are just beyond their existing skills, knowledge and understanding in English, and in ways that allow them to apply this in meaningful and purposeful ways.
3. Actively participating in social interaction is a fundamental way in which ELLs develop both their conversational and academic language skills.
4. Fluency, proficiency and confidence in ELLs' native language skills is directly related to their ability to achieve the same linguistic proficiency in English.
5. Creating a learning environment with a safe and welcoming ethos, and a culture which promotes a sense of belonging for ELLs and minimises feelings of anxiety, is essential for learning.
6. Teaching which makes explicit an understanding of form and function within the language usage and learning in the classroom is key to the development of linguistic proficiency for ELLs.

The following case study demonstrates how these key principles for teaching multilingual learners can be applied within the classroom. It draws on the voice and experiences of a primary student teacher, Rachel (a pseudonym), who I worked with as a senior lecturer during her PGCE course. As you read, consider how Lucas et al.'s (2008) principles are reflected in the approach Rachel took and the ways in which she developed her practice.

CASE STUDY FOCUS

Magic moments of linguistic inclusion

Rachel was working in a Year 4 class and wanted to develop her support for two Ukrainian children during English lessons. The case study is organised into three sections: noticing is an important first step, as teachers need to understand, through careful observation and consideration, which aspects of the language and learning is presenting challenges for EAL learners; acting then focuses on how implementing both pedagogical strategies and a shift in beliefs and attitudes can respond to what has been noticed; finally, reflecting highlights the importance of applying a reflective approach to our own teaching practices, in order to evaluate the impact of these and identify implications for practice going forward.

Noticing

Rachel had noticed that the two Ukrainian children were struggling to engage with the challenging and complex language within whole-class text. Whilst the two children were progressing well with phonics and reading interventions, they were struggling to apply this to the lesson content and text, which was leading to disengagement from the learning and the class community. She identified that the children were relatively confident with sentence structure but needed support to widen and extend their vocabulary knowledge. She also wondered about the impact of the children sitting with strong oral communicators but separately from each other.

Acting

After discussing the issue with a colleague and reflecting on what might be most helpful to support these children, Rachel planned the following approaches to try out in an upcoming lesson:

- Generating a Ukrainian translation of a text extract (using 'tools' in Word), she sent this bilingual text home with the children a week before the lesson, along with a bilingual list of the key spellings for the unit of literacy learning.
- The day before the lesson, Rachel carried out a quick (5–10-minute) pre-teach to embed the grammatical understanding needed and as a formative assessment opportunity.
- She moved the children to sit opposite each other, with confident English speakers as their shoulder partners, and encouraged them to support each other in using their first language knowledge and understanding when accessing the English text.
- At the beginning of the lesson, she revealed an image with the Ukrainian word alongside and asked the two children to teach this to the rest of the class.
- During the lesson, the two children had access to bilingual resources: the text extract, the list of key spellings and a word bank to support descriptive writing.

Reflecting

Rachel reflected that one of the most striking ways in which these approaches impacted on the children was in their sense of belonging. Sharing the Ukrainian vocabulary first and asking them to teach this to the class was simple but effective and generated real excitement for both the Ukrainian children and the wider class. This excitement was also noticeable when they were given the bilingual resources to take home in advance of the lesson. Seating the children opposite each other meant they were able to talk to each other in Ukrainian prior to and during the writing process, to check meaning and develop confidence and independence within the tasks. Importantly, they were accessing the same learning and working towards the same learning objective as the rest of the class, creating a sense of belonging and participation.

Previously, the children had been predominantly writing in Ukrainian and copying some English words. During this lesson and the units of learning which followed (when Rachel applied the same approaches) they were instead able to write full sentences independently in English, which had a significant impact on their sense of success and achievement. Rachel found she was able to withdraw the scaffolding and reduce the pre-teach interventions gradually with a lasting impact on their writing. Whilst she felt a little overwhelmed initially, understanding how technology could help with supporting the children made it manageable and took very little additional time. She reflects that the impact was immediate and significant: visible, tangible and emotive, it was a magical moment for Rachel in her developing practice and for the two children's sense of belonging within the learning environment.

***

This example illustrates the importance of both understanding the particular barriers EAL children might face and establishing a classroom ethos which values and builds on the rich language skills children have in their home languages. Before acting, Rachel built up a picture of these two learners to understand which aspects of English they were finding most challenging, as well as what was already in place to support them. Much of what Rachel then put in place focused on supporting the children to use the proficiency in their native language to develop their English language skills – e.g. the bilingual text and word bank, seating the children together – and, importantly, this approach also created a much stronger sense of belonging. Using carefully planned scaffolding – e.g. the pre-teach and sentence stems – Rachel supported them to work just beyond their existing knowledge and skills, so that the children could develop both their skills and confidence. In the next part, we develop these ideas further by considering how these same key principles can be applied more broadly to our teaching in a language-rich learning environment.

Teaching in a language-rich learning environment

The six principles highlighted by Lucas et al. (2008) can guide your understanding of how to support the progress and development of multilingual and EAL learners. However, these principles can also help us to support all children's development by removing barriers, planning for targeted language development and scaffolding and supporting language development and achievement. The following pedagogical approaches draw on Deb Sanders's insight and experience and aim to provide effective teaching strategies which support the linguistic development of all learners. They offer practical ways to create a language-rich environment within your classroom and to champion this more widely within your school. These pedagogical approaches are organised into five areas: celebrating and valuing linguistic diversity; creating an ethos and culture of talk; scaffolding and supporting linguistic development; targeted language development; and your role as the teacher. For each of these areas, we provide a summary of key aspects to consider, followed by a selection of ideas to support and implement within your classroom practice.

Celebrating and valuing linguistic diversity reflects a core belief that our classrooms should provide a safe, inclusive and language-rich learning environment. To do this effectively, we need to understand what children bring to the learning environment, and so developing your understanding of children's linguistic knowledge, skills and backgrounds is essential. Understanding multilingual learners' linguistic and academic backgrounds is key to effectively supporting their progress and development (Lucas et al., 2008), and The Bell Foundation suggests that getting to know your EAL children and their families and providing opportunities for them to share information about themselves in a range of different ways is an important first step for creating a learner profile. This approach is equally important for understanding how all children within your class engage with language at home, helping to challenge the exclusion of 'unofficial' literacies within our classrooms (Dyson, 2008) and resist a deficit view which marginalises children's home language learning and environments (Cushing, 2022). Once you have built a picture of the linguistic and cultural diversity within your class, you can value and celebrate this within the classroom environment, and ensure multilingualism is seen as an asset within your classroom, a core principle of effective EAL teaching practice according to The Bell Foundation (n.d.).

IDEAS FOR CLASSROOM PRACTICE
Celebrating and valuing linguistic diversity

- Play 'Getting to know you' games and give children opportunities to share information about themselves by creating posters, drawings and collages.
- Language Rivers: children draw, collage and make notes (this could be scribed) about the kinds of reading, writing, speaking and listening activities they engage with at home.
- Create multilingual and multicultural working walls and displays.
- Provide resources for EAL children to access learning in their first language – e.g. books, videos, factsheets, vocabulary banks.
- If possible, provide opportunities for children to work collaboratively with their home language peers.

Creating an ethos and culture of talk within your classroom is fundamental to creating a language-rich learning environment, but we cannot assume that effective talk will simply happen. Developing children's spoken language skills needs to be explicitly planned for and supported, including providing opportunities for meaningful and purposeful talk, which is particularly important for supporting multilingual learners (Lucas et al., 2008). This, of course, can and should be considered in learning across the curriculum; however, the teaching of reading provides rich opportunities for supporting children to engage in talk. Book talk – both informal book talk with peers and more structured, formal opportunities with the teacher – and dialogic reading approaches, such as reciprocal reading, are an extremely valuable way to support a culture of talk and develop children's spoken language skills.

IDEAS FOR CLASSROOM PRACTICE
Creating an ethos and culture of talk

- Co-construct ground rules for talk with your class and revisit these regularly.
- When engaging in talk activities, provide specific roles for children, with particular consideration for how EAL learners can effectively access the task.
- Use structured approaches to organise talk activities and plan time to clearly explain the structure and provide opportunities for children to practice this.
- Set up 'conversation stations' which provide a focused talk topic, key vocabulary and talk frames/sentence stems to support children's dialogue.
- Use concept cartoons to provide a clear focus for discussion around a particular topic.
- Establish book clubs: friendship groups of three choose and read a book together then discuss in weekly structured, but child-led, sessions – e.g. main idea, questions, connections, vocabulary.
- Support children's book talk using Aiden Chambers' 'Tell Me...' approach (Chambers, 1993) by structuring discussion around likes, dislikes, questions and connections.

Scaffolding and supporting children's linguistic development can be effectively achieved in a wide range of different ways – what you use and when will need to be informed by a secure understanding of the language needs within your class. Fundamentally, a language-rich learning environment should be underpinned by high expectations for all children, with appropriate language support rather than simplified curriculum content (The Bell Foundation, n.d.). For EAL learners, it is important to identify the specific language demands inherent in learning tasks and whether scaffolding is required for individual children (Lucas et al., 2008). Establishing the use of language structures and sentence stems is an important way to support all children to articulate, extend and deepen their thinking, by challenging them to share their reasoning and use more complex language structures.

IDEAS FOR CLASSROOM PRACTICE
Scaffolding and supporting linguistic development

- Support EAL learners new to English and SEN (Special Educational Needs) children with particular language barriers with visual cue cards when communicating orally and substitution tables/sentence builders for cross-curricular talk/writing activities.
- Use speaking and writing frames/sentence stems/language structures to support all children to articulate and extend their thinking orally and when writing.
- Use a talk rubric/framework for talk to assess children's spoken language skills and identify next steps – these can be used by the teacher and for self/peer-assessment as a child-friendly version (see The Bell Foundation, n.d.).
- Use graphic organisers to support children to organise and re-construct key information that they have either read or heard.

- Provide vocabulary banks, key questions, key concepts and models to support learning.
- Provide opportunities for EAL children to draw on their home language through the use of pre-teaching, bilingual word banks and texts, and opportunities to first write in their native language.

Example of sentence stems: language of opinion – sharing your views:

Bronze

I think … because …
I prefer… because …
My partner thinks …
I agree because …
I disagree because …

Silver

I agree/disagree because …
I understand x's opinion because … as …
However, I feel … because/as …
My opinion/view is … because/as …
I believe … because …

Gold

I appreciate …'s opinion because/as/due to …
However, I feel differently because/as/due to …
Most reasonable people would agree that … because
Therefore/In my opinion/I believe …

Targeted language development can help to ensure children are given opportunities to develop specific aspects of their language usage. For EAL learners, this should include an integrated focus on content and language, where relevant grammar and language structures are taught in the context of specific subject curriculum content (The Bell Foundation, n.d.). Particular consideration should be given to supporting children's knowledge and understanding of vocabulary: structured approaches to teaching vocabulary and explicitly planning for vocabulary development across the curriculum should consider the selection, teaching, application and reviewing of new vocabulary. Language games play an important role and there are a range of resources to support this in the context of literacy teaching. What we might consider 'traditional' games – e.g. 20 Questions and Simon Says – are also invaluable for supporting children's speaking and listening skills, as well as providing opportunities to apply key vocabulary.

IDEAS FOR CLASSROOM PRACTICE

Targeting language development

- Pre-teach key vocabulary using flashcards with pictures and/or words.
- Create a 'word wall' for adding subject-specific vocabulary, or 'word pots' to collect and revisit key vocabulary.

- Introduce new vocabulary through a targeted '5-minute teach' approach: model, say, act and repeat the word.
- Shades of meaning: using paint swatch colour cards, children order words from 'most' to 'least' – e.g. strongest/weakest, interesting/boring, saddest/happiest, richest/poorest, etc.
- Create vocabulary matching games – e.g. word/picture cards, synonyms.
- Provide opportunities for children to create 'word mats': key word, definition in child's own words, a drawing to represent the word, an example of the word in a sentence, linked words.
- Play 'barrier games' in pairs: one child describes their image (e.g. image of a shape, a map) and the other child identifies and/or draws it.

Your role as the teacher is key to creating a language-rich learning environment: you establish the ethos and principles for learning within your classroom. A fundamental belief, then, must be that the linguistic backgrounds and experiences of each child within your class are valuable and worth celebrating. As the primary language role model in your classroom, you can model this belief by creating a culture and ethos of respect and belonging, supporting children's language needs and scaffolding the linguistic development of learners (Lucas et al., 2008). Through the linguistic opportunities your classroom provides, you can minimise potential anxiety for children and support the positive co-construction of identity (García-Mateus and Palmer, 2017).

Working effectively with parents and carers requires careful consideration, but ensuring your communication with parents – including those of EAL learners – is inclusive supports the principle of social inclusion (The Bell Foundation, n.d.). Fortunately, we now have access to a range of translation software and apps that make providing bilingual newsletters, for example, much easier. For all learners, valuing parents, carers and children's home language environments means authentic and purposeful opportunities for communication and social interactions, access to rich language experiences and equitable opportunities for participation (Lucas et al., 2008) can be extended from your classroom out, to the wider school community.

IDEAS FOR CLASSROOM PRACTICE
Considering your role as teacher

- Reflect on, evaluate and adapt your 'teacher talk': consider whether it is clear and concise, and if you are taking account of EAL learners, remove unnecessary words and make sure instructions and explanations are clear.
- Explicitly plan for 'thinking aloud' within your lessons to model language structures, vocabulary, questions and explanations.
- Rather than continuously correcting children's language usage, rephrase and recast what children say, modelling the language structures and vocabulary you want them to use.
- Plan for opportunities to engage in extended dialogue and shared thinking with children, where you collaboratively explore an idea, text or topic and co-construct knowledge through language.

- Provide language and talk focused newsletters for families which include key vocabulary and talking points.
- Create excitement about words and language, by organising 'vocabulary assemblies' or a dressing up day when children – and teaching staff! – come dressed up as their favourite word.

Useful resources and links

- NALDIC: https://naldic.org.uk/
- The Bell Foundation: www.bell-foundation.org.uk/eal-programme/
- Voice 21: https://voice21.org/
- EAL MESH Guide: www.meshguides.org/guides/node/112
- The Talk-Rich Reading Project: https://research.reading.ac.uk/talk-rich-teaching/
- The Communication Trust's Speech, Language and Communication Framework: www.slcframework.org.uk/
- Talk4Writing: www.talk4writing.com/
- Kagan Co-operative Learning Structures: www.kaganonline.com/
- Word Aware books: https://thinkingtalking.co.uk/word-aware/
- The Lost Words, by Robert Macfarlane and Jackie Morris: www.thelostwords.org/lostwordsbook/
- Descriptosaurus: https://shop.talk4writing.com/products/descriptosaurus
- Collins Cobuild Primary Learner Dictionary: https://grammar.collinsdictionary.com/english-usage

Chapter summary

In this chapter, we have first considered and explored how our own identity as a teacher, and our personal relationship with language, might influence and shape how we think about and enact language within our classroom and teaching practice. From this, we have reflected on the important role that language plays in children's own identities and identity construction, and how the classrooms that they learn in can support a sense of their voice and agency. Understanding wider policy discourses, particularly in relation to standard English, is important if we are to challenge potential deficit views and instead value and celebrate the rich and varied languages and language experiences that the children in our class bring. Finally, we have considered what these ideas and principles might and could look like in practice. This provided a focus specifically on the needs of multilingual and EAL learners, but also demonstrated how embedding these principles within our practice can help us support all children to become confident, critical and effective language users. The examples, illustrations and practical strategies will hopefully support you to also become confident, critical and effective in your approach to teaching, celebrating and valuing language as a teacher.

As we come to the end of this chapter, it is important to reflect on the significance of the different aspects of language, identity, linguistic diversity and language-rich learning environments that we have considered. The fundamental understanding of language being inherently bound up in our identities and language learning as being a social process (Alexander, 2008) demands that we move beyond our thinking about the language within our classrooms as being simply a question of skills and pedagogy. It is much, much more than this. It is our connection with others and the world around us. It is the way in which we think and feel, and it shapes our core beliefs and values. It reflects and shapes our sense of self, as an individual and within the wider community, society and world in which we live.

Consequently, the language learning and environments within our classrooms should aim to reflect the diversity of the world around us and to recognise the power of language to change the lives of the children we teach. The literal silence within schools during the weeks of closure due to Covid-19 highlighted the fundamental role teachers and school communities play in the language development of children across the country and indeed the world. This period in our shared social history clearly demonstrated the benefits of rich linguistic experiences – both within the 'official' and 'unofficial' literacy realms (Dyson, 2008) – and the importance of providing spaces for children to speak, listen, question, wonder and share their thoughts and feelings with others. If anything, this means that, more than ever, understanding diversity and identity as part of language-rich learning environments must be a central purpose within our schools' curriculum provision and culture. As teachers, we must reflect on the privileged position we have in providing rich linguistic experiences for children which enable them to engage critically in a rapidly changing world, use language effectively to work and live with others and with the confidence and power to use their voices and to be heard.

References

Alexander, R. (2008). *Towards Dialogic Teaching: Rethinking Classroom Talk* (4th Ed.). Dialogos UK Ltd.

Ball, S. J. (2013). *The Education Debate* (2nd Ed.). Bristol: The Policy Press.

Bates, J., Lewis, S. & Pickard, A. (2011). *Education Policy, Practice and the Professional*. London: Continuum International Publishing Group.

Bearne, E. & Reedy, D. (2018). *Teaching Primary English: Subject Knowledge and Classroom Practice*. Abingdon: Routledge.

Chambers, A. (1993). *Tell Me: Children, Reading & Talk*. Stroud: Thimble

Coultas, V. (2015). Revisiting debates on oracy: Classroom talk – moving towards a democratic pedagogy? *Changing English*, 22(1), 72–86.

Cushing, I. (2020). The policy and policing of language in schools. *Language in Society*, 49(3), 425–450.

Cushing, I. (2021). 'Say it like the Queen': The standard language ideology and language policy making in English primary schools. *Language, Culture and Curriculum*, 34(3), 321–336.

Cushing, I. (2022). Word rich or word poor? Deficit discourses, raciolinguistic ideologies and the resurgence of the 'word gap' in England's education policy. *Critical Inquiry in Language Studies*, 1–27.

Dyson, A. H. (2008). Research directions: The pine cone wars: Studying writing in a community of children. *Language Arts*, 85(4), 305–315.

Dyson, A. H. (2020). 'We're playing sisters, on paper!': Children composing on graphic playgrounds. *Literacy*, 54(2), 3–12.

García-Mateus, S. & Palmer, D. (2017). Translanguaging pedagogies for positive identities in two-way dual language bilingual education. *Journal of Language, Identity, and Education*, 16(4), 245–255.

Henry, A. (2019). A drama of selves: Investigating teacher identity development from dialogical and complexity perspectives. *Studies in Second Language Learning and Teaching*, 9(2), 263–285.

Hong, J., Greene, B. & Lowery, J. (2017). Multiple dimensions of teacher identity development from pre-service to early years of teaching: a longitudinal study: JET. *Journal of Education for Teaching*, 43(1), 84–98.

Hyatt, D. (2013). The critical policy discourse frame: Helping doctoral students engage with the educational policy analysis. *Teaching in Higher Education*, 18(8), 833–845.

Jones, D. (2017). Talking about talk: Reviewing oracy in English primary education. *Early Child Development and Care*, 187(3–4), 498–508.

Larrivee, B. (2000). Transforming teaching practice: Becoming a critically reflective teacher. *Reflective Practice*, 1(3), 293–307.

Lyle, S. (2008). Dialogic teaching: Discussing theoretical contexts and reviewing evidence from classroom practice. *Language and Education*, 22(3), 222–240.

Lucas, T., Villegas, A. M. & Freedson-Gonzalez, M. (2008). Linguistically responsive teacher education: Preparing classroom teachers to teach English language learners. *Journal of teacher education*, 59(4), 361–373.

McNair, J. C. & Edwards, P. A. (2021). The lasting legacy of Rudine Sims Bishop: Mirrors, windows, sliding glass doors, and more. *Literacy Research*, 70(1), 202–212. https://doi.org/10.1177/23813377211028256

Nordin, A. & Sundberg, D. (2018). Exploring curriculum change using discursive institutionalism – a conceptual framework. *Journal of Curriculum Studies*, 50(6), 820–835.

Rosen, H. (2017). The autobiographical impulse. In J. Richmond (Ed.). *Harold Rosen: Writings on Life, Language and Learning, 1958–2008* (pp. 435–453). London: Institute of Education Press.

Sherry, M. B., Dodson, G. & Sweeney, S. (2019). Improvising identities: Comparing cultural roles and dialogic discourse in two lessons from a US elementary classroom. *Linguistics and Education, 50*, 36.

Solari, M. & Ortega, E. M. (2022). Teachers' professional identity construction: A sociocultural approach to its definition and research. *Journal of Constructivist Psychology, 35*(2), 626–655.

The Bell Foundation (n.d.). *Effective Teaching of EAl Learners*. [online] www.bell-foundation.org.uk/what-we-do/eal-programme/

Villegas, D. F. M., Varona, W. H. & Sanchez, A. G. (2020). Student teachers' identity construction: A socially-constructed narrative in a second language teacher education program. *Teaching and Teacher Education*, 91, 103055.

Wyk, M. M. v. (2011). Student teachers' personal stories-identity, social class and learning: A life history approach. *Loyola Journal of Social Sciences*, 25(2), 141–161.

CHAPTER

5

Dialogic teaching

From theory to getting started in practice

Mark Avis and Lisa Hesmondhalgh

Introduction

This chapter examines the role of talk in teaching and learning. The first part of the chapter provides an overview of some of the different ways in which classroom talk has been categorised by researchers and theorists. We focus on research about the persistence of an 'Initiation-Response-Feedback' form of interaction and on the positive research about the impact of dialogic teaching, particularly its most important components. The second part of the chapter provides a range of practical ideas for classroom practice. Through her work at the Aspire Educational Trust, Lisa discusses teachers' use of strategies to help children to develop their use of talk to facilitate learning. The chapter ends with practical suggestions for teachers interested in getting started with dialogic teaching.

Classroom talk

There is a lot of talk in primary classrooms.

Teachers talk a lot – they ask questions, they answer questions, they explain, they instruct, they model and they 'think out loud'. Children talk a lot – they answer questions, they ask questions, they explain their reasoning and they discuss their ideas in pairs and groups. As well as this formal talk, there is a wealth of talk that contributes to the 'hidden' curriculum – informal interactions and discussions which convey social, cultural and behavioural norms and expectations. So, talk is important.

We begin by providing a number of prompts which you may wish to consider helping you to reflect on your own use of talk in the classroom.

PROMPTS FOR CRITICAL REFLECTION

To what extent do you think classroom talk widens or narrows children's thinking and opportunities for expression?

You might record five minutes of yourself talking to children in the classroom as part of whole teaching or group discussion in different curriculum contexts, following the

DOI: 10.4324/9781003381013-5

school's policy about recording children. Listen back to it (perhaps with a trusted colleague) and consider the following:

- Who does most of the talking?
- How many and what kinds of questions do you ask?

Now focus on the children's responses and consider:

- How long are the children's utterances and what is the quality of these?
- When do you extend children's thinking and when do you close it down?
- To what extent do you build on children's responses in order to extend their thinking?
- What is the impact of your talk on children's learning?

As you read through this chapter, you may wish to reflect back on these points and how you might develop your skill in effective classroom talk.

There has been a significant amount of research into classroom talk and what happens in real classrooms, focusing on helping teachers to make their talk more effective. An example from Howe et al. (2019) in the *Spotlight on research* which follows identifies five key recurring themes underpinning effective classroom talk.

SPOTLIGHT ON RESEARCH

Evidence from Howe's review of literature on effective characteristics of classroom dialogue

Howe et al. (2019) identified five recurring themes from research literature associated with positive student outcomes in classrooms. This suggested the following positive characteristics of verbal interaction:

- Open questions.
- Elaboration – extended discussion, building on previous contributions.
- Differences of opinion acknowledged, probed and reasoned.
- Co-ordination between contributions.
- Participants should value verbal interaction.

Howe et al. (2019) suggested that an underpinning characteristic of effective classroom dialogue included high levels of quality student contribution and the expectation that most children would participate in dialogue.

Littleton and Mercer argue that spoken language is 'the most important mode for enabling us to think collectively' (2013, p7). Talk, when it works well, allows us to share ideas, creatively and productively, back and forth between individuals and in larger groups. Littleton and Mercer refer to this as 'interthinking' (2013, p1). The authors contend that this collaborative use of talk is one of the 'most important characteristics of our species' (Littleton and Mercer, 2013, p6). In primary classrooms, 'interthinking' through talk facilitates teaching and learning.

In recent years, the discussion of theories and research into talk as an effective tool for teaching and learning has become a prominent feature of Initial Teacher Education and teacher professional development programmes.

In this chapter, we will share some of the key research about talk. Despite widespread acceptance of its importance, its practical use in the classroom is worthy of further exploration. Therefore, this chapter will discuss key skills that you may wish to build into your teaching repertoire.

Talk and 'oracy'

The term 'oracy' was first used in the 1960s (Wilkinson,1965) to highlight the importance of developing children's ability to use spoken language as well as their ability to read, write and count. The All-Party Parliamentary Group on Oracy defines it as 'the ability to speak eloquently, to articulate ideas and thoughts, to influence through talking, to collaborate with peers and to express views confidently and appropriately' (OAPPG, 2021, p9). Voice 21, the national oracy charity, suggests that oracy is 'a set of teachable skills that are essential for life, but it is also a pedagogy' (Gaunt and Stott, 2018, p8). They see oracy as an important way in which teachers' teaching and learners' learning can intersect. Alexander discusses the different definitions of the term 'oracy' and highlights that each of them focuses on 'the development of the child's capacity to use spoken language' (Alexander, 2020, p26) and that is the way in which we will use the term in this chapter.

Oracy is not the same as dialogic teaching. Oracy education can be seen as teaching specific skills to children to aid learning. Mercer (2019a) likens oracy education to the teaching of algebra skills in maths, i.e. as an integral component of a wider curriculum. Whereas dialogic teaching might be seen as the acquisition of talk skills by teachers to aid teaching in any subject, oracy is something that whole schools – teachers and children – work to develop together.

It is important to note that some conceptions of oracy are reductive and present a 'deficit' view of many children's ability to use spoken language (see, for example, Cushing, 2024, and Smith and Sanders, this volume). Such conceptions see oracy as primarily being about ways in which children can be persuaded to speak 'properly', always using full sentences and conforming to the norms of spoken language which are representative of white, middle-class populations.

Teacher talk has been under scrutiny for decades. In particular, the ways in which teachers ask questions and the lack of opportunity for children to contribute their ideas and thinking has been seen as problematic. For example, Hardman et al. (2003) found that open questions, those which elicit longer, more considered answers, made up just 10% of questioning exchanges, while 15% of the exchanges in the study did not ask any open questions at all. More sustained discourse between a teacher and child made up 11% of exchanges. The answers from most children were very short, typically five seconds, and 70% of the answers consisted of just three words. The study concluded that most of the questions asked were of a low cognitive demand, requiring a pre-determined answer. The nature of teacher questioning has been a long-standing problem. This is explored in the *Spotlight on research* which follows.

SPOTLIGHT ON RESEARCH
'Typical' teacher talk

In 1992, Sinclair and Coulthard's seminal research described a typical interaction between a teacher and child as following the sequence 'Initiation-Response-Feedback' (IRF).

'A typical exchange in the classroom consists of an initiation by the teacher, followed by a response from the pupil, followed by feedback, to the pupil's response from the teacher' (Sinclair and Coulthard, 1992, p3).

The teacher's **initiation** (I) would most often be a closed question. The learner's **response** (R) would usually consist of a short correct or incorrect answer. The teacher's **feedback** (F) would then usually indicate a positive affirmation or an indication that the answer was not correct.

An example might be:

Teacher: In the story, how do you think Sally is feeling? (I)
Child: Sad. (R)
Teacher: Yes, well done. (F)

Or perhaps:

Teacher: In the story, how do you think Sally is feeling? (I)
Child: Sad. (R)
Teacher: Well, maybe not sad…. (F)

This IRF exchange has often been compared to asking the child to guess what is in the teacher's head. You may consider that those studies from over two decades ago portray a situation which has long since been supplanted by typically more open, discursive and collaborative exchanges, but more recently Alexander has noted that patterns of recitation are difficult to change (see Alexander, 2020). In synthesising studies from UK and US classrooms he notes that:

- Interactions are still typically brief rather than sustained.
- Teachers rarely develop sustained lines of thinking and understanding.
- Closed questions still predominate.
- Children concentrate on giving correct answers rather than using questions as stepping stones to understanding.
- Talk which encourages speculation, hypothesising and thinking aloud is relatively rare.
- Children are still encouraged to 'play the language game'.

Much more recently, the Oracy All-Party Parliamentary Group (OAPPG, 2021) found that while 8 in 10 (78%) young people say schools should prioritise oracy 'a lot', only a third (32%) say their school/education did so.

This deteriorated during and following the Covid-19 pandemic. The OAPPG found that 66% of primary teachers said that school closures had had a negative effect on the spoken language development of children.

The discussion in this chapter about oracy and getting started with dialogic teaching is in contrast to this narrow view. It concentrates on oracy as a tool to help children find and use their own voice in order to express their ideas in their own way. Dialogic teaching incorporates a repertoire of skills which teachers might develop to improve their teaching.

IDEAS FOR CLASSROOM PRACTICE

The Oracy Framework

A new school set up in East London in 2012 wanted to give children's spoken communication skills the same importance in the curriculum as maths and English. The benefits of this to children's learning were soon apparent. Wanting to share their approach to oracy pedagogy, teachers from the school set up Voice 21 as the national oracy charity. Working with researchers from Cambridge University, they constructed the Oracy Framework to help teachers and children to understand what constitutes good communication in different contexts.

Voice 21 has broken down the capacity to use spoken language into four constituent strands in their Oracy Framework (Gaunt and Stott, 2018). Each strand represents an area of oracy that teachers can help learners to develop. They are:

- The Physical Strand – This includes aspects of talk such as intonation, fluency and pace, clarity and body language. These are often the most noticeable aspects of the way that someone speaks. They liken the development of skills in this strand to becoming more adept at playing a musical instrument.
- The Linguistic Strand – This includes aspects such as appropriate vocabulary choice, grammar, register and rhetorical techniques such as the use of metaphor. Being able to adapt our way of speaking to fit different situations and contexts is an important skill. They make the point that this is just one of the four aspects of oracy and should not be prioritised above the other strands, thereby avoiding a narrow representation of high-quality talk (Voice 21, 2024).
- The Cognitive Strand – This includes aspects such as the choice of content, building on the ideas of others, structuring and organising talk effectively, summarising, seeking information and clarification through asking questions, giving reasons for opinions and critically examining ideas. Bringing the appropriate content to talk is essential.
- The Social and Emotional Strand – This includes aspects such as working with others, listening and responding, confidence in speaking and awareness of the audience. Being able to conduct themselves appropriately in discussion and dialogue is an important part of learners developing their skills in oracy.

The Framework highlights that good oracy is not just about 'speaking well'. It's about understanding that there are different skills involved. A person might have good physical speaking skills but need to develop cognitive skills. Gaunt and Stott (2018, p17) remind us that although a person can be an amazing performer, if what they are saying makes no sense or lacks a basis in reasoning, then they cannot be a good speaker. Different skills are needed to a greater or lesser degree in different contexts. Speaking to a large audience about a big idea is different from talking to one other person in order to achieve a compromise.

Types of talk

In the 1980s and 1990s, Neil Mercer was part of a team researching classroom talk, observing the ways in which children used talk when working in pairs or groups. As a result of their research, they identified three types of talk which occur in classroom groups (Littleton and Mercer, 2013, p15):

- Disputational talk – Talk in which there are frequent disagreements. Learners make up their own minds and there is little attempt to co-construct or share ideas.

- Cumulative talk – Talk in which there is a lot of agreement between speakers and repetition of ideas but little evaluation or critical consideration of them.
- Exploratory talk – Talk in which speakers engage critically but constructively with each other's ideas, value everybody's contribution, visibly reason, ask and answer questions and try to reach agreement before moving on.

Initially, they found that most children's talk in their study was unproductive and did not lead to improvements in learning. For instance, some children talked across each other or loudly disagreed or, where talk was respectful, the children did not address or solve the problem that they had been set. However, they also observed others who were 'thinking together', using exploratory talk. These children solved problems effectively and made the best individual progress in their learning.

These three types of talk serve as a simple guide for teachers. The more teachers can create the conditions for exploratory talk in the classroom, the more likely it is that talk will be effective.

Robin Alexander (2008, p38) offers a further perspective on talk, distinguishing between types of talk for teaching and types of talk for learning.

He breaks talk for teaching into two groups. The first group comprises:

- Rote – Talk focused on memorising facts and routines through repetition.
- Recitation – Talk which uses short teacher–learner answer sequences to recall what has previously been encountered or to test what is presumed or required to be already known.
- Instruction – Talk aimed at telling learners what to do and/or how to do it.
- Exposition – Talk aimed at imparting information, explaining ideas or procedures.

This first group involves necessary types of talk for teaching but, if teacher talk is restricted to these, learners' talk is unlikely to develop into a rich, collaborative exchange of ideas.

Alexander's second group is:

- Discussion – Talk which fosters the exchange of idea and information, uncovers and juxtaposes viewpoints.
- Deliberation – Talk which weighs the merits of different ideas, opinions or evidence.
- Argumentative – Talk which makes or tests a case by reference to reasons or evidence.
- Dialogue – Talk which works towards a common understanding through structured questioning, in which responses are probed and elaborated and which has an interactive dynamic that strives to be collective, reciprocal and supportive as well as deliberative and purposeful.

Alexander (2008, p39) suggests that expanding their repertoire to include the second group leads to more productive classroom talk. For example, teachers can encourage children to narrate, explain, ask different types of questions, analyse and solve problems, speculate and imagine, explore and evaluate ideas, negotiate, argue, reason and justify.

Alexander's second group links closely to Mercer's 'exploratory talk' and represents what might be understood as 'dialogic talk'. By adopting an approach of dialogic teaching, teachers may positively affect children's cognitive outcomes and their linguistic, physical, social and emotional aspects of oracy. Evidence of the effect on dialogic teaching is outlined in the *Spotlight on research* section which follows.

SPOTLIGHT ON RESEARCH

Evidence from Education Endowment Foundation (EEF) on the impact of dialogic teaching

The EEF conducted a large-scale randomised control trial of Alexander's particular approach to dialogic teaching (Jay et al., 2017). This approach used video review, print materials and in-school mentoring to support teachers' practice across English, Maths and Science lessons for 20 weeks. The study found consistent, positive effects in English, science and maths for all children in Year 5 (9–10-year-olds), equivalent to about two months additional progress on average.

During the trial, as well as focusing on the overall, average effects on test scores, Alexander's project team also studied classroom processes and teacher perceptions revealed by interviews and coded lesson videos. This highlighted a number of productive and effective ways in which teachers used talk, including greater use of:

- Open questions.
- Wait or think time.
- Revoicing to clarify what a child had said.
- Rephrasing of children's contributions.
- Challenging and seeking justification.
- Extended exchanges between teachers and children and children and children.

The Education Endowment Foundation produced a 'Toolkit' based on oral interventions. Recommendations for effective practice were as follows:

- Targeted reading aloud and book discussion with young children.
- Explicitly extending children's spoken vocabulary.
- The use of structured questioning to develop reading comprehension.
- The use of purposeful, curriculum-focused dialogue and interaction.

Before the talking starts

As with anything worth doing, good preparation is essential. There are some things you can do to set the scene for improving talk in the classroom.

Lesson planning

Ask a balance of open and closed questions

Closed questions are not 'bad' and open questions 'good'. At times, teachers need to ask closed questions that require one word or short answers. But we know that it is important to balance the proportion of open and closed questions in a lesson. When planning lessons, it is a good idea to think in advance of some open questions that you might use to get dialogue going so that you don't need to think them up on the spur of the moment.

Identify key vocabulary

Vocabulary choice is part of the Linguistic strand of the Oracy Framework. As part of lesson design, it is common to plan small but important examples of key vocabulary that you want children to use in the lesson. This might be vocabulary which is precise to the subject matter of the lesson. Sharing this key vocabulary during the lesson, as well as making it visible on working walls and in word banks, will help to scaffold its use in dialogue.

Decide on the talk 'structures' you will use

'Talk to your partner' and 'talk in your groups' are ubiquitous 'structures' seen in primary lessons across all subject areas. These can be effective ways to get talk going but they may represent a lost opportunity to develop dialogue. Too often, children talk about anything other than what they have been asked to discuss or one or two children dominate the discussion and talk becomes cumulative or disputational.

When planning lessons, it's a good idea to plan alternatives to 'talk to your partner', which will result in better quality talk. Planning for how children will structure talk and not just what they will do can help initiate dialogue.

There are useful structures for talk which are at the heart of Kagan's Cooperative Learning. They are simple to understand and quick to introduce to the class. They include:

- Numbered Heads Together.
- Think, Pair, Share.
- Timed Pair Share.
- Round Robin.
- Inside/Outside Circle.

You might look here to begin to find out more about these structures: www.kaganonline.com/free_articles/

Philosophy for Children

Philosophy for Children (P4C) is a way of structuring enquiry. It is based on children working through a discussion of 'big ideas' in a set P4C format that includes: Getting set, Introducing a stimulus, Thinking time, Question making, Question airing and Question choosing, First thoughts, Building, Last thoughts and a Review. There are suggestions for how children, at each of these steps, can be helped to express their ideas effectively and positively. A P4C approach was evaluated by Gorard et al. (2015) and found to impact on progress in Maths and Reading.

It takes time and training to use P4C in the classroom but these simple structures can serve as alternatives to 'talk to your partner'. Find out more about P4C here: www.thephilosophyman.com; https://p4c.com/; www.sapere.org.uk.

Establishing talk rules

If children are to use talk to learn, the teacher needs to establish a culture where dialogue is the norm – used across all subjects and understood and valued by all members of the class community. There are many aspects to helping children to develop their talk skills, one of which is agreeing guidelines or 'rules' for classroom talk.

Phillips and Wegerif (in Manalo, 2020) suggest that most sets of talk rules include these expectations:

- Sharing relevant knowledge.
- Listening to everyone's ideas attentively and treating them respectfully.
- Accepting that claims should be challenged and that the reasons underpinning claims and challenges should be shared and explored.
- Actively seeking and considering alternatives before any decisions are taken.
- Taking shared responsibility for decisions.
- Reaching agreement whenever possible.

The 'Thinking Together' Project suggested that 'child friendly' rules for exploratory talk might be:

- We will talk together to think about what to do.
- We will share what we know with each other.
- We will ask everyone to say what they think.
- Everyone will listen carefully to others and consider what we hear.
- We will give reasons for what we say.
- We will pay attention and try to think of good ideas.
- We will decide what to do only when everyone has said all they want.
- We will try to agree about what we think.

(Mercer, 2019b)

Voice 21's (Gaunt and Stott, 2018) list is simpler:

- Always respect each other's ideas.
- Invite others to contribute.
- Demonstrate active listening.
- Be prepared to change your mind.
- Try to come to a shared agreement.

Talk repertoire

Having considered the importance of the co-construction of classroom talk rules, we turn our attention to the teacher's talk repertoire. What follows should not be seen as a blueprint or a recipe of things to do in each lesson or in each day, but rather as a repertoire of skills that you can deploy when each is most appropriate and, in this way, build into your practice some key talk strategies identified by the research discussed earlier (see, for example, Alexander, 2020; Howe et al., 2019; Littleton and Mercer, 2013). To do this, we use 'Talk Tactics' of Voice 21.

Voice 21 Talk Tactics

Voice 21 (2024) suggests a number of 'Talk Tactics' to be modelled by teachers and then used by children. Here are some examples:

Invite instigation

You might get a dialogue going by asking:

- *Has anyone considered...?*
- *Let's think about...*
- *Who would like to begin our discussion...?*

At a point in the discussion where you want to introduce a different point, you might ask:

- *Does anyone have another idea...?*
- *Would anybody like to share a different point?*

Invite clarification

Sometimes when a child answers a question, their meaning is not clear. So, teachers may 'revoice' their answer. This is different from repeating it. You might verify what you think they have said by saying something like:

- *So, are you saying...?*
- *Let me get this right, what you're saying is...?*
- *Can you clarify what you mean by...?*

This provides the child with a model which may in turn support them in elaborating upon their ideas. You might add in some subject-specific vocabulary or a particular stem sentence to make the child's answer clearer.

You might throw this task open to the rest of the class:

- *Could anybody clarify what X is saying?*
- *Can you repeat what X has said using our stem sentence?*
- *Would anybody like to ask a clarifying question?*

Invite probing

We want children to justify their answers and to elaborate on them so you might model some 'probing' questions such as:

- *Why do you think...?*
- *Could you provide an example of...?*
- *How do you know that?*

You might throw this task open to the rest of the class:

- *Would anyone like to probe what X said?*
- *Who would like to ask a probing question?*
- *Does this remind you of anything we've learned before?*

Invite challenge

Challenge is at the heart of dialogue. The ability to respectfully challenge a point of view is a key life skill that many adults could do well to develop! You might respond to children's opinions by asking:

- *Have you considered...?*
- *You mentioned X but what about...?*
- *What if...?*

You might throw this task open to the rest of the class:

- *Would anybody like to challenge X's idea?*
- *Does anybody have a counter argument?*
- *Who disagrees with that point?*

Invite summary

At certain points in a dialogue, it is helpful to summarise and recap where the discussion has taken us so far. You might do this by saying:

- *So far, we have talked about...*
- *The main points raised today were...*
- *To summarise X's idea...*

You might throw this task open to the rest of the class:

- *Can anybody summarise the main points so far?*
- *Could you summarise what X is saying?*
- *Who can recap the main ideas?*

Invite building

Children elaborating on their own and building on others' ideas is another important aspect of dialogue. You might model it by saying:

- *Building on X's idea...*
- *X's idea made me think...*
- *To develop X's idea...*

And then invite children to do the same:

- *Would anybody like to build on X's idea?*
- *Could you tell me more about...?*
- *Who can tell me why they might agree with X?*

Additional moves: e.g. marking

You might 'mark' that a particular idea or contribution is important by saying:

- *That's an important point.*
- *Did everyone hear what X just said? How does that help move us on?*
- *Did you notice how X just probed Y's idea?*
- *What did X say to challenge Y's idea politely?*

Having modelled the tactics and invited children to use them, they will naturally begin to use them in their discussions with each other in classroom activities. You can encourage this by praising their use:

- *Well done X, you asked Y to clarify her idea.*

Dialogic teaching – from theory into practice

So far, in this chapter, we have explored some of the key research about talk, focusing particularly on supporting you in getting started with dialogic teaching, developing your repertoire of talk skills (in particular by using Voice 21's 'Talk Tactics') and establishing the routines and curriculum ethos that help children to develop their oracy skills. This chapter now presents real-life examples from schools. Collected by Lisa, these examples show schools beginning to work with the Voice 21 approach in the classroom.

It is important to note here that some children will have speech or other communication needs that mean that you will need to adapt the suggested *Ideas for classroom practice* presented in the next section. For example, when working with children with phonological/pronunciation difficulties, it may not be appropriate to ask them to speak clearly, and some children are not comfortable in being asked to maintain eye contact or be in close proximity with other children or adults. As with any classroom practice suggestion, always use your knowledge of the children you work with to ensure you are sensitive to their individual needs and preferences.

The children in these examples have been introduced to the idea of talk guidelines and thinking time early on so that they get used to them and accept turn-taking, active listening and showing respect for others' ideas as a normal part of classroom expectations. In each year group, procedures for agreeing, disagreeing and challenging other children's ideas are developed. These are the bedrock on which exploratory talk is built. Using gestures at the beginning can help children to signal their intention to build on or challenge ideas.

Participation is a fundamental component of good classroom talk. In the examples that follow, teachers use structures such as 'Envoys' and 'Traverse' to facilitate talk. When it is working well, the children rather than the teacher are taking the lead.

IDEAS FOR CLASSROOM PRACTICE

Example 1: Introducing talk guidelines, thinking time and building on others' ideas (nursery class)

In this session, eight children were sitting around the whiteboard with sentence stems written about a book they were already familiar with – *Jasper's Beanstalk* by Nick Butterworth and Mick Inkpen.

Before beginning the session, the teacher reminded the children of their talk guidelines, e.g. 'What is good talking? What do you have to do?' She shared a picture/icon to remind them: 'This picture is for taking turns. One at a time.'

Each child was given a talk token (small plastic counter or coin) to help them with turn-taking. The teacher presented three pictures, one picture for 'I agree...', one picture for 'I disagree...', and one picture for 'I think the same...' The teacher and children rehearsed each sentence stem carefully. She then introduced the problem: 'Jasper thinks he needs to pick up all the slugs and snails to help the beanstalk grow'. The teacher gave the children some individual thinking time, referring to it as being in your 'nest'.

Once children had had their individual thinking time in their nest, she asked them to show their talk token when they were ready to speak. Children held their talk token in the air. Children then began the discussion using the sentence stem, 'I think he needs to ... so they don't eat the slugs and snails'.

The teacher modelled how to challenge talk sensitively, e.g. 'I agree with this because...' She prompted other children to think about whether they thought the same or different, using a physical action to show this (fingers apart for different, fingers crossed for the same, similar to Makaton). She also used the language of talk tactics, e.g. 'Can anyone build on XXXX's ideas?'

Children placed their talk tokens on the corresponding sentence stem after they had spoken, e.g. 'I agree...'

Children who spoke quietly were reminded to use a louder voice – the teacher referred children to their talk tactics and showed the picture/icon again.

At the end of the session, the teacher praised the children specifically on their oracy skills rather than giving general feedback. For example, rather than saying 'well done', she praised children for using a clear and loud voice (where appropriate) and trying to look at the person speaking.

IDEAS FOR CLASSROOM PRACTICE

Example 2: Talk guidelines, agreeing and disagreeing (Reception class)

Children were arranged as a 'hoop group' (4–5 children sitting around a hoop on the carpet), facilitated by the teacher. They were reminded of the rules for talking and listening, using the agreed talk rules, e.g. 'Good looking' ('pair of eyes' icon) and 'We have to look at the person talking'.

The teacher asked, 'How do we show good listening? 'We take turns to talk'. Children were given a talk token (small plastic counter or coin) which would be placed in the hoop when they spoke. The teacher referred to the talk guidelines icons. 'Speak clearly and loudly. Don't be shy, think of your own ideas'.

The teacher introduced a sentence based on a book they had been reading: 'All dragons are scary'. On the board were written two sentence stems:

> *'I agree with Miss XXX because...'*
> *'I disagree with Miss XX because...'*

The children placed their token to take turns. Children were prompted to take part and reminded of the basic skills for listening (this links to the Physical Strand of the Oracy Framework discussed earlier in this chapter), e.g. 'Remember to use a loud voice so we can hear you'.

Children were prompted to use sentence stems, e.g.:

> *'I disagree with Miss XXXX because...'*
> *'I challenge what XXXX said...'*
> *'I agree because they...'*

Once each child had participated, the teacher praised the oracy skills they had used, e.g. 'You were looking at XXXX when you were talking' or 'You looked at XXXX when you spoke'.

This kind of group is facilitated in different ways in the Early Years Foundation Stage (EYFS), depending on the activity or the needs of the group. Sometimes a group with a specific oracy focus is taught as a small group whilst the rest of the class is accessing continuous provision. This allows for focused talk and enables the teacher to target specific children to develop their Personal, Social and Emotional Development (PSED) and oracy skills.

In a different activity with EYFS, children were asked to think about whether the dragon was always the baddie in the story (*There is No Dragon in this Story* by Lou Carter and Deborah Allwright). The children were already very familiar with the story and the term 'baddie'. As well as being reminded of the talk guidelines before the session, children were then asked to talk to their partner. They moved their bodies, so they were 'touching knees' face-to-face. They could then look at each other and begin the conversation with their partner, e.g. 'He steals'. 'He makes bad choices'.

Similar to the earlier activity, the teacher reminded the children of the talk tactics. 'What does BUILD mean?' and 'What does CHALLENGE mean?' ('I agree' and 'I disagree', etc.). She clarified what thinking the same and thinking something different meant, using finger symbols to demonstrate (similar to Makaton). Two fingers together (the same), fingers apart (different). Children were then supported to orally rehearse the sentence stems, 'I disagree because...'

IDEAS FOR CLASSROOM PRACTICE

Example 3: Categorising through collaborative talk (promoting exploratory talk)

As a whole class, children were presented with pictures of familiar objects and asked to think of something that linked them. The question was open ended and, although linked to some previous knowledge, gave children the opportunity to make their own choices without the fear of there only being one right answer. By planning this activity, the teacher was enabling exploratory talk (sometimes called Messy Talk) into the classroom.

Children were seated around tables in pairs or threes, giving them the opportunity to talk about the links they could see, e.g. 'My phone uses electricity by I don't always have to plug it in'. 'My TV remote is electric, but I never plug it in'. 'For something to be electric you need to plug it in'.

The teacher tuned into each group's exploratory talk and then began the discussion with an open-ended invite. 'Would anyone like to start a conversation about the links they talked about?' Children were then invited to use the talk tactics to extend the conversation. 'Building on your idea...'

The teacher praised children for projecting their voices and for being respectful when listening to each other. He didn't offer judgement on children's ideas and let the children shape the initial discussion. He then asked children to sort the appliances into groups, 'What could the title of each category be?'

Again, the teacher asked children to come up with their own groupings – leaving this open ended would allow for lots of exploratory talk linked to children's knowledge of electrical appliances. The skill of the teacher is tuning into the conversations each group were having and teasing out the ideal groups at the end of the session, addressing possible misconceptions whilst teaching. Once children had shared their thoughts using the talk tactics, the teacher then asked one child from each group to move to a different table and asked them to look at the new groups, e.g. 'Do you agree with the groupings from this table?'

This is an activity from co-operative learning, sometimes called 'Envoys'. It introduces another child's opinion to the group, extending the thinking process and widening participation even further.

IDEAS FOR CLASSROOM PRACTICE

Example 4: Building and challenging – children taking ownership of the talk (science)

The teacher began the lesson by reminding the children of the stem sentences they were going to use. These were displayed in the classroom and were already familiar to the children:

> *'I would like to start by saying...'*
> *'I disagree with XXX because....'*

The lesson began with specific talking points linked to science. The purpose was to revisit concepts children had already been taught and address any misconceptions and recall prior learning. The first talking point was introduced by the teacher: 'Freezing is the same as a solid'.

Children were given thinking time (at least ten seconds of silence) and then asked to contribute their ideas to a whole class discussion facilitated by the class teacher. Children who wanted to start the discussion used the 'instigate' sign to show they wanted to start talking.

(As well as a symbol for INSTIGATE, children also used a hand signal which had been agreed in previous lessons and was very familiar to the children.) The child who instigated the discussion stated, 'You freeze water, but it is not a solid'.

The teacher did not comment or jump in to correct the child's misconception. Instead, he allowed the next child to build on this comment. The next child indicated they would like to speak by using the familiar hand signals for 'BUILD' (one fist over the other like one potato two potato). He said, 'I would like to add that freezing is a change, but water is a state of matter.'

Children continued to build and/or challenge the initial thought until they had a consensus that water in its frozen state is a solid. The children co-constructed the answer using their previous knowledge and arrived at the consensus without the need for the teacher to intervene except for managing the discussion. The teacher offered comments such as 'interesting' or 'tell me more' but did not correct initial misconceptions.

The second talking point was then introduced by the teacher: 'In a narrative, we should use a character, setting and description.' Children instigated the discussion in the same way. The child who contributed first used the physical hand signal and was chosen by the teacher to start. Children then built on or challenged the points using language such as, 'I agree with what XXXX said and want to build on their point further by saying ...'

Again, the teacher didn't jump in to offer his opinion or correct the children's responses. He clarified some of the points for discussion or stated, 'That's an interesting point. Can you tell me more?' He also praised children for listening to each other and building on the discussion.

IDEAS FOR CLASSROOM PRACTICE

Example 5: Using a traverse to facilitate participation (maths)

The teacher presented children with four different statements, asking children to look for patterns and connections. Children were seated in tables of four. They were asked to talk to their partner. Children turned to face their partner (after being reminded of the discussion guidelines to look at each other and listen). They began their discussion using the sentence stem, 'I would like to start by saying....' The teacher clarified what the child was saying, and children continued the discussion by using the 'BUILD' action to build on what each child was saying.

As well as using pairs and small groups to manage the discussion, the teacher skilfully used a *traverse* to enable children to talk about a common misconception. A traverse enables children to hear lots of different opinions on the same subject. The teacher presented children with the sentence opener: 'When we add fractions with the same denominator, we should...'

Children then moved along the traverse, listening to each other explain what they should do when they add fractions with the same denominator. The teacher then asked children to explain their thinking and rationale, addressing any misconceptions quickly.

These examples show how schools might approach helping children to begin to use structures to develop the effectiveness of their talk. You will notice that this does not only occur in English lessons but in lessons across the curriculum. Oracy is a whole curriculum pedagogy.

In using some of these strategies, teachers will be sensitive to the varying needs and diversity of children. They may consider the use of augmentative or alternative communication strategies or tools which help children who have difficulties with speech. These may range from picture cards, gesture and communication boards to digital speech generating devices.

Building teachers' dialogic teaching skills

Howe et al. (2019) identify high participation as an underpinning principle of developing good dialogue. Using the previous tactics will serve to widen participation but this can also be facilitated by simply asking, after a child has made a contribution, 'What do you think about what they think?' It's also important to 'track' participation and ideas. You might, at times in the lesson, consider whether there has been a wide range of contributors. You might track those by saying something like, 'So, over here, Sally suggested that ... and then Dave thought ... but Mia thought ...' or you might ask a child to summarise the discussion so far.

Becoming a dialogic teacher is not a 'quick fix'. It takes time to develop the skills and establish the routines and curriculum ethos that help children to develop their oracy skills.

PROMPTS FOR CRITICAL REFLECTION

Reflect on some of the activities and suggestions earlier in the chapter. Select one or two to try with your class. What went well? What was getting in the way?

Consider children's participation. Did the strategy facilitate participation. Which children participated and how?

Go back to your recording from the first task in this chapter. Which strategies do you need to consider first to impact on children's use of dialogue and participation?

> Begin to identify talk tactics and strategies in your lesson planning. Which ones would help to support the lesson learning outcomes. Remember to plan in opportunities for talk.
>
> A pair or small group of teachers might take one strategy and use it where appropriate for a week, and then discuss how well it worked in their classes.

There is a lot more to developing oracy and dialogic teaching than we have presented here. There are lots of aspects that we haven't even mentioned such as how we might group children in different ways for talk and how children might assume different talk roles in discussions. But hopefully, we have presented a few key ideas and the research behind them that will enable you to get started with dialogic teaching.

Chapter summary

Research, in general, supports the idea that talk is the most important mode of communication which mediates teaching and learning. It facilitates connections between areas of experience, knowledge and culture. Most research also suggests that the ways in which teachers and schools use talk can be improved.

We have examined some whole school strategies, based on the Oracy Framework (Gaunt and Stott, 2018), that schools might use and develop over time in order to help children to use talk more effectively. We have also considered how individual teachers can, even in the absence of a school wide drive to improve oracy, plan to improve their own use of talk and build a repertoire of dialogic teaching skills to use across the curriculum.

References

Alexander, R. (2008). *Towards Dialogic Teaching: Rethinking Classroom Talk*. Dialogos.

Alexander, R. (2020). *A Dialogic Teaching Companion*. Oxon: Routledge.

Cushing, I. (2024). *Social (In)Justice and the Deficit Foundations of Oracy*. Oxford Review of Education.

Education Endowment Foundation (2021). Oral Language Interventions https://educationendowmentfoundation.org.uk/education-evidence/teaching-learning-toolkit/oral-language-interventions [Accessed 05/05/2024].

Gaunt, A. & Stott, A. (2018). *Transform Teaching and Learning Through Talk: The Oracy Imperative*. London: Rowman & Littlefield.

Gorard, S., Siddiqui, N. & See, B. H. (2015). *Philosophy for Children: Evaluation Report and Executive Summary*. London: Education Endowment Foundation.

Hardman, F., Smith, F. & Wall, K. (2003). 'Interactive whole class teaching' in the National Literacy Strategy. *Cambridge Journal of Education*, 33(2), 197–215.

Howe, C., Hennessy, S., Mercer, N., Vrikki, M. & Wheatley, L. (2019). Teacher–student dialogue during classroom teaching: Does it really impact on student outcomes? *Journal of the Learning Sciences*, 28(4-5), 462–512.

Jay, T., Willis, B., Thomas, P., Taylor, R., Moore, N., Burnett, C. & Stevens, A. (2017). *Dialogic Teaching: Evaluation Report and Executive Summary*. London: Education Endowment Foundation.

Littleton, K. & Mercer, M. (2013). *Interthinking: Putting Talk to Work*. Abingdon and New York: Routledge.

Manalo, E. (2020). *Deeper learning, dialogic learning, and critical thinking: Research-based strategies for the classroom*. London: Routledge.

Mercer, N. (2019a). *Language and the Joint Creation of Knowledge: The Selected Works of Neil Mercer.* London: Routledge.

Mercer, N. (2019b). *Thinking Together: Ground Rules for Exploratory Talk.* Available at: https://thinkingtogether.educ.cam.ac.uk/resources/Ground_rules_for_Exploratory_Talk.pdf [Accessed 06/02/2024].

OAPPG (Oracy All-Party Parliamentary Group) (2021). *Speak for Change: Final Report and Recommendations from the Oracy All-Party Parliamentary Group Inquiry.*

Sinclair, J. & Coulthard, M. (Ed.) (1992). *Advances in Spoken Discourse Analysis.* London: Routledge.

Voice 21 (2024). https://voice21.org/response-to-itt-and-early-career-framework/?s [Accessed 06/02/2024].

Wilkinson, A. (1965). The concept of oracy. *Educational Review, 17*(4), 11–15.

CHAPTER

6

Stories of writing in the classroom

Lynsey Wigfull

Introduction

Writing is AMAZING! It allows us to express our thoughts, share our stories and connect with ourselves and others in ways that transcend time and space. From the shopping list scribbled on the back of an old envelope, to the highly researched university dissertation; from a short text message inviting a friend to meet for a coffee, to a heartfelt, emotional letter explaining the reasons for ending a relationship, writing offers us the chance to have a voice and shape it in the best way to communicate meaning through a chosen, purpose-driven form. This versatility makes writing an indispensable tool for self-expression and communication in our everyday lives, enriching our interactions and allowing us to share our unique perspectives on and with the world.

Writing gives us a tool with which to play and create. It allows us to explore the perspective of others, trying out new roles and exploring made up worlds before safely returning to the comfort or reality of our own lives. It allows us to test out alternative realities and experience other perspectives, taking on the voice of others, and gives us the opportunity to be someone else within a different time or place. Through writing, we can be anyone, anywhere, transcending time and space and our own day-to-day existence.

Through writing, we have the power to inspire and be inspired; to share the depths of our hearts, our minds and our imagination, capturing our thoughts at a particular moment in time. Writing offers us the opportunity to process and work our way through our thoughts and return to our experiences time and time again, enabling the chance to reflect with fresh eyes, to learn, to change and to grow.

Writing gives us the chance to inform others, to educate and explain, to persuade and develop understanding. The topics about which we can do all this are never-ending, and the situations and contexts for what we write can be fact or fiction. The potential of what we can do and achieve through the medium of writing has no bounds, no limits and no end.

For us as teachers, then, the potential which we are able to offer children through writing is immense. As Young and Ferguson (2021, pix) powerfully state: 'No other subject allows us to give children a voice to tell us who they are, what they know, what they think and what they believe in.'

However, despite all these incredible benefits and the infinite potential which writing opens up to us, The National Literacy Trust's most recent research into children and young people's writing makes for stark reading. Levels of writing enjoyment amongst children are at their lowest since 2010 and the number of children involved in daily writing activities in their own free

DOI: 10.4324/9781003381013-6

time has decreased by a quarter since their research into writing began (NLT, 2023). In addition, primary school assessment data from 2022 suggests that one in three of all 11-year-olds and almost half of all disadvantaged children in England left primary school unable to write at the expected level.

In this chapter, we will explore writing and how it pertains to the primary classroom. Drawing on research and the real-life experiences of children, student teachers and teachers in the early years of their career, we will consider writing at school, being a writer in the classroom and being a teacher of writing. We will think about how we might approach teaching writing and the importance of having an identity as a writer for both our children and ourselves.

Thinking about what we mean by 'writing', we will look at ways in which we as teachers can inspire, support and guide young writers in and beyond the classroom, drawing on work which has been done in a number of schools to try and develop writers and writing. We will share ways in which we can develop our own skills and confidence as authors to ensure that our teaching is the best quality it can be and consider the important role that being part of a writing community in and outside the classroom has on the enjoyment and enthusiasm for writing.

This chapter draws on classroom research including work conducted as part of Lynsey's doctoral study about the experiences of Key Stage 2 writers (aged 7–11 years). It includes examples of how schools have focused on specific aspects of writing to affect change. The chapter includes examples of lived experiences in the classroom from both children and adults, along with reflections on how these might influence and inspire our practice in the classroom as writers, learners and teachers.

What is writing?

Writing is both a noun and a verb. It is something we produce – a 'thing' or 'product' – and also something that we do – a 'process'. We go through the process in order to shape and create the product. When we write, we engage in a series of actions which form a complex cognitive and linguistic process that involves generating ideas, organising thoughts and translating them into written language which eventually becomes our product to achieve our goal: the written text.

'Writing' as a noun

'Writing' as a noun refers to the text that is created. As a product, it encompasses a wide range of text types or forms, from simple labels and jottings to essays and stories, and from emails of complaint to persuasive letters, blogs and social media campaigns. Pieces of writing can be handwritten, print-based or, increasingly in the modern world, digitally produced and multimodal in their make-up, incorporating graphics, video, transitions and sound as well as text. The range of written forms is vast, and it is essential that children in our classrooms experience as many different text types as both stimuli and product as well-rounded readers and writers.

Reflection as a writer

Reflecting on our own practices as writers can help us to understand and make sense of our experience and can help us to connect our own experience with both the theory of writing and of the teaching and learning of writing. By considering some of the questions that follow in the *Prompts for critical reflection*, and completing the critical reflection tasks throughout the chapter, you will begin to appreciate the role that writing plays in your own life and begin to shape your identity as a teacher of writing (see also Smith and Sanders, this volume).

PROMPTS FOR CRITICAL REFLECTION

- Which of the written texts at the bottom of the box do you produce? Why?
- What is their purpose in your life? Who sees them?
- Are there some that you create and use more often than others?
- Which are print-based and which are digital? Which can be both?
- Which ones do you find most difficult to create and why?
- Can you think of any other text types you might add?

Text types

Lists	*Labels*	*Greetings cards*	*Diary entries*	*Blogs*	*Letters*
Emails	*Social media posts*	*Text messages*	*Stories*	*Poetry*	*Journal entry*
Academic writing	*Reports*	*Aide-memoires*	*Notes*	*CVs*	

- How might you find these reflections useful in the classroom?
- What might this mean for you as a teacher when ensuring children produce a range of text types and print-based and digital forms?

During your reflections, you will have identified many different kinds of texts that you produce in your own life and the ways in which you use them. With each piece of writing or text we create, we attempt to communicate and express our meaning to and with our audience, be that another person or people, or just ourselves. We produce a piece of writing to serve and achieve a purpose, seeking specifically to express thoughts, entertain, inform or persuade whoever the intended audience is for our work. Even the first time a young child makes marks in the sand or on a piece of paper, they are trying to communicate something with the world. In these early stages, there are no legible formal letter shapes or sounds which correlate to formal written language, but to that young child – the author – there is meaning attached to the piece that they have produced. In this sense, the earliest marks made by young children and emergent writers should be considered 'writing' even if the writers themselves have not yet learnt about the correlation between sounds, written symbols and letters.

The written product can be a simple reminder on a post-it note to 'Ring Mum!' or a complex, multi-media discussion about the pros and cons of recycling complete with moving images, sounds and imported video clips providing information from both sides to encourage the audience, perhaps a class of younger children, to help them decide what their own feelings are on the subject. At their heart, both texts are created to communicate something specific to an identified audience and achieve their intended purpose using an appropriate text type. The post-it note is a quick reminder to prompt the memory of either myself or perhaps a family member (maybe with a slightly more nagging tone!) whereas the multi-media presentation would require much more thought about the content, the different ways of organising the writing as well as considering the way in which it seeks to inform and potentially to persuade and how this might be achieved. When we seek to produce a piece of writing, in whatever form, it is therefore essential that we know:

- WHAT we are writing – the text type or intended form.
- WHO we are writing for – the audience.
- WHY we are writing – the purpose.

In the *Case study focus* which follows, you will see how concentrating on just one of these aspects – audience – has resulted in improvements to writing overall.

CASE STUDY FOCUS

Developing real audiences – Primary School A

As part of their focused work to develop children's writing, Primary School A decided to focus on the concept of audience to see if having an authentic audience for each written task could impact positively on the quality of children's writing.

In an interview, the Deputy Headteacher outlined what they had developed:

> We now ensure every single writing unit has a real-life audience. This can be anything from creating a book of stories for the reading corner so that the children themselves are the audience, performing poetry in assembly, creating a Wikipedia page with an intended target audience or even writing to MPs, authors and actual people. Having a real, authentic audience has allowed children to see how important their writing is and how much their writing is valued. This has given their writing real purpose and they love it. Even though audience was our targeted area, it has simultaneously made us ensure the purpose for the writing is authentic too.

Applying what you have just read

Use the *Prompts for critical reflection* which follow to help you connect what you have just read about audience and purpose with your own experience and then consider how you might use this in your classroom.

PROMPTS FOR CRITICAL REFLECTION

Go back to your earlier reflection about text types. What was the purpose of the writing in each situation? What prompted you to write? Who was the audience for your writing? Was it something just for your own eyes or was it to communicate with someone else? Think about how easy you found each situation and the things which helped or made it more difficult to write.

Putting it into practice in your classroom

How can you make writing tasks authentic and purposeful? What different audiences are there in your school and how can you use the local community as an authentic audience?

How could you encourage children to connect with their audiences? How might they write differently if they were writing to the King, the headteacher or a group of younger children in school?

Every time you come to plan a writing task, think about purpose, audience and text type or form at the start. Your writers need to know these things if they are to be successful.

'Writing' as a verb

'Writing' as a verb can be viewed in two interconnected ways. Firstly, it involves the physical action of creating the written outcome or product, be it with pen or digital tools. It requires hand-eye co-ordination, or the use of assistive technology designed to support writers where hand-eye movement might be difficult or restricted. It demonstrates at these initial stages the essential links between physical movement and many aspects of literacy and reinforces the links between gross and fine motor skills, and the emergence of the physicality connected with writing. In school, it might typically involve the print-based actions of writing on paper with pencil or pen, with particular attention being given to emerging letter formation, moving into legible handwriting of letters, words and sentences, and then developing individual fluency and style. In digital terms, it might initially involve developing basic keyboard and word-processing skills and build to the development of a toolbox of publishing and multi-media techniques.

The second way of viewing writing as a verb encompasses various stages or actions within a process. These stages usually include some combination of generating ideas, planning, drafting, revising, editing and publishing, with each of these having its own set of aims, skills and practices. Not every piece of writing will include every stage in its entirety, and it is important to realise that each stage does not necessarily follow in linear progression. Furthermore, the parts of the process do not have to be in written form. All are essential to know about and for our young writers to value, experience and be able to use.

Let's look at what each stage in the process involves.

Generating ideas

The writing process begins with generating ideas in some way. It gives the writer the chance to be playful, to explore ideas for writing and to gather useful information about language and the features of the kind of writing they are going to do so that they can begin to create a useful writer's toolkit ready to use on the writing journey. It might involve brainstorming, freewriting or mind mapping to explore potential topics, themes and concepts. It could also involve discussion with others or undertaking creative activities like drama or art to explore a theme or to gain a personal insight that might then be transferred into a later piece of writing.

Planning

Once ideas have been generated, the next stage is, or can be, planning. This involves organising thoughts, outlining main points and structuring the writing piece. A well-constructed plan provides a roadmap for the writing process, guiding the writer through the development of their ideas and ensuring coherence and logical flow.

Drafting

With a plan in place, the writer begins the drafting stage. This should be deliciously messy, where ideas are fleshed out, sentences are formed and paragraphs are developed. The focus during this stage is on getting thoughts down on paper without worrying too much about handwriting, presentation, grammar, spelling or punctuation. The goal is to create a rough draft that serves as the foundation for the final piece.

Revising

Once the draft is complete, the writer moves on to the revising stage. This involves reviewing and refining the content, structure and organisation of the writing piece. The writer may change words for more powerful or preferable ones, reorganise paragraphs, clarify ideas, strengthen arguments and improve overall coherence and clarity. Revising is an iterative process, allowing for the writer to consider their writing with fresh eyes, reading their work more critically and testing out how effective they think it is in fulfilling its purpose and its aim.

Editing

After revising, the writer moves on to the editing stage. Here, the focus is on polishing the writing piece by changing sentence structure/syntax to support meaning and effect, or correcting errors in grammar or punctuation, spelling and style. The writer may also pay attention to sentence structure and overall readability. Editing ensures that the writing is clear, concise and error-free, ready to be shared with an audience.

Publishing

The final stage of the writing process is publishing; sharing the writing piece with its intended audience. Depending on the context, publishing may involve publication in a book or on a display, posting a piece on a blog or website, or presenting it to a particular audience in a letter, email or debate. Evaluating and reviewing is an important step, followed by publishing, which marks the culmination of the writing process, allowing the writer to share their ideas, insights and creativity with the audience for whom it was intended.

The simple view of writing

And so the whole process of writing as a verb has been done. The two elements of writing as a verb we have just discussed align well with two of the components within the 'Simple View of Writing' (Berninger et al., 2002), which is a theoretical framework that suggests that writing is the product of three main components: transcription, composition and executive function. This view underpins the National Curriculum for English (DfE, 2013):

- Transcription involves the mechanical aspect of writing, such as spelling, punctuation and handwriting, while composition involves the ability to generate and organise ideas into coherent written text.
- Composition involves the generation and organisation of ideas, selecting from an increasingly sophisticated number of techniques with which to put those ideas into an appropriate structure and form. It connects back to purpose, making writers select the most appropriate ways to achieve the aims of their writing, and requires an awareness of the audience, known or unknown, to whom the writer must learn to connect. Each product requires a complex combination of knowledge, skills, experiences and techniques to be applied, meaning that lessons in all these aspects of writing must have taken place in the classroom before each task commences.
- Executive Function is commonly thought to involve some of the processes outlined in the previous stages, such as planning and reviewing.

Although it can be a useful tool for thinking about the components of a writing programme for children, this framework can potentially mislead us and reduce the very complex interplay of experiences and skills involved in writing to something much too simplistic. We know that the product and process of writing which we have already considered are both evident and revered in writing theory and in curriculum documents. However, writing is about much more than just subject knowledge. Writing is also about being a writer, having a writing identity and exhibiting and developing writerly behaviours. To omit these crucial elements is to ignore some of the most important factors which influence the product and processes and suggests that a curriculum without them can never be fully successful.

Although the National Curriculum refers to 'Reading for Pleasure', there is no mention or suggestion of any such pleasure being attributed to writing. As part of their 'Writing for Pleasure' pedagogy, Young and Ferguson (2020) identify and highlight the importance of the affective domains which impact on writerly emotions, behaviours and identity. They cite these as:

- Motivation (I know why I write).
- Agency (I have a say in what I write).
- Volition (I want to write and am motivated to write).
- Self-regulation (I know what to write and how to write it).
- Self-efficacy (I can write).
- Writer identity (I am a real writer).
- Enjoyment and satisfaction (happiness when writing and pride in what I have written).

The importance of these elements can be seen in the next *Spotlight on research* which draws on research conducted as part of Lynsey's doctoral study. The study explored the experiences of Key Stage 2 writers, with data collected through a series of child voice activities.

SPOTLIGHT ON RESEARCH

Exploring the experiences of Key Stage 2 writers

Using a range of creative methods, I worked with a group of Key Stage 2 children to create a range of artefacts exploring their thoughts about writing, being a writer and their experiences of writing at school. Creating word clouds, taking photographs in the school environment and creating Lego characters to represent themselves as writers, the participants also engaged in discussion with their classmates about their thoughts and experiences of writing and of being writers. The children were positioned as experts in their own lived experience, and I sought only to illuminate what they said and created.

In the creation of their word clouds, the children were keen to share their thoughts and to compete with each other to find the most negative word or phrase they could about how 'boring' writing was. It was interesting that this was when they were in earshot of each other, whereas when they were working on their own, they were much more positive. This seemed to suggest a perceived need to be 'seen' to be negative about writing when in a public domain.

The photographs that the children took were very interesting. Each child was given a digital camera or iPad to use individually to take ten photos of things they believed represented writing to them. Many of the photographs were of phonics charts or spelling charts but not a single child took a photograph of their own writing or of that of any other child. During discussion, many of the children spoke about being made to produce writing in a certain way decided on by the teacher and having little control. On the occasions where they did have some input to the subject or context, they found it difficult to think of their own ideas. As one child put it, 'It's like the ideas part of my head has seized up because I don't get to use it very much'.

The Lego writers they created also revealed that many of the children saw writing as a battle, with many of the characters carrying weapons along with expressions of anger or distress.

If children don't feel these emotional and behavioural connections with themselves as authentic writers, then a fundamental part of the jigsaw of writing is missing. They might be able to go through the process of writing and produce a piece of text, but they do not feel moved or emotionally connected to what they are writing. The act of writing becomes simply a 'task to be completed' and a redacted version of what it has the potential to be. Although this might mean children can still 'succeed' in relation to curriculum expectations, crucially, it misses the vital motivated empowerment and amplification of the child's voice, which is its most powerful, future-self gift to take beyond the classroom into that young person's adulthood. As teachers, why would we want to leave out the most important piece of the writing puzzle and leave our children with only two-thirds of the jigsaw complete?

We need to think about subject knowledge for writing as being both text-oriented AND writer-oriented. The following *Case study focus* shows how thinking in this way can impact hugely on writing in a school.

CASE STUDY FOCUS

Love and competition improve outcomes – Primary School B

The headteacher of Primary School B was interviewed as part of a study around developing and improving writing. The school had decided not to look just at the mechanics of writing, but how they could motivate and inspire children to write for both purpose and for pleasure. Looking at their curriculum, they realised that children were not having any opportunities to choose for themselves what they wrote about.

The school introduced weekly Writing for Pleasure sessions where children were free to write about whatever they wanted and could do so using special notebooks and pens. Almost immediately, teachers noticed an enormous shift in the children's enthusiasm for writing with many children transferring new skills from lessons into their own work.

Such was the success that the school then launched a termly school writing competition to showcase the enthusiasm and improvement in quality of writing. A specially selected panel of judges gave the competition a feeling of importance and formality and the competition cumulated in an awards ceremony where the winners and runners up were given certificates and prizes. Writing is now prized in more ways than one!

The teaching of writing – an array of approaches

As we now take the chapter into the teaching of writing, it seems obvious that this must also be as multi-faceted as the subject itself. This requires careful consideration and the planning of a whole range of elements to ensure children experience high-quality, well-rounded writing instruction.

It is imperative that children have the experiences and opportunities which teach them to see themselves as authentic authors writing with a genuine purpose and to develop the skills and attitudes needed to become effective writer.

In their *Handbook of Research on Teaching Young Writers*, Young and Ferguson (2020) identify a range of different approaches to the teaching of writing found in research, each of which is based on its own perception of what writing is and what it is for. They outline the key approaches as being:

- A presentational or skills-based approach to writing.
- Naturalistic self-expressionist.

- Structuralist and genre-based approach.
- The literature-based model.
- Critical literacy and multiliteracy perspective.
- Environmental and community orientation.

The diversity of approaches to the teaching of writing further reflects the complexities of the subject and illustrates the different pedagogies which can underpin teaching in the writing classroom.

A presentational or skills-based approach to writing

A presentational or skills-based approach to writing focuses on teaching specific writing skills and techniques through direct instruction and practice. This approach emphasises the mastery of writing conventions such as grammar/sentence structure, punctuation and spelling. Children are taught to write by learning and practising these skills in isolation before applying them to their own writing. The presentational approach typically involves structured lessons, guided practice and feedback to help students develop proficiency in the mechanics of writing. It aims to build a strong foundation of writing skills that students can apply across various writing tasks and genres.

Naturalistic self-expressionist

The naturalistic self-expressionist approach to writing, often associated with the 1960s and 1970s, emphasises the idea that writing is a natural outgrowth of the individual's thoughts, feelings and experiences. This approach prioritises personal expression, creativity and the exploration of individual voice over the mastery of writing conventions. Writers are encouraged to express themselves freely and authentically, drawing from their own experiences and emotions. This approach is often contrasted with more traditional, skills-based approaches to writing, as it focuses less on the mechanics of writing and more on personal expression and creativity. Techniques such as freewriting and journalling to encourage personal expression and creativity in writing feature in this approach and have strong links to personal growth and mental health.

Structuralist and genre-based approach

The structuralist and genre-based approach to writing emphasises the importance of understanding and analysing the structures and conventions of different types of texts or genres. This approach views writing as a social practice influenced by specific contexts and purposes. It teaches students to recognise and analyse the common features and structures of various genres, such as narratives, reports, essays and poems. By studying these genres, students learn to identify the typical organisation, language and style used in each genre and how to effectively produce texts within these conventions. The structuralist and genre-based approach aims to help students become proficient writers by providing them with the knowledge and skills needed to navigate different writing tasks and contexts successfully.

The literature-based model

The literature-based model of writing integrates the study of literature with the practice of writing. In this approach, children learn to write by reading and analysing a variety of literary texts, including fiction, nonfiction, poetry and drama. By studying literature, children are exposed to different writing styles, techniques and genres, which they can then incorporate into their own writing. This approach emphasises the importance of reading as a foundation for developing writing skills and encourages students to emulate the techniques and styles of the authors they study. Through close reading and analysis of literature, our young writers learn about narrative structure, character development, descriptive language and other elements of effective writing. The literature-based model of writing aims to develop critical thinking skills, literary appreciation and writing proficiency simultaneously.

Critical literacy and multiliteracy perspective

The multiliteracies approach to writing expands traditional literacy education to encompass the diverse range of literacy practices in today's digital and globalised world. Developed by the New London Group in the 1990s, this approach recognises that literacy is not limited to reading and writing printed text but also includes a wide range of communication practices, including visual, digital and multi-media forms. The multiliteracies approach emphasises the importance of teaching students to critically analyse and produce texts in various modes and media. It also encourages students to develop the skills needed to navigate and communicate effectively in different cultural and social contexts. In writing instruction, the multiliteracies approach involves teaching students to compose and interpret texts in multiple modes, such as print, visual, digital and multimodal forms, and to understand how meaning is constructed differently across different modes and media.

Environmental and community orientation

An environmental and community-oriented approach to writing focuses on connecting writing instruction to real-world contexts and community needs. This approach emphasises the importance of engaging students in writing tasks that are relevant and meaningful to their lives and communities. Students are encouraged to explore and write about environmental issues, community events and local concerns, as well as to take action through writing to address these issues. This approach often involves collaborative writing projects, service-learning activities and community-based research projects that allow students to apply their writing skills to make a positive impact in their communities. By connecting writing instruction to environmental and community issues, this approach helps students develop a sense of civic engagement, social responsibility and environmental awareness while also improving their writing skills.

In the *Prompts for critical reflection* which follows, we reflect on everything we have just read about the different approaches and invite you to consider what it might mean in your classroom.

PROMPTS FOR CRITICAL REFLECTION

Think about a writing lesson you have seen or delivered recently. Which of the previous approaches feature within the lesson?

Which of the approaches have you seen most when you have been in school? Why do you think that might be? What drives the approaches used?

Do you feel that any of the approaches are more important than any other? For what reason?

Putting it into practice in your classroom

Think of five writing tasks that would be faithful to each of the previous approaches in turn. Don't forget to be clear about the purpose and audience for each task. Which do you think would excite children? Which would excite you as the teacher?

Although each approach has its benefits, adopting any one approach faithfully to the exclusion of all other approaches seems to give a rather stilted view of writing and would lead to children missing out on the richness and multiplicities that are actually the joy of writing and of the writing experience. Rather than advocate any one singular approach, let us now instead consider taking elements from each and combining them to create a 'best of the best' series of principles to incorporate into our teaching, ensuring our children's experiences of writing and being a writer are just as multi-faceted as theory and research suggest. These principles are presented in Table 6.1.

Table 6.1 illustrates the importance of the teacher in the success of the writing classroom: as the central column suggests, the role of the teacher in the 'process' or 'doing writing' and 'being a writer' is paramount. The development of structured lessons with guided practice is further supported by Rosenshine's principle of providing models as part of direct instruction. Along with carefully planned models, it is essential for teachers to narrate the writing process as they demonstrate, create and shape the text, explaining why they are making certain language choices or why particular grammatical structures are being used to provide a certain effect on the reader (see also Helks and Myers, this volume). This guided practice is extremely important, has huge potential to impact on children's writing but requires a certain confidence along with regular practice.

Applying what you have just read

Using the *Prompts for critical reflection* which follow, consider the different examples of ways in which teachers can support and guide writing in class. Reflect on how confident you would be to use each of them in the classroom.

Table 6.1 Key principles taken from the different approaches to writing

'Writing as a noun' – Product (Task)	'Writing as a verb' – Process (Teacher/Writer)	Affective Domain – Person (Child/Writer)
Tasks connected to real world and children's experience	Connection between reading and writing continually emphasised	Use of freewriting and journalling
Tasks which help develop a sense of civic engagement, social responsibility and environmental awareness	Analysing and interpreting texts in print, visual, digital and multimodal forms and in different genres	Opportunity to write freely and authentically
Different kinds of writing tasks in a range of social and cultural contexts	Balance of composition and transcription	Collaborative writing projects
Purpose and audience clear for each task	Structured lessons, guided practice and feedback	
Compose a range of visual, digital and multimedia forms	Practising skills	
	Grammar/sentence structure, punctuation, spelling and sentence structure (with a focus on their impact on meaning and effect)	
	Activities organised to promote working with others	
	Critical thinking skills	

PROMPTS FOR CRITICAL REFLECTION

Different ways of guiding writing in the classroom

Modelling – as outlined earlier, this is where the teacher writes a piece of high-quality text explaining the choices they are making as a writer.

Guiding – the teacher provides specific verbal prompts for the children as they write, enabling the teacher to guide children towards particular writing targets or using specific techniques or focuses.

Coaching – the teacher asks questions to support the children making choices of their own in their writing.

These ways of directing practice can be used with whole classes, targeted groups working on similar targets in writing or with individuals. Each way allows you to adapt your teaching to best meet the needs of the children and can therefore be a key part of your inclusive and adaptive teaching toolkit.

Reflecting on what you have seen and what you can do next

Which of the previous approaches have you seen or used yourself in school?

Which would you feel most confident to use and why?

Think about how you would need to prepare to model, guide and coach. What can you do in advance to support you with this? Are there any resources you could prepare or any aspects of subject knowledge that you could research?

Teachers as writers

It is clear from what we have discussed so far that the role of the teacher and the teaching in school-based writing is pivotal. We will now move our focus on to consider the way in which writer identity, writerly behaviours, pedagogy and practice are all interconnected for the teachers themselves as well as influencing the children within their classroom writing communities. In the following *Spotlight on research*, we reflect on research that suggests that where teachers are confident as writers, this will have a positive influence on the children they teach.

SPOTLIGHT ON RESEARCH

Debra Myhill, Teresa Cremin & Lucy Oliver (2021) Writing as a Craft: Reconsidering Teacher Subject Content Knowledge for Teaching Writing, Research Papers in Education

This research draws on the 'Teachers as Writers' project which looked at the value of teachers working with professional writers to increase their confidence as writers and to examine the subsequent impact on classroom practice and on children's outcomes. Participants expressed that they were much less confident teaching writing than they were teaching reading. The project involved a residential writing retreat for teachers to work with writers in workshops and writing activities developing their skills and confidence as writers with ongoing feedback from the professionals to develop their 'craft knowledge'. Three main themes emerged as being important for teachers to develop as skills or to explore further in their teaching than they had previously:

> The writing process – specifically the 'preparing to write' stage:
> Creative experiment.
> Drafting.
> Revision.
> Writing process as a whole is messy, complex, rarely linear.
> Knowledge of language choices.
> Knowledge of text level choices.
>
> Being an author involves:
> Drawing on experience.
> Authorial intention.
> Emotional connections.
> Authentic voice.
> Drawing on reading.
> Ownership of writing.
>
> Reader–writer relationship:
> Help the reader understand.
> Techniques to engage and affect the reader.
> Reader–writer interaction.

These then shaped the practice and the way in which these teachers began to operate in more writerly ways within the classroom, planning activities which allowed children to explore some of the aspects of writing their teachers had discovered by being 'real writers'.

CASE STUDY FOCUS
Developing high-quality model texts – Primary School C

As part of discussions with staff, the Literacy Lead in at 'Primary School C' explained:

> As a staff, we have developed the modelling part of the writing process. Teachers now use a carefully pre-prepared model with explicit teaching points alongside all writing expectations for each year group. Children then watch the teacher think, write and edit the model in real time before then using the model to construct their own and apply what they have heard and learned. The impact has been phenomenal as the cognitive load on children has decreased, the expectation is crystal clear and they are able to take a structure and make it their own. It has been such a worthwhile thing to do and has led to writing of a much higher quality. It has also supported staff.

Although the conclusions were drawn from serving, qualified teachers, the same lack of confidence in teaching writing may be present in student teachers. Some of this lack of confidence is linked to the task of modelling writing to children.

SPOTLIGHT ON RESEARCH
Linking research with practice – student teachers as writers

The difference in confidence with reading and writing explored by Myhill et al. (2021) was certainly very true of a group of PGCE Primary and Early Years student teachers, the vast majority of them reporting that they were incredibly worried about modelling writing. As a result, Lynsey's school set up an online 'Teachers as Writers' group where students could come and develop their own writing once a month and consider ways in which they could apply the activities and exercises done in the group into their teaching. Their feedback was 100% positive and all the student teachers said that by practising and developing their own skills and understanding as writers, they were better placed to begin to model more effectively to their children, explaining their word choices and sentence construction more confidently.

Here are two comments from participating students:

> I dreaded writing in front of children because I didn't really know how to explain why I was writing what I was writing. Now that I have practised making choices as a writer, I understand more and the quality of my explanations to children is much better. I also see the value of practising as writing isn't something I do a lot of.
>
> (PGCE Primary Student)

> I have only ever written at school and hated it. I realised I would struggle on placement in the classroom if I didn't have a go at doing my own writing. The difference that a few games and activities for me to take part in as a writer myself has made is incredible. I might go as far as saying I even enjoyed it!
>
> (PGCE Primary Student)

It is clear from this *Spotlight on research* that student teachers and qualified teachers can benefit from developing their own confidence as writers, and that this is likely to impact positively on their confidence to teach writing in school.

Chapter summary

Although it would be impossible to cover every aspect of writing in just one chapter, we hope that by considering aspects of theory, research and practice, and identifying some of the most important factors involved in the writing process in developing effective writing provision, you feel ready to take the following summary list of principles and begin to build your own successful writing classroom community.

Writing is complex and children will need to orchestrate a number of different skills when writing. The following principles would seem to be key:

- There are many parts to the process, and all parts of this process are important and need to be valued and authentic – drafting does not require best handwriting, but publication requires care and to fulfil the purpose and suit the audience.
- The role of the teacher in modelling writing is vital; children need to see you write and hear from you as a writer explaining your writerly choices. At other times, you will need to direct, guide, scaffold and coach before children can be fully independent.

- Children need to use talk, discussion, collaboration and interaction with others at different parts of the writing process. Writing is a social practice and the classroom should be a writerly community.
- Finding out what children think about writing through child voice activities can provide insights to inform writing pedagogy.

References

Berninger, V., Vaughan, K., Abbott, R., Begay, K., Coleman, K., Curtin, G. & Hawkins, J. (2002). Teaching spelling and composition alone and together: Implications for the simple view of writing. *Journal of Educational Psychology*, 94(2), 291–304.

DfE (Department for Education). (2013). *The National Curriculum in England: Key Stages 1 and 2 Framework Document*. London: DfE.

Myhill, D., Cremin, T. & Oliver, L. (2021). Writing as a craft: Reconsidering teacher subject content knowledge for teaching writing. *Research Papers in Education*, 38(3), 403–425.

NLT (National Literacy Trust) (2023). *Children and Young People's Writing in 2023*. https://nlt.cdn.ngo/media/documents/Writing_in_2023.pdf [Accessed 12/07/2024]

Young, R. & Ferguson, F. (2020). *Writing for Pleasure: Theory, Research and Practice*. London: Routledge.

CHAPTER

7

Exploring the teaching and learning of grammar

Marie Helks and Julia Myers

Introduction

In this chapter, we explore the challenges inherent in the teaching and learning of grammar in the primary classroom. We identify grammatical terminology as an area of particular difficulty and ask how the development of understanding of grammar and its terminology can be effectively achieved within a curriculum which aims to promote children's enjoyment of literature and language.

The chapter is organised into three sections. Section 1 explores the meaning of grammar and subsequent challenges, issues and debates surrounding classroom practice. Section 2 focuses specifically on grammatical terminology (as the labels for grammatical concepts) and its impact as a potential aid or barrier to children's learning. Drawing Sections 1 and 2 together, Section 3 proposes a pedagogical model of practice, illustrated by two example texts. These examples offer ideas for teaching strategies to support effective grammar learning, including the purposeful and accessible integration of appropriate grammatical terms.

This chapter covers a wide area, but it is not intended as a study guide. Its purpose is to develop your understanding of grammar as a meaning making resource and the complex challenges of teaching it. Through reading it, we hope you will increase your awareness of the exciting potential for grammar to be taught within meaningful, motivating contexts which encourage the development of creativity, criticality and confidence in language use.

Section 1: Exploring the meaning of grammar and grammatical terminology

We begin by asking, 'What is grammar?' The *Prompts for critical reflection* which follow are intended to help you unpack your thoughts and feelings about what grammar means to you, as these may well influence your current practice on teaching grammar in the classroom.

PROMPTS FOR CRITICAL REFLECTION
What does 'grammar' mean to you?

How do you feel when you hear the word, 'grammar'?

- *A sense of achievement? A feeling of inadequacy? Enthusiasm? Interest? Boredom? Worried about getting it wrong?*

DOI: 10.4324/9781003381013-7

What does 'grammar' mean to you? Try to unpack what you understand by the word.

- *An awareness of rules to be followed? A focus for exercises and tests? A puzzle? A structure within a language that you've recognised when learning other languages? An expectation of accuracy?*

Where have these perceptions come from? Try to recall experiences that may have shaped your perceptions of grammar, particularly outside of school.

Did you find this critical reflection activity difficult? Research suggests that experienced teachers struggle to define grammar, noting confusion between grammatical rules and usage and linguistic etiquette (Watson, 2015). Watson (2015) found that some teachers could only manage to articulate grammar in vague ways as an 'airy concept', while other teachers approached it by reflecting on what grammar was not.

How vague or specific were your reflections? Perhaps you immediately thought of grammatical terminology, such as 'nouns', 'adjectives' and 'verbs'. This would not be unusual. Notions of grammar are often to do with explicit grammar teaching dominated by grammatical terminology which is, in turn, dominated by the recall and identification of that terminology.

And what of your feelings? Research suggests that grammar is often associated with negative feelings such as anxiety, confusion and boredom (e.g. Alderson and Horak, 2001; Myhill, 2005). Of course, it may be that you feel positive and enthusiastic about this area of the curriculum (see Bell, 2016). But, if this is not the case, please be reassured you are already an expert in grammar! If reading this chapter is making sense to you (and if others can typically make sense of what you say and write), your understanding of how language works grammatically is very complex indeed.

Learning grammar implicitly

As humans, we have the ability to learn the grammar of our language without any instruction. If you spend time with young children, you will be aware of their ability to communicate from an early age. As soon as they begin to string two or three words together, they demonstrate implicit understanding of the structure of the language/s of their home environment. For example, a young child whose own/home language is English might say, 'Me draw it!'. This shows awareness of word order in English through the sequence: **subject** + **verb** + **object**. In this case, the child uses the pronoun 'me' when at a later stage they will use 'I', but the sequence is still followed.

Later, reporting on the event, the child may say, 'Me drawed that'. The child recognises that the past tense is often formed by adding the suffix '-ed', showing understanding of how individual words are structured (known as morphology). They have not yet learned that the verb, 'draw', does not follow this pattern and 'drew' is the appropriate form. In overgeneralising, they have demonstrated their understanding of how the past tense is often indicated in English.

Grammar is acquired and used at an unconscious level without any meaningful labelling. By being immersed in language structures naturally as part of real-life conversation, many young children come to understand and use complex verbal grammatical structures within language – and all this well before starting school!

However, this reveals a key paradox: the child can already 'use' grammar despite not yet having been formally 'taught' it. Vygotsky cites 'arithmetic' as a contrasting example. Arithmetic is a taught concept and so, when a child is taught arithmetic, it seems to provide the child with more obvious 'new abilities' – i.e. the child has learnt something new which they can now use. However, grammar teaching is unusual in that it 'does not seem to provide the child with new capacities in this sense' (Vygotsky, 1987, p205).

Teaching grammar explicitly

The ability to learn grammar in these ways leads to the following familiar – but wholly reasonable – question: If young children can acquire grammar implicitly, why do we need to teach it? Here, grammar is perceived as a means of representing a system 'already known' – even to the young child. As teacher educators, we have encountered this question on many occasions and this whole chapter could be seen as our extended response to it. Should we study grammar? Is it relevant today? Absolutely, yes, and perhaps more so now than ever before.

Given the ubiquitous and powerful role of language in our lives, we believe that an understanding of language structures and an appreciation of how they work can enable and empower us as language users in many far-reaching and significant ways. For example:

- From a linguistics perspective, knowledge about grammar enables us to know how words and sentences work, to understand structures, to see patterns, to appreciate language differences and to use this to help us learn other languages.
- From a literary perspective, knowledge about grammar gives us the tools to comprehend and create texts, critiquing too our own language use and the choices we make to create meaning and effect.
- From a social-cultural perspective, knowledge about grammar enables us to learn about ways in which meaning is constructed for different purposes and audiences, enabling people to feel pride in the linguistic diversity of communities and to consider how assumptions about accuracy are linked to social prestige and power.
- From a cognitive perspective, knowledge about grammar challenges us to think hard about complex ideas, manipulating language explicitly and working at a high level of abstraction.

Ultimately, knowledge about grammar provides a particular lens to explore, to interrogate and to question, to understand how and why meanings are shaped and interpreted, thereby developing children as critically literate language users (Janks et al., 2014).

Before we embark on the consideration of how to teach grammar, we need to give some thought to what grammar means within the academic field. That said, texts are never neutral, and this chapter is no exception. The *Spotlight on research* which follows reflects our combined perspective as the authors of this chapter. We hope that through reading this chapter, alongside many other sources, and reflecting on your own experience as a learner and a teacher in the classroom, you will begin to develop your own.

SPOTLIGHT ON RESEARCH

Exploring the meaning of grammar

'Grammar' is not easily defined. This single word represents an extensive field of study. Within the discipline of linguistics, 'grammar' has multiple definitions and terms, reflects different schools of thought and crosses over different disciplines. Indeed, Crystal (2008, p217) reminds us that there are different 'grammars'.

For Crystal, grammar is 'the study of how sentences are structured and how they connect with each other' (Crystal, 2004, p18). Traditionally, these structures have been divided into two areas: the structure of sentences (syntax) and the structure of words (morphology) (Aarts et al., 2019). But this only takes us so far. We also need to understand the purpose of teaching grammar within the context of the school curriculum to understand what 'grammar' might mean to teachers and children.

However, alongside different grammars, there are also different views on the purpose of grammar teaching. This is reflected in the long-running debate about grammar education that has raged unresolved over decades. Locke (2010) uses the metaphor of 'the grammar wars' to describe the many opposing arguments of teachers, linguists, educationalists, politicians and the general public. For example, a lack of attention to grammar is often equated with a decline in standards, behaviour and social discipline by politicians (Locke, 2010) and an increase in attention to grammar may be regarded by educationalists 'as stifling and limiting of children's engagement with language' (Myhill, 2018, p2).

These two contrasting views ('a decline in standards' versus 'children's engagement with language') reflect something of the 'prescriptive' and 'descriptive' debate. A prescriptive approach to language tells people how they should read and write. Seen prescriptively, grammar is the embodiment of rules and accuracy and the 'fix-it approach to weak writing' (Micciche, 2004, p716). In contrast, a descriptive approach aims to describe how people do use language. Seen descriptively, grammar is concerned with the patterns and variations in actual use in varying contexts and for varying purposes.

When these contrasting approaches are reflected in the same curriculum, there is the potential to create confusion and conflict for teachers over the purpose of knowledge about grammar. As Bell asks, 'Is the aim to develop confidence and offer children "control and choice" in language use, or to improve their written accuracy?' (Bell, 2016, p158).

Within this chapter, we take a descriptive view of grammar. We see grammar as involving words, sentences and texts in 'a process of making meaning in context' (Halliday and Matthiessen, 2014, p3). We advocate the principle of seeing language through a grammatical lens, to enable children to analyse, evaluate and create meaning and effect in texts – and to do so with confidence and enthusiasm.

However, this is not to the exclusion of learning about grammar as a system and how that system operates in both standard and non-standard forms. In English, standard English is often presented as a model, as in the prescriptive view of grammar. Confidence in the use of standard English is clearly important in formal assessment and in the wider world (e.g. employment). However, in life, language users draw from a wider range of language forms according to their regional background and social groups, but also their purpose and audience. A descriptive view of language encourages the recognition and exploration of such differences.

Therefore, a key question is how best to realise – or reconcile – these two perspectives as part of classroom practice, enabling children to develop pride in their own language/s, as well as confidence and accuracy in the use of standard English and independence and autonomy as critical and effective language users.

Considering the grammar curriculum

At this point, we invite you to consider your own experiences of being taught grammar at school. The *Prompts for critical reflection* which follow are intended to help you to reflect on your memories of school grammar. Given the often-prescriptive nature of this area of the curriculum, we also ask you to consider the place of the language/s of your home and community.

PROMPTS FOR CRITICAL REFLECTION

Memories of grammar teaching at school

Reflect on what you remember of learning grammar at school:

- What can you recall from your own time as a child in the classroom about your experiences of the teaching and learning of grammar?

- Did the grammar taught in school reflect the patterns of English language used in your home or did you feel the need to adapt your use of language to conform to those presented in the classroom?
- What impact do you feel any of your classroom experiences in relation to the teaching of grammar had on your use of language, spoken or written, and on your attitudes to language and literature?

If you were educated in a state-maintained school in England, it is likely that you followed the grammar curriculum of the National Curriculum. We will now use the National Curriculum for English as an example of 'schooled grammar'. This reflects the key principles and practice which would seem to be evident in other curricula in various Anglophone countries, including America, Australia and New Zealand. Over recent decades these countries have moved, albeit in different ways, towards a more focused and explicit teaching of grammatical terminology and an increased emphasis on the assessment of related knowledge.

The current 'National Curriculum for English: Key Stages 1 and 2 framework' document (DfE, 2013a) represents the most extensive grammar curriculum of all previous iterations. Largely prescriptive in design, the depth and detail of the statutory requirements and non-statutory guidance are substantial, dwarfing many other aspects of the curriculum for English. For example, the statutory 'Appendix 2' provides a year-by-year list of 'terminology for children' (DfE, 2013a) which is then defined and exemplified by a non-statutory glossary (DfE, 2013a). While the glossary does bring some consistency to grammar knowledge, a formally assessed 'right or wrong' national test on grammar also brings high stakes accountability (DfE, 2013b).

In comparison, content relating to grammar pedagogy is thin. The predominant message seems to be one of a 'teach-practise-apply' approach, reminiscent of decontextualised 'drill and skill' exercises. Giovanelli (2015, p38) refers to it as the 'here's the term, now explore it' pedagogy that typifies traditional, prescriptive grammar approaches. For example: 'The grammatical terms that children should learn are labelled as "terminology for children". They should learn to recognise and use the terminology **through discussion and practice**' (DfE, 2013a, p74) [our emphasis in bold].

There is also an assumption that initially children will be *unfamiliar* with the target grammatical concept. This can be seen in the following example:

> **Once children are familiar** with a grammatical concept [for example 'modal verb'], they should be encouraged to apply and explore this concept in the grammar of their own speech and writing and to note where it is used by others.
>
> (DfE, 2013a, p74: our emphasis in bold)

This perceived lack of necessary grammar knowledge presents as something of a 'deficiency pedagogy' (Carter, 1990, pp105–106). It returns us to earlier discussions about the acquisition of implicit grammar and the young child's ability to communicate verbally using a wide range of sophisticated grammatical structures even before starting school. Therefore, it can be argued that new learning at school lies not so much in children acquiring *familiarity* with a grammatical concept but in them coming to explicitly know and name a schooled grammar version of it.

Seeing the child in this way, as something of a 'blank grammar slate', also raises questions of the place of linguistic diversity, in particular regional dialects which, although they differ from standard English, are still rule-following forms. Any content-heavy, prescriptive curriculum which is predicated upon the teaching and assessment of accuracy and 'correctness' in standard English presents challenges for teachers keen to value the languages and cultures of their children. (For a closer consideration of linguistic diversity, see Smith and Sanders, this volume.)

Focusing on grammatical terminology

The prevalence of grammatical terminology within the curriculum requires us to take seriously the principles, purpose and classroom practice associated with it. Myhill et al. (2012, p162) underline its significance, describing it as an aspect which has been 'systematically overlooked at both policy level and in research' and for which there is 'neither understanding nor agreement about how best to explain grammatical terminology'. In the next *Spotlight on research*, we present views from the literature about the role and value of teaching grammatical terminology in the classroom.

SPOTLIGHT ON RESEARCH

The role and value of grammatical terminology in the curriculum

Grammatical terminology reflects our human preoccupation with naming things – in this case, the naming of grammatical structures. 'Knowing grammar' (implicitly) is not the same as 'knowing about grammar' (explicitly) which is not the same as 'knowing grammatical terminology'. (Indeed, 'knowing about grammar' could be achieved without ever learning the labels of 'verb', 'adjective' and 'noun', etc.). Keith (1997, p12) maintains that 'terminology and rules are pointless if your mind hasn't grasped the concepts behind the terminology'.

Berry maintains that access to complex grammatical concepts is 'difficult, if not impossible, without the term', even if the concepts exist in someone's mind without having a term (2010, p21). Therefore, any grammar curriculum in which grammar is taught explicitly would seem to require a language to talk about it. In this way, the teaching of grammar is potentially no different from most subjects and their associated specialist terminologies.

For Carter (1990, p119), grammatical terminology is potentially an aid to learning, providing children with a pathway to acquiring 'conscious control and conscious choice over language' and enabling them to 'see through language in a systematic way and to use language more discriminatingly'. But Krashen (1983, cited in Hartwell, 1985) suggests that the sheer challenge and complexity of this level of formal learning for children at this age and stage of development creates a barrier to learning instead.

For Hudson (2001), grammatical terminology is a worthy and relevant body of knowledge, of interest in its own intellectual and aesthetic right. This is reminiscent of Halliday's 'Grammatics', a term coined to denote 'a way of using grammar to think with' (Halliday, 2002, p416). In this way, understanding grammatical terminology can enable children to consider, discuss and create texts with clarity, economy and control and have a positive effect on their intellectual development.

Within this chapter, we advocate there is real value in teaching carefully selected, developmentally appropriate grammatical terminology over time and as part of a whole school approach. If taught well, with the priority on the development of grammatical concepts first and terminology second, it stands to become 'an efficient and precise way of accessing and discussing functions and purposes' (Carter, 1990, p109). As the children's awareness, knowledge and ownership increases, it stands to become a tool to better understand and use meaning and effect. However, in the worst cases, it becomes 'an alternative to clear thinking instead of an aid to it' (Halliday, 1967, p87). Therefore, the challenge is one of *how*. How can grammatical terminology be effectively integrated into teaching and learning about grammar, literacy and language?

This challenge is exacerbated by the current statutory requirement for children in Year 6 (10–11-year-olds) to take a grammar test. Prescriptive in form, the 'Grammar, Punctuation and Spelling' test (GPS) (DfE, 2013b) threatens to impose an overfocus on traditional teaching approaches, characterised by the recall of definitions and the identification of grammatical terms in texts.

In the next section we step directly into the classroom, asking the question: What can we learn about the teaching of grammatical terminology by listening to children and their teachers?

Section 2: Grammatical terminology and the perspectives of children and their teachers

In Section 2, we explore two of Marie's key findings from her doctoral research study. This study focused on the investigation of the perspectives of Year 5 and Year 6 children and their teachers. Given the abstract nature of grammatical terminology, this study adopted an exploratory approach and incorporated a wide range of research methods. These included semi-structured questionnaires, teacher interviews, child group interviews (e.g. using video elicitation; playing and inventing grammar games), lesson observations and children's writing conferences. This research design supported the detailed triangulation of qualitative and quantitative data which, in turn, enabled the complex and abstract nature of grammatical terminology to be comprehensively explored.

Given the scope of this chapter, we focus on two key findings which suggested that grammatical terminology created barriers rather than aids to children's learning. We present these as: (i) 'struggling to remember it' and (ii) 'struggling to use it'.

SPOTLIGHT ON RESEARCH

'Struggling to remember it' (Helks, 2019)

When Marie's doctoral research study asked, 'What do you think is hard about grammatical terminology?', children's responses were overwhelmingly in agreement – it was about trying to remember what the different grammatical terms mean:

Child 1: In remembering what they mean.
Child 2: You can't remember.
Child 3: Can't remember it the next day.
Child 4: It is hard to remember the meaning of the word.

This was also reflected in teachers' responses and included concern about the stress and anxiety that recall caused for some children. For example, following a lesson observation, one teacher commented:

> *I mean I don't know if you noticed, the boy sat here was really stressed with himself that he couldn't remember what a subordinate clause was.*

This was despite a well-established, daily, discrete grammar skills session in which the children routinely recapped definitions and practised target grammatical features in decontextualised exercises. For example, here the teacher recaps the meaning of 'adjective', using the familiar simplified, semantic definition of 'describing word':

Teacher: What's an adjective, [child's name]?
Child: It's a describing word.

Teacher: And what does it describe?
Child: A noun.

Alongside discrete grammar skills sessions, grammatical terminology was routinely modelled or practised in the context of reading and writing activities. For example, here we see a teacher using grammatical terminology in discussion with a child during independent writing:

> *That's a subordinate clause [child's name]. You need a main clause to go with it. Do you want some help with it?*

However, despite grammatical terminology being commonplace in the classroom and the children feeling confidently familiar with a range of grammatical terms (particularly those relating to the word classes of adjectives, nouns and verbs), the children still maintained that recall was the hardest thing of all. Follow-up child interviews revealed something of their difficulty. For example:

> *Well, there's loads of different ones, for example, an adjective and then like a verb and an adverb, because they both start with the same thing and you get a bit confused.*

When asked, 'Is grammatical terminology harder than the technical terminology of other subjects?' the children and their teachers all responded with a resounding 'yes', though articulating why was difficult (even for the teachers). One child tried to put it into words, saying, 'You have to think more harder than normal.'

This puzzling situation is summed up well by Crystal (1997, p24) when he asks, 'What is so special about linguistic terms that prompts people to react in this way? It cannot be just a matter of "long words"...'

Examining the nature of grammatical terminology

Have you ever considered the nature of grammatical terminology and wondered why it might feel problematic? As Myhill et al. (2012, p162) explain, research here is limited: 'This is an aspect of grammar teaching which has been systematically overlooked at both policy level and in research; there is neither understanding nor agreement about how best to explain grammatical terminology.'

So, before considering how best to teach grammatical terminology, we need to understand the unusual nature of grammatical terminology. This takes us into the field of linguistics and is explored in the *Spotlight on research* which follows.

SPOTLIGHT ON RESEARCH
The unusual nature of grammatical terminology

Grammatical terminology is unusual. This is for a number of reasons, including:

- All subjects have their specialist terminology, but grammatical terminology is more than just 'content vocabulary' (Berry, 1997, p136). It is language to talk about language and, as such, it does not normally occur incidentally in everyday contexts and conversation.

- Terms such as 'adjective, 'verb' and 'subordinate clause' do not denote simple things or ideas. They act as labels to denote categories of language concepts. Trask refers to these categories as 'lexical categories' (1999, pp38–39). Given that language is already a symbolic system and that written language constitutes second-order symbolism, grammatical terminology is therefore highly abstract.
- A word (or phrase or clause) can have a different grammatical label, depending on how it is being used in a sentence. For example, on its own, we are unable to deduce the grammatical category of the word 'light'. To do that, we must know the role the word is playing within a sentence. For example, in the sentence, 'The shopping bag was light', the word 'light' is being used as an adjective. However, in the sentence, 'She turned on the light', the word 'light' is being used as a noun, whereas in 'They light the fire', it functions as a verb.

The glossary of the English National Curriculum (DfE, 2013a) demonstrates something of the complexity of trying to define a grammatical term ('subordinate clause' in this case) through its grammatical properties and, because grammar is a network, by its connections to other grammatical concepts. (Underlining signals hyperlinks to other definitions within the glossary.):

> **Subordinate clause**: A clause which is subordinate to some other part of the same sentence is a subordinate clause; for example, in *The apple that I ate was sour,* the clause that I ate is subordinate to apple (which it modifies). Subordinate clauses contrast with co-ordinate clauses as in *It was sour but looked very tasty.* (Contrast: main clause) However, clauses that are directly quoted as direct speech are not subordinate clauses.
>
> (DfE 2013a)

Here we have words describing words, all of which are at a high level of abstraction.

Myhill et al. (2013) argue that such definitions are unlikely to be conceptually robust enough for children's application in authentic language contexts. For this reason, Kolln and Gray (2017) suggest that definitions need to go beyond word meaning to consider word form, i.e. to know the defining and limiting characteristics (e.g. 'A verb is a word that can take an -s or an -ing form'). So, although simplified semantic definitions (e.g. 'describing word' and 'doing word') can be a useful starting point (and even a handy mnemonic for later years), more linguistically functional explanations will better serve application and support the ongoing development of conceptual understanding.

The development of children's ability to use specialist terminology alongside the acquisition of new concepts is a lengthy and complex process. Thus, the teacher's task of making grammatical terminology 'intelligible and useful' to children (Beard, 2000, p207) is a very challenging one indeed.

Teaching grammatical terminology within the context of real texts

The need for grammatical terminology to be made 'intelligible and useful' to children (Beard, 2000, p207) brings us to the notion of context. Having considered the unusual nature of grammatical terminology and the implications of this for teaching and learning, we now consider the challenges posed by grammatical terminology when we endeavour to teach grammar explicitly in the context of reading and writing texts.

SPOTLIGHT ON RESEARCH
'Struggling to apply it' (Helks, 2019).

Within Marie's doctoral research study, the children's struggle with recall seemed significantly harder when using grammatical terminology in the context of a reading or writing task (e.g. discussing a class novel or their own writing).

Examples of typical reading and writing tasks included feature-spotting in reading (e.g. 'Underline all the nouns in green') and practising a grammar feature formulaically as 'display writing' (e.g. 'Try to put some more adjectives in'). Suddenly, children who had been previously articulate, and confident in their simplified semantic definitions and practice examples, needed to double-check their subject knowledge. For example, one child checked whether a verb was a 'doing word' when reviewing his own writing and another child confused adjective with verb, despite previously having been adamant that adjectives were 'easy!', having learned them in Year 3.

The teachers were confused by this, especially when the grammatical term should have been familiar to the children, having been taught for at least three years as part of the primary school curriculum. As one teacher explained: 'We have been doing adjectives forever and they still can't identify them in a sentence.'

For many children, trying to both remember and apply grammatical terminology in the context of real language use caused confusion and anxiety, seemingly impacting their working memory, creating cognitive overload and reducing their attentional capacity for the higher order thinking involved in the consideration of meaning and effect. Thus, reading and writing tasks involving a sequence of steps, the first of which was dependent upon recall (and, of course, conceptual understanding), were particularly demanding.

Some children seemed aware of the issue. For example, one child announced in a group interview that he preferred 'to have one thing to do' at once. He stressed the word 'one' by jabbing his index finger in the air, at which point the other children in the group readily agreed.

The need to recall grammatical terms, alongside 'feature-spotting' in reading and/or formulaic practice in 'display writing', seemed to reduce time for children to explore the impact of grammatical choices on meaning and effect. 'Contextualised' activities were almost entirely focused upon the recall and identification of grammatical features and terminology in the context of a literary text, rather than consideration of 'choices'. This was in line with the findings of Cushing & Helks (2021, p248) who found that decontextualised approaches of 'feature spotting and the arbitrary insertion of grammatical features into their writing' were actually in 'stark opposition' to the contextualised pedagogies that teachers reported to be enacting. This raises the question of what we mean by 'contextualised' approaches, a point explored by Myhill (2005, p82) who argues, there has been 'little genuine discussion or consideration of what "in context" means'.

What more does this tell us about how to best teach grammatical terminology? Should this finding lead us to reconsider the value of contextualising grammar in authentic texts? Our answer would be a resounding 'no'. As one teacher said, '...with no context, they [the children] actually wouldn't see the point to it'.

It is clear from the points made earlier that teaching grammar is complex. The next section considers what might be a suitable pedagogical strategy for teaching of grammar, given its complexity. We illustrate this through the design of a five-staged pedagogical model, exemplified through two examples of application to texts.

Section 3: Implications for classroom practice

Crystal argues that grammar has a fundamental role to play in the development of reading, writing, speaking and listening, 'But only if we take on board that ever-so-critical clause: if it's taught well' (2013, p28). While it is beyond the scope of this chapter to discuss in detail the range of research examining causal relationships between explicit grammar teaching and language learning, we draw your attention to the work of key researchers in this area whose work has pointed to the benefits of a contextualised grammar pedagogy, explicit grammar teaching and children's writing and/or reading. For example, the teaching of grammar in the context of authentic texts with a focus on how textual patterns and linguistic choices serve to create meaning has been shown to improve writing ability (Myhill et al., 2012) and the use of reader-response theories has been shown to provide an effective contextualised, concept-driven approach to the teaching of grammar and meaning in secondary classrooms (Cushing, 2018; Giovanelli, 2016).

As we move on to consider the implications for classroom, it may be useful to reiterate key points presented in the chapter, as these underpin the practice we aim to exemplify. These are:

- Children have implicit understanding of grammar which they use to communicate, even if they do not have explicit knowledge of grammatical features.
- Grammatical terminology is an unusual and highly abstract body of specialist terms.
- The development of children's ability to use grammatical terminology alongside the development of grammatical concepts is a lengthy and complex process.
- The overarching aim of teaching grammar is to develop the understanding of how grammar creates meaning and effect in spoken and written texts (in standard and non-standard forms), supporting a critical and analytical understanding of form, purpose and audience in language use.

Pedagogical model

The pedagogical model we propose is based on the principle of conceptual development over time as a back-and-forth process within which grammatical terminology becomes an increasingly efficient and effective tool for children to engage with text analysis (reading) and text creation (writing).

The model is organised as a sequence of learning (see Table 7.1). This five-staged sequence could take place within a single lesson or a series of lessons, as deemed appropriate by the teacher. Although it has a linear presentation, in practice it is fluid. It is intended as a loose framework, to be used flexibly according to the needs of the children. The two examples of classroom practice focus on written texts: one literary (picture book) and one non-literary (real-life poster), although, of course, grammar can be studied in the context of oral texts (e.g. speeches, news reports, adverts and storytelling performances).

Throughout this sequence of learning, the role of talk is essential. This draws on a wealth of research which highlights the importance of talk, particularly dialogic talk, in promoting learning (Alexander, 2008; Mercer and Littleton, 2007). Children move from conversations where they share their responses to a text 'in their own words' to engaging in discussions which are more 'grammatically dialogic' (Myhill, 2018, p16) and in 'dialogic metatalk' to explain and justify the choices made in their own writing (Myhill, 2021, p271). (For a closer consideration of dialogic talk, see Avis and Hesmondhalgh, this volume.) They draw upon their growing conceptual understanding and their increasing ownership of specialist grammatical terms in understanding, creating and critically evaluating texts. Interacting collaboratively with others,

Table 7.1 A five-staged sequence of learning for the teaching of grammatical concepts and terminology in context		
Stage	**Title of stage**	**Focus**
1	Responding to text through book-talk TEXT	Engaging interest and sharing responses through an open discussion.
2	Exploring patterns IN TEXT	Exploring language patterns or characteristics in the text, focusing on the target grammatical feature and discussing its impact on the reader.
3	Spotlighting a grammatical concept and its terminology OUT OF TEXT	Giving spotlighted attention to the grammatical feature (e.g. its properties) away from the text and then introducing the grammatical term.
4	Contextualising the new grammatical learning APPLIED TO TEXT: READING	Applying the grammatical feature and using the grammatical term in the context of discussion to support deeper textual exploration and analysis in this and similar authentic, real-life texts (reading).
5	Increasing ownership APPLIED TO TEXT: OWN WRITING	Deepening learning of the grammatical feature and use of the grammatical term through application to critical reflection and analysis of own linguistic choices and language use (own writing).

they deepen their learning through structured activities, the use of mediated resources and teacher support, improving both spoken and written language.

The following two examples take place in classrooms in which language and creativity are valued and literature and authentic texts play a key role in the teaching of English. The first example is in a Key Stage 1, Year 2 classroom and has a focus on the conceptual understanding and terminology of 'adjective'.

IDEAS FOR CLASSROOM PRACTICE
Example 1: Year 2

Context

As part of a whole school focus on encouraging reading, the Year 2 class (6–7-year-olds) are reading to children in Reception (4–5-year-olds). Some children have expressed a preference for *Where the Wild Things Are* by Maurice Sendak (1963) and are planning dramatic readings, supported by props and puppets they have created. In the following sequence, this text is used as a focus for grammar study.

Stage 1: Responding to text through book-talk

The children re-read *Where the Wild Things Are*, sharing their memories of this book from when they were younger. The teacher encourages open discussion of their interpretations of the meanings and themes of the text, including its suitability for younger children.

Stage 2: Exploring patterns

The class read aloud expressively an extract from the text and give their initial thoughts on its meaning and effect.

> "And when he came to the place where the wild things are they roared their terrible roars and gnashed their terrible teeth and rolled their terrible eyes and showed their terrible claws."

The teacher leads the children to focus on the language, giving prompts about word order and structure if necessary, but without using technical terms. The children note the repetition of 'terrible' which the teacher underlines. They discuss the impact of this repetition.

> "And when he came to the place where the wild things are they roared their terrible roars and gnashed their terrible teeth and rolled their terrible eyes and showed their terrible claws."

The teacher asks the children whether they think Maurice Sendak should have/could have varied his word choice here. He then invites the children to suggest different words that Sendak could have used instead of 'terrible' to describe the sounds and features of the Wild Things. He lists their suggestions on the screen and then asks the children to select words from this list to insert into the text in which each use of the word 'terrible' has been removed.

> "And when he came to the place where the wild things are they roared their _____ roars and gnashed their _____ teeth and rolled their _____ eyes and showed their _____ claws."

The children produce the alternative text.

> "And when he came to the place where the wild things are they roared their horrible roars and gnashed their razor-sharp teeth and rolled their bulging eyes and showed their curly claws."

The children read this text and the original aloud and discuss their preferences and the reasons for them. The teacher encourages consideration of the repetition of the adjective, 'terrible'. (What does this do? What meaning and effect do you think he was trying to create?) Discussion includes the use of repetition for dramatic effect, particularly for reading aloud and the choices made by all writers according to the impact they wish to create.

The teacher comments that repetition is a common feature in young children's literature and asks how this relates to their independent story reading and writing.

Stage 3: Spotlighting a grammatical concept and terminology

Focusing on a list of adjectives, including 'terrible' and alternatives previously suggested, the teacher asks the children to consider the role that these words are playing in the text and their position in relation to other words. The children agree that these words describe things. The teacher then names the grammatical feature as 'adjectives' and gives a brief explanation. (The teacher may choose to use 'describing words' as a proxy definition here, but the ongoing development of the grammatical concept is the priority and will continue.)

The teacher draws key points together into a summary of, *what we know about adjectives* (i.e. the typical properties of an 'adjective'), avoiding lengthy technical explanations. (Later, the children will learn that adjectives may be placed after the noun and that other word classes 'describe things', not just adjectives.)

The teacher gives the children time to record the word 'adjective' and their understanding of it in their notebooks. They are encouraged to do this in whatever ways make most sense to them (e.g. words, sketches, diagrams).

Stage 4: Contextualising the new grammatical learning

The teacher then presents a poster for a lost toy, inviting the children to discuss why the adjectives, already highlighted in the text, are important in the description. The children recognise that the adjectives in this context are needed for a different purpose than creating dramatic effect.

The teacher and the children discuss where else they might (or might not) find adjectives being used in other texts, particularly those from everyday life (e.g. to describe – in stories; to persuade – in adverts). The teacher encourages them to collect examples to bring into class to be shared and reviewed in future sessions.

Stage 5: Increasing ownership

The teacher explains that the children are going to create a guessing game for the Reception class to play, based on the Wild Things. It will involve the Reception children in matching descriptions (written and read aloud by the Year 2 children) with large pictures of the Wild Things. The children discuss how they will need to use adjectives for the purpose of a guessing game, choosing their words carefully and precisely.

The children draft their descriptions and try them out with their peers. With teacher support, they review whether they are effective and consider how they can be improved. They are encouraged to use the grammatical term, 'adjective', to facilitate their discussions and their thinking. They then refine their descriptions and present them to the younger children.

The second example is in a Key Stage 2, Year 6 (10–11-year-olds) classroom and has a focus on the conceptual understanding and terminology of 'passive voice'.

IDEAS FOR CLASSROOM PRACTICE
Example 2: Year 6

Context

The Year 6 teacher is aware that the children in her class lack confidence in using or identifying the passive voice. To focus attention on this, she selects a poster which is displayed outside the building site close to the school.

Stage 1: Responding to text

The class discuss the purpose of the poster and its style of presentation. The children comment on its use of colour, font, images and language and note the formal tone of the language. The teacher encourages them to identify examples from the text which illustrate this formality and ensure that the children understand the meaning of the vocabulary used.

Stage 2: Exploring patterns

The teacher asks the children whether they have noticed any patterns in the language of the text. She then draws their attention to the use of the passive voice, presenting them with a list of statements from the poster containing this feature (e.g. Safety helmets must be worn. Unauthorised entry to this site is strictly prohibited.) and asking them to identify any common characteristics. They note the impersonal and authoritative tone. They then discuss how the message of each sentence could be changed to make it more personal and informal in tone, for example as a more personal command, using the second person, 'you' (you must wear a safety helmet. etc).

Stage 3: Spotlighting a grammatical concept and its terminology

The teacher presents a range of examples of short sentences containing either the passive voice or the active voice. She asks the children to work together to sort the sentences into two groups based on how they are structured, justifying their selection. Focusing on the examples of the passive first, the teacher provides the label and reinforces the properties of the passive voice as per the children's suggestions and drawing out the significant purpose of hiding the agent or moving it to the end of the sentence. Using blank strips of paper, the children work together to generate pairs of passive and active voice sentences.

The children are then encouraged to record their understanding about the 'passive voice' in their notebooks in whatever ways makes most sense to them (e.g. words, sketches, diagrams), including examples discussed during the session. This process is repeated with the 'active voice'.

Stage 4: Contextualising the new grammatical learning

The teacher then introduces a text previously seen by the children in their geography topic on Natural Resources, with examples of the passive voice already highlighted. The teacher reinforces the characteristics of passive voice and the children discuss why they think it has been used in that context. The process is then repeated with other texts (e.g. official documents). They consider where else the passive voice might be found in school and in everyday life. The teacher encourages them to collect examples to share and review in future sessions.

Stage 5: Increasing ownership

The teacher challenges the children to produce a formal poster modelled on the original text discussed in Stage 1 for visitors to their classroom, incorporating the use of the passive voice as appropriate. The children later share their texts, comparing the tone and impact of their sentences. They are encouraged to use the grammatical term, 'passive voice', to facilitate their discussions and their thinking.

In Section 3, we explored a pedagogic model (a five-stage sequence of learning) designed to contextualise the teaching of grammatical concepts and terminology in purposeful and meaningful ways. These examples illustrate a number of key pedagogical features. These can be summarised as:

- An initial focus on children's understanding of and response to an authentic text.
- Exploration and identification of grammatical patterns to develop children's understanding of a grammatical feature.
- The analysis and exploration of a chosen grammatical feature following the broader critical appreciation of the text.
- Use of grammatical terminology, at first spotlighted 'out of text' alongside examples of the feature and then integrated and applied 'within text', with working definitions and examples being developed and recorded with the children.

- Consideration of a specific grammatical feature moves beyond the initial text to other real-life examples and includes consideration of the reasons for its use in the child's and others' writing.

Within these examples, children are supported and challenged to apply their understanding to the production, review and development of their own related texts and to the critical evaluation of texts used in other contexts. This process is encouraged through using carefully chosen texts (literary and non-literary) which are authentic and reflective of real life in teacher-led sessions. There is an emphasis on the use of dialogic talk, structured and supported by the teacher through a variety of practical, interactive approaches and resources.

This sequence provides teachers with opportunities to use formative assessment to plan and build children's conceptual development over time.

Chapter summary

This chapter has explored the challenges inherent in teaching and learning grammar, identifying grammatical terminology as an area of particular difficulty. It has considered a number of key issues created by grammatical terminology, given its highly abstract nature and the challenges of teaching it in meaningful, motivational and accessible ways. This is especially significant within a curriculum and assessment system that attaches substantial importance to recall of subject knowledge and the identification of grammatical features.

These issues sit within the wider context of the 'grammar debate' and differences in principles, purposes and practice in teaching grammar. We have explored this debate and have contributed to it by proposing a pedagogical model comprising a five-staged process in which teacher-led interactive sessions and collaborative talk enable children to develop understanding of grammatical concepts first and increase their confidence in the use of grammatical terminology second. Crucially, this process takes place within the context of the investigation and production of a range of authentic literary and non-literary texts (paper-based or digital).

Clearly, within this process, teachers need to be secure and confident in their knowledge about grammar and how it works but, as Bell (2015) writes, there is also a pressing need to contextualise this grammatical knowledge and to support teachers in knowing how to teach it in class. Therefore, as we draw this chapter to a close, it is important to highlight the need for professional development opportunities which equip, empower and enthuse teachers in their understanding and investigation of pedagogical approaches. More widely, we advocate a reconceptualisation of grammar and its pedagogy and a change in curriculum design to prioritise conceptual understanding within a descriptive approach to language learning, which incorporates attention to the acquisition of associated grammatical terminology.

Finally, we hope this chapter has enabled you to develop your understanding of teaching grammar as a meaning making resource within the context of varied and authentic texts, discussion and language play and production. By developing a grammatical lens on language, we enable children to explore, discuss and create texts with purpose, insight and clarity. In an ever-changing, language-rich world, this is more important than ever. We therefore hope that this chapter has encouraged you to reconsider the nature of grammar and its pedagogy and that you will continue to investigate this area and contribute to a new and different grammar debate – one which discusses and explores the best pedagogical models for equipping and empowering children to become confident, critical and enthusiastic language users within and beyond the classroom.

References

Aarts, B. Cushing, I. & Hudson, R. (2019). *Oxford Teaching Guides: How To Teach Grammar.* Oxford: Oxford University Press.

Alderson, J. C. & Horak, T. (2001). *Metalinguistic Knowledge of Undergraduate Students of English Language and Linguistics.* Lancaster: Subject Centre for Languages, Linguistics and Area Studies in Higher Education.

Alexander, R. (2008). *Towards Dialogic Teaching: Rethinking Classroom Talk* (4th Ed.). York, UK: Dialogos.

Beard, R. (2000). *Developing writing 3–13.* London: Hodder & Stoughton.

Bell, H. (2015). The Dead Butler revisited: Grammatical accuracy and clarity in the English Primary Curriculum 2013–2014. *Language and Education,* 29(2), 140–152.

Bell, H. (2016). Teacher knowledge and beliefs about grammar: A case study of an English primary school. *English in Education, 50*(2).

Berry, R. (1997). Teachers' awareness of learners' knowledge: The case of metalinguistic terminology. *Language Awareness,* 6/2 & 3: 136–146.

Berry, R. (2010). *Terminology in English Language Teaching: Nature and Use.* Bern: Peter Lang AG.

Carter, R. (Ed.). (1990). *Knowledge About Language and the Curriculum: The LINC Reader.* London: Hodder.

Crystal, D. (1997). The linguistic identity of English-language dictionaries of linguistics. *Lexicographica,* 13, 17–33.

Crystal, D. (2004). *Making Sense of Grammar.* London: Longman.

Crystal, D. (2008). A Dictionary of Linguistics and Phonetics (6th Ed.). Oxford: Blackwell.

Crystal, D. (2013, May 5). [Web Blog post]. Retrieved from http://david-crystal.blogspot.com/2013/05/on-testing-time.html

Cushing, I. (2018). 'Suddenly, I am part of the poem': Texts as worlds, reader-response and Grammar in teaching poetry. *English in Education,* 52(1), 7–19.

Cushing, I. & Helks, M. (2021). Exploring primary and secondary students' experiences of grammar teaching and testing in England. *English in Education,* 55(3), 239–250.

DfE (Department for Education) (2013a). *The National Curriculum in England: Key Stages 1 and 2 Framework Document.* London: DfE.

DfE (Department for Education) (2013b). *2013 Key Stage 2 Tests: English Grammar, Spelling and Punctuation Tests.* London: DfE.

Giovanelli, M. (2015). *Teaching Grammar, Structure and Meaning.* London: Routledge.

Giovanelli, M. (2016). Text World Theory as cognitive grammatics: A pedagogical application in the secondary classroom. *World Building: Discourse in the Mind,* 109–126.

Halliday, M. A. K. (1967). Linguistics and the teaching of English. In J. Britton (Ed.), *Handbook for English Teachers: 2. Talking and Writing* (pp. 80–90). London: Methuen.

Halliday, M. A. K. (2002). On grammar and grammatics. In J. Webster (Ed.), *The Collected Works of M. A. K. Halliday (Vol.* 3, pp. 384–417). London: Continuum.

Halliday, M. A. K. & Matthiessen, C. M. I. M. (2014). *Halliday's Introduction to Functional Grammar* (4th Ed.). Abingdon: Routledge.

Hartwell, P. (1985). Grammar, grammars, and the teaching of grammar. *College English,* 47(2), 105–127. National Council of Teachers of English.

Helks, M. (2019). *What, Why and How: The Policy, Purpose and Practice of Grammatical Terminology – An Exploratory Study of Grammatical Terminology Through the Perspectives and Practices of Year 5 & Year 6 Pupils and Their Teachers.* Doctoral thesis, University of Huddersfield.

Hudson, R. (2001). Grammar teaching and writing skills: The research evidence. *Syntax in the Schools*, 17, 1–6.

Keith, G. (1997). Teach yourself English grammar. *The English and Media Magazine*, 36.

Kolln, M. & Gray, L. (2017). *Rhetorical Grammar: Grammatical Choices, Rhetorical Effects* (8th Ed.). New York: Pearson Education Inc.

Janks, H., Dixon, K., Ferreira, A., Granville, S. & Newfield, D. (2014). *Doing Critical Literacy: Texts and Activities for Students and Teachers*. New York: Routledge.

Locke, T. (2010). Introduction: 'Grammar wars' and beyond. In T. Locke (Ed.), *Beyond the Grammar Wars* (pp. 1–18). New York: Routledge.

Mercer, N. & Littleton, K. (2007). *Dialogue and the Development of Children's Thinking: A Socio-Cultural Approach*. Abingdon, UK: Routledge.

Micciche, L. (2004). *Making a Case for Rhetorical Grammar*. The National Council of Teachers of English.

Myhill, D. (2005). Ways of knowing: Writing with grammar in mind. *English Teaching: Practice and Critique*, 4(3), 77–96.

Myhill, D., Jones, S. M., Lines, H. & Watson, A. (2012). Re-thinking grammar: The impact of embedded grammar teaching on students' writing and students' metalinguistic understanding. *Research Papers in Education*, 27(2), 139–166.

Myhill, D., Jones, S. & Watson, A. (2013). Grammar matters: How teachers' grammatical subject knowledge impacts on the teaching of writing. *Teaching and Teacher Education*, 36, 77–91.

Myhill, D. (2018). Grammar as a meaning-making resource for language development. *L1 – Educational Studies in Language and Literature*, 18, 1–21.

Myhill, D. (2021). Grammar re-imagined: Foregrounding understanding of language choice in writing. *English in Education*, 55(3), 265–278.

Sendak, M. (1963). *Where the Wild Things Are*. New York: Harper.

Trask, R. L. (1999). *Language: The Basics* (2nd Ed.). Oxon: Routledge.

Vygotsky, L. S. (1987). Thinking and speech. Trans. N. Minick. In R. W. Rieber and A. S. Carton (Eds.). *The Collected Works of L.S. Vygotsky: Vol. 1: Problems of General Psychology: Including the volume Thinking and Speech* (pp. 167–241). New York: Plenum Press.

Watson, A. (2015). Conceptualisations of 'grammar teaching': L1 English teachers' beliefs about teaching grammar for writing. *Language Awareness*, 24(1), 1–14.

CHAPTER

8

Children as critical consumers and producers of multimodal texts

Susan Borland, Karen Daniels, and Siobhan Hunt

Introduction

The chapters in this book carefully frame children's activity in ways that see them as active participants in literacy, who bring a wealth of cultural knowledge shaped by their home and community experiences to the classroom. In this chapter, we consider the implications of this when we think about an effective way to support children in becoming critical consumers and producers of both print-based and digital texts. From an early age, young children are often confident when exploring and producing multimodal and digital texts and these may be very much part of children's cultural life and home and community experience. However, this confidence with digital tools may detract from the need to explicitly teach critical digital literacy that can protect and empower young people online.

The evolution of literacy

Literacy, like any social and cultural activity, continually changes across place and over time. We certainly don't 'do' literacy today, in the same way as we did 50, ten or even five years ago. One of the significant ways in which literacy changes is shaped by the kinds of literacy materials and resources to hand; in particular, advances in digital technologies have meant seismic shifts in the ways in which we do literacy (see also Merchant, this volume). Likewise, our understanding of literacy has evolved and is now much broader than the traditional understanding of literacy, associated with the ability to read and write the printed word. The word *literacy* itself is applied to a growing number of conceptual competencies (Barton, 1994), such as 'Health literacy', 'Media literacy' and 'Emotional literacy', to name but a few. These metaphorical uses of *literacy* describe desirable competencies, but otherwise have no connection to the more traditional understandings of literacy. In education, the concept of *literacy* is often used interchangeably with *English*, and this is true of the National Curriculum, where the overarching aim of the Primary English National Curriculum is to 'promote high standards of language and literacy' (DfE, 2013, p3). The Early Years Foundation Stage (EYFS) statutory framework (DfE, 2023a) identifies literacy as a specific area of learning but there is no mention in either curriculum of the development of literacy to be interpreted broadly, or through the inclusion of digital texts. Broader societal use and the significance of the kinds of literacies that are produced using digital

DOI: 10.4324/9781003381013-8

tools, such as mobile phones, iPads and laptops, are not yet recognised as significant in school contexts. Indeed, the assessment of both Primary English for children aged 5–11 years, and in the EYFS for children aged 0–5 years, the specific area of learning, 'literacy', focuses on the traditional literacy forms of written and print-based texts. In some respects, the omission of digital literacy in the Early Years Foundation Stage statutory framework (2023a) reflects the tensions that many early years educators express. Concerns that digital technologies sit in opposition to print literacy goals, and that such technologies detract from basic skills associated with early literacy development, are prevalent (see Daniels et al., 2019).

Comprehension of print literacies is very often more highly valued in classrooms than other forms of 'reading'. This seems particularly at odds in a society where digital communication – drawing from texts where combinations of print, moving and still images and sound – work together in a kind of orchestration to produce meaning. However, when we think of 'text' we often think purely of a book, or some print-based publication or other. Kress (2003) argues that we must question our understanding of the nature of literacy considering its digital multimodal evolution. Like Kress, Evans (2004) recognises the multimodality of 'text' and the ways in which this can produce diverse written and oral forms. Casey and Bruce (2011) describe how literacy can enable participation as new technologies facilitate new (plural) literacies. Within this broader, 21st Century understanding of literacy and of 'text', the ability to use and produce information digitally is an ever-increasing part of our lives. As socially situated 'literacies', these digital ways of producing text enable communication and meaning making (Lankshear and Knobel, 2008) which are contextual, reciprocal and ever-changing (Cazden, 1996; Casey and Bruce, 2011). Despite the focus on print literacy competencies in schools, the ways in which digital tools and technologies shape our evolving literacy practices have been an interesting area of exploration in literacy research (see, for example, Monkhouse and Bailey, this volume). However, *digital literacies* have proved difficult to define.

SPOTLIGHT ON RESEARCH

Digital literacy in literature: What is it?

Within literature, you will find many different models or explanations of what digital literacy is. The systematic, qualitative literature review by Tamborg et al. (2018), with its modest study of 55 papers, offers an interesting analysis of the range of uses of digital literacy as a concept. They identify eight main usages of digital literacy to describe *how* differences in digital literacy as a term exist. They also discuss *why* it is ambiguous and used in different ways, by identifying a lack of definitions within literature, in addition to a wide range of theoretical approaches to defining digital literacy as a concept. Tamborg et al. identify a range of different conceptualisations in literature, in addition to those studies about digital literacy which do not provide a definition of what it is. This includes:

1. Reading and writing with digital technology.
2. Communication.
3. Access to and acquaintance with digital tools.
4. Attitude toward technology.
5. Digital skills and knowledge.
6. Social practice and classroom culture.
7. Ethics.

8. Critical thinking.
9. No definition/no uses of the term.

(Tamborg et al., 2018, p7)

Within literature that does not define digital literacy, Tamborg et al. (2018) identify two main features, which they refer to as *tacit replacements* and *tacit definitions*. They use *tacit replacements* to describe where the term digital literacy is used in the title or body of the text but is then replaced by a similar term. *Tacit definitions* describe the way that digital literacy is referred to in studies, but not defined. The range of theoretical conceptualisations of digital literacy, in addition to the tacit use of the definitions identified in the study by Tamborg et al., exemplifies the complexity associated with understanding what digital literacy is, what it includes and how it is then framed.

Belshaw (2010) questions the need to create a new digital 'literacy' and Casey and Bruce (2011) remind us that although we may seek to name and define the new literacies associated with digital literacy, it is not new to the children we teach: it is simply literacy as they know it today. Within the wider understanding of literacy as socially situated and enabling communication and meaning making (Lankshear and Knobel, 2008), many children's home literacies are increasingly digital (Ofcom, 2023) and often more so than the traditional print-based literacies they are taught in school. This raises the question of whether there should be more inclusion of these digital literacies to engage children with literacy learning in a way that is not only relevant to their lives and experiences, but necessary in the digital age.

Digital literacy and the evaluating multimodal texts

The evolving nature of digital tools and their affordances has provided a challenge for academics seeking to classify this new form of literacy. In 1997, Paul Gilster first coined the term 'digital literacy' to describe the way that digital texts have revolutionised the way that we interact with information online: 'Digital literacy is the ability to understand information and more important-to evaluate and integrate information in multiple formats that the computer can deliver' (Gilster, 1997, p6).

Gilster's concept of 'digital literacy' is a general explanation of the abilities that are necessary to be able to understand, evaluate and combine the multimodal information that computers present, with a particular emphasis on the need to evaluate its source and context. Glister's definition predates Web2 technologies that utilise user-based content and merge users as both consumers and producers of information (Jenkins, 2006), but because his definition is quite general, and he does not try to list all the skills that it encompasses, it has stood the test of time reasonably well.

In this chapter, we take forward Glister's definition of digital literacy, and think further about how we can evaluate the 'source and context' of digital and non-digital texts. Firstly, we look more closely at multimodality and its implications for children's comprehension of digital texts.

Multimodality and digital literacies

Multimodality, in a broad sense, is used to describe the use of different modes of communication that produce meaning: for example, using words, still and moving pictures and images, art or music. It is important to remember, however, that multimodality is not exclusive to the digital realm, and it has long been considered good practice to interweave children's traditional literacy learning with diverse, non-digital modalities such as art and drama (Evans, 2004). Examples include the use of visual story maps to aid writing composition, the 'hot seating' of characters and the scrutiny of illustrations, to support and develop children's comprehension. Multimodality also acknowledges the embodied nature of human communication – and how the orchestration of words, bodily movements, gestures, sounds, as well as objects around us, come together to produce meaning.

The multimodal nature of digital texts expands the processes incorporated in their comprehension. Walsh (2018) describes how digital information can be 'read' in different ways, including by being viewed or listened to. The author describes how digital writing too has expanded and can encompass talking, interacting or producing and designing digital texts. Consequently, Walsh highlights the importance of research into new literacy pedagogy that combines traditional print-based literacy practices with an understanding of how to design and use digital modalities, the aim of which is to enable children to develop the skills needed to evaluate multimodal texts. There is also the opportunity to support and engage children who find traditional literacy practices challenging, by embracing the use of multimodal reading and writing to enable them to communicate in the mode that they find most accessible.

Digital agency and some of its problems

Facilitators of multimodality, the agency of digital technologies themselves, are the focus of a growing number of studies. From a semiotic technology perspective, Knight et al. (2020) highlight the impact of digital technology on the creation of meaning and discuss the importance of educating children about 'hidden agents' acting within the digital interface and making them more salient to users. For example, Dooly and Darvin (2022) describe the danger of social media algorithms that facilitate the spread of misinformation and manipulate the information we are presented with, based on who we like or dislike, leading to the production of insular communities or *echo chambers*. These echo chambers allow users to share common views free from opposition or challenge, and can foster intolerance and social fragmentation by race, gender, ethnicity and social class. They also have the power to negatively impact on the self-esteem of children and young people by measuring the value of users' interactions in terms of likes, comments and shares.

SPOTLIGHT ON RESEARCH
Digital equality

It is not always the simple case that children's home literacies are more digital than their school literacies. Some parents may choose to minimise their children's screen time or access to digital devices, but for many families this is not a choice. The inequality of access to digital information was underlined during school lockdowns in 2020 and schools became more aware of the children in their communities who did not have the resources to access appropriate digital devices, the internet and even a quiet space to study at home (Piggott et al., 2022). In their report on digital exclusion, Holmes and Burgess (2021) identify that digital exclusion is more likely amongst lower income households (Office for National Statistics [ONS], 2019). Although people within these households may have internet-linked devices (i.e. a phone), access to information may be hampered by a lack of digital skills, a suitable device, e.g. a laptop, or a reliable internet connection.

Research from EU Kids (Smahel et al., 2020) finds that children who engage with a wider range of online activities develop better digital literacy skills than those who do not. This highlights the issue of inequal access to digital resources and the associated outcomes – the so-called 'digital divide' or 'participation gap' (Jenkins, 2009; Lythreatis et al., 2021). Back in 2008, Lankshear and Knobel discussed the early evidence of an alignment of digital literacy inequity with traditional literacy inequity. More recently, Hu et al. (2018) correlate a link between academic achievement and digital capability, through the exploration of Programme for International Student Assessment's (PISA) data from the Organization for Economic Co-operation and Development (OECD) in 2015.

Schools have an opportunity to address this inequity and enable children to develop their understanding of digital affordances to empower them to interact effectively and responsibly online. This is also particularly the case with children who have special educational needs or disabilities (SEND) or who have had adverse childhood experiences (ACE), as research shows that just as these children are more vulnerable in the real world, they are also particularly vulnerable online (HM Government, 2021).

Where are digital literacies in the EYFS and primary curriculum?

Merchant (2020) argues in favour of broad agreement on the kinds of practices we value and wish to support in classrooms. However, within the Early Years Foundation Stage framework (DfE, 2023a) and the Primary National Curriculum (DfE, 2013), digital literacy does not have its own subject curriculum. This is perhaps particularly surprising in the English National Curriculum, as it asserts in its purpose that 'All the skills of language are essential to participating fully as a member of society' (DfE, 2013, p3). The only formal references to digital literacy in the Primary National Curriculum are vague online safety-related references within the Computing curriculum about recognising acceptable/unacceptable behaviour and knowing how to report concerns about *Content* and *Contact*. In the current 'Keeping Children Safe in Education' (DfE, 2023b) guidance, there are *four* areas of risk, including *Commerce* and *Conduct*: demonstrating a greater awareness and understanding of evolving risks and highlighting the need to update the Computing curriculum.

In 2019, additional statutory guidance regarding online safety was introduced in the Relationships Education, Relationships and Sex Education (RSE) and Health Education curriculum (DfE, 2019), but there has been no revision to the Primary English curriculum to include digital literacy. This is despite concerns being raised about the ability of children and young people to identify correct information online, with a National Literacy Trust survey (Picton, 2018) indicating that only 2% of children have the critical literacy skills to be able to identify fake news or misinformation. In response to the findings by the National Literacy Trust (2018), the Digital Culture, Media and Sport Select Committee (2019, p19) recommended that a comprehensive framework for digital literacy be created within Personal, Social, Health Education (PSHE) as a 'fourth pillar of education, alongside reading, writing and maths'. Whilst agreeing that digital literacy is key to tackling disinformation, this was dismissed by the government who asserted that digital literacy was already taught across the curriculum. The government is currently working to prevent children's exposure to harmful information, particularly on sites designed for their use, through the Online Safety Act (Department for Digital Media, Culture and Sport, 2022). This will hopefully reduce children's exposure to misinformation, but it does not remove their need to be taught the critical digital literacy skills to effectively evaluate content across *all* digital platforms. However, when the statutory curriculum does not give specific reference to digital literacies, it may be difficult for teachers to include a focus on these within their practice. Furthermore, as found by Susan, next, some teachers seem unsure of the value of digital literacy and how to teach it. This is interesting as teachers are very likely to use digital technologies in their own lives but may not be aware of the significance of these in children's developing repertoires.

SPOTLIGHT ON RESEARCH

Susan's recent research into the way that digital literacy is understood by teachers, and the extent to which primary literacy is digital, suggests that digital literacy is not well understood by primary teachers. It also suggests that the lack of curriculum guidance and the expectation that digital literacy is taught across the curriculum (Secretary of State for Digital, Culture, Media and Sport, 2020) is in fact hindering teachers in their ability to empower young users with the skills and knowledge needed to navigate the digital world. This seems particularly significant as many children are already accessing digital resources before they start school.

The small-scale, but in-depth, case study research, conducted across two primary schools, found that despite a lack of clarity around the identification and understanding of what digital literacy is, amongst the teacher participants, digital literacy is an embedded part of cross-curricular literacy practice in both schools. However, whilst the digital literacy skills of teachers were evident in the study (to a greater or lesser extent), in their use of digital tools to facilitate learning, the extent to which digital literacy skills are developed by the children is unclear.

Further research is needed to measure the impact of current practice on the development of children's digital literacy. There is evidence to suggest that digital literacy is used widely to support traditional literacy practices such as reading, phonics and to a lesser extent writing. However, it is unclear whether digital literacy is taught discretely and the extent to which the link between digital literacy and English, within the wider multimodal view of literacy (Cazden, 1996), is understood.

A word about digital natives

Young, confident users of digital technologies can be assumed to be 'digital natives' because they have grown up with new technology, unlike their older 'digital immigrant' teachers and parents (Prensky, 2001). However, Dooly and Darvin (2022) describe the danger of this assumption, which can be a barrier for some teachers, as it risks moving the responsibility for critical reflection onto younger users who are unaware of its ability to marginalise or promote exclusion. Although written before the introduction of the current National Curriculum (DfE, 2013), Hague and Payton (2010) describe how adults and teachers, who may potentially lack confidence or functional digital skills, can still support children to develop the critical analysis skills to allow them to question digital information and assess its reliability. Teachers are also able to support collaboration, effective communication and understanding of social and cultural factors to allow them to effectively evaluate all forms of information, both digital and non-digital. For decades, concerns have been raised about children's access to books in the home (see also Sharpe and Taplin, this volume). Access to suitable digital tools and content has in many ways complexified this concern, as children have unequal access to these. This foregrounds the issue that children's success in literacy can be impacted by not just social and cultural factors, but by economic ones too.

Adults in education settings therefore have an important role in helping children to navigate the print and digital landscape, and children's confidence with the technology in itself should not be mistaken for the complex understandings needed to critically reflect on both print and multimodal texts. The *Spotlight on research* that follows illustrates some concerns of researchers of digital literacies in early years classrooms, and how even very young children can be influenced in significant and often concerning ways, through their interactions with digital technologies.

SPOTLIGHT ON RESEARCH

K. Wohlwend & T. Hall (2017) Race and Rag Dolls: Critically Engaging the Embodiment of Diversity in Lalaloopsy Transmedia. In G. Enriquez, E. Johnson, S. Kontovourki & C. A. Mallozzi (Eds), *Literacies, Learning and the Body: Putting Theory and Research into Pedagogical Practice* (pp.155–169). London: Routledge

Wohlwend explores how children's engagement with literacy takes place in a commercialised world. In her book chapter, she discusses how children's interests in favourite characters can often be propelled by media franchises who link products across platforms that influence how children live their daily lives, from what they say, what they eat, how they sleep. In addition, very particular representations of race and gender are portrayed through the products and merchandise.

> As children watch television programs and DVDs, tap through games and apps on tablets and phones, play with dolls and action figures, they can also be clothed in licensed apparel, snack on character gummies, tote school supplies in themed backpacks, and so on. These franchises of branded products grounded by a media narrative, or transmedia, produce far-reaching, ubiquitous, and pervasive flows of merchandise but also circulate discursive messages attached to media narratives.
>
> (Wohlwend and Hall, 2017, p155)

What is critical literacy and why is it important?

The previous sections clearly indicate that critical digital literacy is an important educational goal for life in a digitally mediated world. Parents, teachers, policy makers and researchers cannot take it for granted that children have equal access to digital literacy, or that their experiences with it as 'digital natives' will equip them with the skills to consume and produce digital texts in ways that are beneficial to their lives, and to their broader communities.

Texts are ideological, that is, they contain the ideas, beliefs and values of the text producer (see Street, 1995). Texts are never neutral and Wohlwend's work clearly demonstrates how they can shape children's understandings of their world and the people in it, and that children are often the target audience for media franchises. The youngest children can be drawn into the ideas, thoughts, markets and ideological positions of the producers of digital texts. Texts can assert immense power positions, and they are always produced with an intention or purpose; to argue, to share information, to entertain, to discuss, to persuade, for financial gain or customer 'loyalty'. These beliefs, values and intentions are often 'hidden' or implicit. By reflecting on the affordances of digital texts, we may be better equipped to support children in developing their own critical literacy skills when 'reading' online texts. Firstly, it is worth identifying some of the key features of digital and print texts.

When we compare a digital text to a print text, we can generally assume the following:

Print texts convey meaning through drawing on the alphabetic code, read from left to right (in English) and from the top to the bottom of the page. Print can have different fonts, styles and sizes, but generally it is assumed to be of a form that is conducive to tracking with the eyes, and follows conventions of punctuation, spelling and grammar for the purposes of clarity of expression. Authorship of print and 'published' texts tends to be acknowledged and have been through a process of commission and review. Published, print-based texts tend to take time to produce and distribute to readers, although both digital and print versions of texts may be published rapidly.

Digital texts may have some or most of the previous features. They may also draw on the affordances of combinations of modes: sound, moving images, print, colour, still images to convey meaning. The digital reading pathway may be guided by hyperlinks to other content and websites, including advertisements. Authorship of digital texts may be acknowledged, but very often it is hard to determine who has produced the text. Often there are opportunities for readers to respond and comment, so becoming 'co-authors'. Digital texts are often instantly published, readily and widely available to readers, and may be quickly editable.

In considering the previous distinctions, children require critical literacy skills whether working with both print-based and digital texts, and though print and digital texts raise similar issues, they also raise some quite different challenges. In Chapter 7, for example, Helks and Myers discuss the teaching and grammar. Developing children's knowledge about how language works in written texts can empower them to make specific language choices to create impact on meaning, and also support children in identifying specific linguistic devices in texts used to persuade or inform, for example. Digital texts have a different kind of 'grammar' that involves the impact of multiple modes in orchestration, that creates very particular kinds of effects. It is essential, therefore, that children are equipped with understandings of how they respond to (or consume) and create (or produce) both print and digital texts.

Maine and Shields (2015) noted how often the use of digital texts, such as film, has the potential to support and enhance traditional print-based comprehension skills. Their small-scale research study demonstrates the potential for alternatives to written texts, such as film, to enhance children's comprehension skills by focusing on the development of oral language. The study suggests that by focusing on a range of texts, including film, children's print-based comprehension skills can be quantifiably increased.

Critical literacy is a key element of digital literacy, identified in a range of literature (Tamborg et al., 2018), but it is not a new concept, and it can be argued it has been fundamental to literacy education over generations. Indeed it is closely linked to critical thinking, which, it could be reasonably argued, should be an overarching aim of education.

Critical literacy and some of its theorists

Next, we present several theorists and how they have explained critical literacy.

Louise Rosenblatt's Transactional Theory of reading

In understanding how we can develop critical literacy, Rosenblatt's Transactional Theory of reading presents a useful description of what happens in the reading process. Rosenblatt (1995) described comprehension as what he termed a transaction between the reader and the text, within a particular cultural context. This is significant, as it implies that the meaning is not purely in the hands of the author but is shaped by the reader and the ways in which they make sense of the text, from their own cultural position and experience. In the light of this, key to Rosenblatt's position is that developing reader response through discussion around texts is essential to literacy education. This positions the reader as an active participant in the reading process and acknowledges that readers both individually and socially construct meanings and impressions from the texts they read. Our own experiences and cultural backgrounds, therefore, influence the kinds of ways in which we understand and interpret the texts we read.

Rosenblatt's work originally referred to print-based texts, but the implications of the transactional view of reading have a similar resonance when we reflect on the ways in which we 'read' and make sense of digital texts.

Paulo Freire and the workings of power

In 1970, in his landmark thesis, Paulo Freire hailed that critical literacy should be a key feature of education and include an examination of how power works in language. Freire's work was driven by an understanding that learners should be co-creators of knowledge, and active participants in the reading process, moving beyond passively accepting the text's message. Freire argued that this involves questioning, examining and disputing the power relations that exist between readers and authors (and indeed teachers). His work was specifically about considering the ways in which readers should ask the following questions:

- Who produced this information? Why did they produce it?
- Where was it published?
- What does it really say?
- Who is it aimed at?
- What is it based on?
- Is there evidence for it, or is it just opinion?
- Is it verifiable elsewhere?

Recent concerns over the proliferation and consumption of digital texts, however, have heightened concerns for educators, parents and policy makers. These range from challenging issues such as online safety; children accessing biased, inaccurate or inappropriate content; to concerns about the mental health and wellbeing of children and young people. It is also clear that children and young people are not always able to sufficiently evaluate the texts that they encounter.

Margaret Mallett and the questioning of authorship

Response to texts, stimulated by discussion, and asking critical questions about authorship is key to critical appreciation of texts. Mallett (1992) highlighted that discussing texts and encouraging children to respond to texts was crucial in developing critical literacy. This also included the teaching of inference and encouraging children to provide reasoned justification of their views about texts. Mallett (1992) also describes the importance of discerning fact from opinion (where this is overt – if we are to assume that language and literacy is ideological). Mallett also suggested that children needed to look closely at the structure of language and language choices made by the author, and the ways in which this contributes to the meaning of a text.

Hillary Janks – texts as potent ways of reading, seeing and acting

For Janks (2014), being a critical reader is more than just not passively accepting a text message, but it is an issue of social justice, and being able to understand the workings of power and influence in texts. According to Janks, texts have social effects and always present a version of 'truth' that can be used for good and ill, and texts produce identity positions in readers, and impact on who has access to opportunities for a better life. Janks asserts that critical literacy can give us potent ways of reading, seeing and acting in the world. To achieve this, the teacher's role is to encourage children to become *resistant readers* who do not blindly buy into the meanings and positions that texts offer. This necessitates supporting a child's growing understanding that texts are not neutral, and to recognise the ways in which language can be a powerful way of influencing.

PROMPTS FOR CRITICAL REFLECTION

Consider the ways in which Rosenblatt, Mallett, Freire and Janks describe texts and reflect on the following:

Does anything surprise you about the positions held by these authors?

Which ones particularly appeal to you and why?

Reflect on your own practice when teaching literacy. Do you encourage children to:

- Give their views about the texts they read and discuss why they hold these views? (Mallett)
- Reflect on their differing interpretations and responses to the texts they read? (Rosenblatt)
- Be resistant readers? (Janks)
- Ask children how the text is positioning them as a reader? (Janks)
- Discuss with children how the text is positioning people and places in the text? (Janks)
- Talk about the language choices used in texts? (Mallett)
- Ask critical questions about the source, context or author of the texts they read? (Freire)

Developing critical literacy in digital texts.

In the section that follows, we summarise some of the thinking about critical literacy that can help guide thinking and practice. This includes ensuring children are not passively accepting the messages in texts and that they develop an understand of the ways in which texts exert power and influence. While we are arguing that some critical literacy skills can cross both print-based and digital texts, there are also some different challenges, as explored by Lim and Toh (2020) in the *Spotlight on research* that follows.

SPOTLIGHT ON RESEARCH

Lim and Toh and Information Literacy

Lim and Toh (2020) identify the ability to read digital texts critically and make balanced judgements about the information they provide as a part of Information Literacy (IL). They identify the key skills and awareness needed for digital reading as including the ability to strategically explore information, for example by using navigation buttons and hyperlinks and the understanding that the creation of information is both a process and a product. They also highlight the importance of understanding and being cognisant of how meaning is created by the multimodal element within digital texts. These multimodal elements enable digital reading to be a social experience that can be engaged with both continuously and asynchronously, at a time that suits the reader. Multimodal elements such as hyperlinks also enable a level of agency and interactivity, with readers able to decide what and how they read.

Lim and Toh (2020) suggest learners who do fully understand the knowledge conveyed by digital multimodal texts are disadvantaged by their inability to critically evaluate what they read and recognise nuances of meaning. They also highlight digital readers' frequent divergence from print reading processes, and the use of shallow processing strategies such as skimming and scanning, that limit their ability to comprehend. Lim and Toh therefore advocate the development of linear print reading strategies to support knowledge building.

Suggestions for practice in early years and primary

Lim and Toh clearly illustrate how digital texts can create challenges and may require some quite different critical literacy skills than those associated with print-based texts. Next, we present suggestions for practice, written by teachers, which can enhance children's awareness of how both print and digital texts work, and support the development of their critical literacy skills.

The first example is from Susan and illustrates how working with film clips can enhance children's understanding of how the modes of film work to produce meaning and effect.

CASE STUDY FOCUS

Using wordless film to develop comprehension

I used Wallace and Gromit films, as part of an intervention to support the oral language skills of a group of Year 4 children, whose difficulty with word reading was a barrier to comprehending print-based texts. The children watched parts of the film together and then used discussion and hot seating to develop their understanding of characterisation.

Although the character of Gromit does not speak in the films, he is physically expressive, and this was used to help the children to explain how they could infer what he was thinking through his actions. 'Gromit is scared because his ears are up!' and 'I think Gromit is thinking that Wallace is being silly because he is shaking his head and rolling his eyes.'

This approach as an intervention certainly engaged the children and allowed them to develop their comprehension of characters' feelings and intent, separately from developing their word reading.

The next example, by Siobhan, Key Stage 1 teacher, illustrates the way that KS1 children's comprehension can be scaffolded using small play which can develop their reader responses. You will notice how what plays out allows the children to challenge assumptions made in texts and the value of exploring children's evolving ideas through moments when they are engaged in play.

CASE STUDY FOCUS

Small world play in KS1

> *We use small world play to support our texts especially in KS1. The play allows children to understand the text in a different way as they think about it and imagine themselves in the story. I remember once in a Year One literacy session we were looking at alternative fairy tales. Two boys were building towers and I encouraged them to use the figures to retell Rapunzel. There were not enough figures, so the boys decided to use a female doll to rescue Rapunzel as one child suggested 'some women marry women'. This led to a class discussion about different kinds of families. The children questioned why fairy tales traditionally have a Mum, Dad and children structure. The conversations about representation that followed were high level for the age group and I don't think such analysis would have come about without the children having time to mull the story over through play.*

Siobhan's example shows how retelling of stories in different ways can often help children think more critically about the assumptions presented within them. Exploring different versions of traditional stories and comparing the differences helps children to understand how authors make choices and shape narratives differently. Some authors deliberately subvert character stereotypes and again this draws attention to the kinds of decisions that authors make when presenting characters, and the kinds of messages that these presentations convey. For example, Robert Munsch's book, *The Paper Bag Princess*, presents a princess very different to the ones in traditional tales. *The True Story of the 3 Little Pigs*, by Jon Scieszka and Lane Smith, provides an alternative story that challenges the idea of the stereotypical villain of the original Three Little Pigs story by using the device of an unreliable narrator. *Mr. Wolf and the Pancakes*, by Jan Fearnleigh, embellishes the character of the wolf; rather than being a hunger driven beast, he is a vulnerable and struggling character, trying to get help from his friends. The shocking and surprising ending to the story is very subtle, and open to multiple interpretations and so is useful for class discussion of what happened and why.

CASE STUDY FOCUS

Fake news and Year 5

To develop Y5 children's ability to discern fake news, I presented the children with a number of short news articles, including some that were true and some fake news stories. We went through each of the articles together and discussed ways that we could evaluate whether they were true, for example by fact checking using reputable news websites. It was interesting to hear the children's discussion of the plausibility of each of the texts. Several children based their evaluations on their own prior knowledge and some of the fake images persuaded some children that they might be true. It became clear that some children were unclear about what fake news is, and the fake news stories that contained an element of truth were harder to spot. This helped the children to realise that although there may be an element of truth in some fake news stories, it can be sensationalised or exaggerated, so that it becomes false.

As a follow-up activity, the children were also given the opportunity to work with programmes that allow images to be manipulated, to develop their understanding of how digital tools can create fake images. This is particularly important because of the proliferation of fake images on social media.

CASE STUDY FOCUS

Webpages at Key Stage 2: Multimodal news

> *I remember my Year 4 class enjoyed reading the Newsround webpage and I used it as an opportunity to talk about how we could navigate to different stories and information by clicking on hyperlinks or images that enabled videos to play. We identified the multimodal features on the homepage, and how they enabled different reading pathways and understanding of the information on each webpage. We explored different pathways to find out more information and then the children used this analysis of multimodal elements to design a multimodal 'news' bulletin in PowerPoint that included features such as sound buttons and embedded videos. We used our print writing and reading skills to construct the information within the news and the children really engaged with the digital format of this activity. The finished news pages were uploaded to the internet, so that they could be shared with parents, and the children enjoyed having their work published in an authentic way.*

Some further thoughts about strategies to develop critical literacy skills

The previous case studies demonstrate how critical literacy can be embedded into teaching to draw children's attention to the ways in which texts work and provide them with tools for evaluating the texts they come across at home and at school. Of course, online safety plays a key part in stakeholders' responsibilities to children and equipping them with an understanding of the workings of power in texts is key to keeping them safe as they grow. In many ways, supporting the development of children's inference and deduction skills will enhance their skills in reading critically. Next are some additional *Ideas for classroom practice* to draw on:

IDEAS FOR CLASSROOM PRACTICE

- Encourage children to find out about the authors of the text (this is not always possible on online texts).
- Teach children how to use retrieval devices (contents, indexes, online searches, glossaries) to locate information.
- Identify the purpose of the text and whether it is good at achieving this purpose.
- Look for clarity in organisation and presentation of information.
- Present children with a wide range of print and digital texts written for a range of purposes and encourage them to draw on these to create their own texts.
- Talk about the multimodal affordances of digital text, and consider how the various modes (e.g. sound, colour, moving images, text) work together to create meaning.
- Learn how to navigate (safely) the reading path of digital texts and the use of hyperlinks.

An eye on the present and into the future – 'fake news' and AI

In 2018, the National Literacy Trust commissioned an inquiry into critical literacy and fake news, concerned by the increasing concerns that 'the new digital media landscape can be bewildering and overwhelming even for experienced media consumers' (Picton, 2018, foreword by Lucy Powell MP). The commissioned study involved written evidence submitted by a range of stakeholders, surveys of 388 primary-aged children and 1,832 secondary students, and 414 teachers in the UK. The report called for the need to teach critical literacy skills in primary and secondary schools and showed that:

- Almost half of children interviewed were worried about not being able to spot fake news.
- Two-thirds of teachers believe fake news is harming children's wellbeing, increasing their anxiety levels.
- Half of teachers believe that the national curriculum does not equip children with the literacy skills they need to identify fake news.

Defining 'fake news', however, is far from uncontentious, and Picton drew on Rubin (2017) who defined five types of fake news as follows:

1. That which is intentionally deceptive.
2. Jokes taken at face value.
3. Large-scale hoaxes.
4. Slanted reporting of real facts.
5. Stories where the truth is contentious.

The final report (Picton, 2018) provides a comprehensive review of the inquiry and a framework of strategies to work towards ensuring that children and young people are supported in a digital era (see also Merchant, this volume). This endeavour necessitates collaboration by industries, web designers, policy makers, parents, educators and children themselves. The report also includes a range of resources for teachers to develop critical literacy in their classrooms.

https://literacytrust.org.uk/policy-and-campaigns/all-party-parliamentary-group-literacy/fakenews/

Critical literacy and artificial intelligence (AI)

The advent of generative AI, and its 'ability' to create original text, images, videos, sound and music, has meant that it is even more important to talk to children about how they can evaluate the texts they encounter. The rapid growth of artificial intelligence (AI) is impacting on the digital information landscape, with language models such as ChatGPT and Google Bard capable of producing high-quality 'original' writing in different styles and purposes. With the look and feel of a chatbot, these language models can respond to prompts and answer questions, providing information formulated from large internet-based datasets, including Wikipedia, which means that they are not always 100% accurate. The quality of the writing (if not always the information) is proving challenging for both human readers and plagiarism tools, such as 'Turnitin', to discern AI generated text from human authored writing. However, it is important to note that AI powered chatbots lack the ability to reflect, and the writing produced can be impersonal. Therefore, collaboration with AI still requires human criticality to add depth and personalisation. Other forms of AI are being used to produce 'deep fake' pictures, videos and sounds that can mimic human voices, adding to the need for young consumers and producers of digital content to develop their evaluative literacy skills to interact with AI tools appropriately and safely. To address the issue of AI, it is quite simply necessary to educate children about what it is, what it can do and explore ethical implications associated with its use. Children from a young age are using these digital tools to learn about aspects of literacy such as phonics, reading and writing. The implications of AI are still emerging and currently nations, institutions and organisations are working through the implications of AI to both the integrity and safety of communications and production of texts.

Kervin and Mantei (2016) describe how the expanded understanding of *text* requires a reconceptualisation of traditional writing practices and review of the processes by which digital texts are created. It is important that as teachers we enable children to have opportunities to produce their own digital *texts*, to develop their understanding of how digital modes can be used to create meaning and develop their ability to critically evaluate the digital texts that they encounter.

Chapter summary

Children, often from a very young age, are consumers and producers of digital content both in school and at home (Ofcom, 2023), and there is a strong body of research that generates understandings of the ways in which children's lives and literacy practices are influenced by digital media (Burnett and Merchant, 2018). Literacy education 'lags behind' and its focus is predominantly on the developing of reading and writing. This is concerning, particularly where the need to have good skills in critical literacy and critical digital literacy is more pressing than ever. Many of the strategies to support critical literacy of print-based texts are still important when consuming and producing digital texts. However, the need for children to understand how power and influence works in texts, and to effectively manage or 'deal with' the proliferation of multimodal texts in flow in the media landscape, is crucial.

References

Barton, D. (1994). *Literacy: An Introduction to the Ecology of Written Language*. London: Blackwell.

Belshaw, D. (2010). *Digital Literacy: A Function of Poor Design?* https://dougbelshaw.com/blog/2010/06/03/digital-literacy-a-function-of-poor-design/

Burnett, C. & Merchant, G. (2018). *New Media in the Classroom. Rethinking Primary Literacy*. London: Sage.

Cazden, C. (1996). A pedagogy of multiliteracies: Designing social futures. *Harvard Educational Review*, 66(1), 60.

Casey, L. & Bruce, B. (2011). The practice profile of inquiry: Connecting digital literacy and pedagogy. *E-Learning and Digital Media*, 8(1), 76–85. https://doi.org/10.2304/elea.2011.8.1.76

Daniels, K. (2017). Young children in an education context. In N. Kucirkova & G. Falloon (Eds), *Apps, Technology and Young Learners. International Evidence for Teaching* (pp. 280–292). London: Routledge.

Daniels, K., Bower, K., Burnett, C., Escott, H., Hatton, A., Ehiyazaryan-White, E. & Monkhouse, J. (2019). Early years teachers and digital literacies: Navigating a kaleidoscope of discourses. *Education and Information Technologies*, 25, 2415–2426.

Department for Digital Media, Culture and Sport (2023). *Online Safety Bill*. https://publications.parliament.uk/pa/bills/cbill/58-03/0121/220121.pdf

DfE (Department for Education) (2013). *National Curriculum in England: Primary Curriculum*. https://www.gov.uk/government/publications/national-curriculum-in-england-primary-curriculum

DfE (Department for Education) (2019). Relationships and Sex Education (RSE) and Health Education. www.gov.uk/government/publications/relationships-education-relationships-and-sex-education-rse-and-health-education

DfE (Department for Education) (2023a). Statutory Framework for the Early Years Foundation Stage. Retrieved from https://foundationyears.org.uk/files/2023/09/EYFS_framework_from_September_2023.pdf

DfE (Department for Education) (2023b). Keeping Children Safe in Education: Statutory Guidance for Schools and Colleges. https://irp.cdn-website.com/9df3e6f8/files/uploaded/KCSIE%202023.pdf

Digital Culture, Media and Sport Select Committee (2019). *Disinformation and 'Fake News': Final Report.* https://publications.parliament.uk/pa/cm201719/cmselect/cmcumeds/1791/179111.htm

Dooly, M. & Darvin, R. (2022). Intercultural communicative competence in the digital age: Critical digital literacy and inquiry-based pedagogy. *Language and Intercultural Communication*, 1–13.

Evans, J. (2004). *Literacy Moves On: Using Popular Culture, New Technologies and Critical Literacy in the Primary Classroom.* Oxon. David Fulton Publishers. https://doi.org/10.4324/9780203963272

Freire, P. (1970). *Pedagogy of the Oppressed.* New York: Continuum.

Gilster, P. (1997). A new digital literacy: A conversation with Paul Glister. *Educational Leadership*, 55(3), 6–11.

Hague, C. & Payton, S. (2010). *Digital literacy across the curriculum* [PDF file]. Bristol, England: Futurelab. Retrieved July 5, 2017, from https://www.nfer.ac.uk/publications/digital-literacy-across-the-curriculum/

HM Government (2021). *Tackling Child Sexual Abuse Strategy 2021* [online]. https://assets.publishing.service.gov.uk/media/605c82328fa8f545dca2c643/Tackling_Child_Sexual_Abuse_Strategy_2021.pdf

Holmes, H. & Burgess, H. (2021). Digital exclusion and poverty in the UK: How structural inequality shapes experiences of getting online. *Digital Geography and Society*, 3, 1–9.

Hu, X., Gong, Y., Lai, C. & Leung, F. (2018). The relationship between ICT and student literacy in mathematics, reading, and science across 44 countries: A multilevel analysis. *Computers & Education*, 125, 1–13. https://doi.org/10.1016/j.compedu.2018.05.021

Janks, H. (2014). *Doing Critical Literacy. Texts and Activities for Students and Teachers.* London: Routledge.

Jenkins, H. (2006). Convergence culture. In *Convergence Culture.* New York: New York University Press.

Jenkins, H. (2009). *Confronting the Challenges of Participatory Culture: Media Education for the 21st Century.* Cambridge, MA: MIT Press.

Kervin, L. & Mantei, J. (2016). Digital writing practices: A close look at one grade three author. *Literacy*, 50: 133–140. doi: 10.1111/lit.12084.

Knight, J., Dooly, M. & Barberà, E. (2020). Getting smart: Towards critical digital literacy pedagogies. *Social Semiotics*, 1–24.

Kress, G. (2003). *Literacy in the New Media Age.* London: Routledge.

Lankshear, C. & Knobel, M. (Eds) (2008). *Digital Literacies: Concepts, Policies and Practices* (Vol. 30). Oxford: Peter Lang.

Lim, F. V. & Toh, W. (2020). How to teach digital reading? *Journal of Information Literacy*, 14(2).

Lythreatis, S., Singh, S. & El-Kassar, A. (2021). The digital divide: A review and future research agenda. *Technological Forecasting and Social Change*, 121359.

Maine, F. & Shields, R. (2015). Developing reading comprehension with moving image narratives. *Cambridge Journal of Education*, 45(4), 519–535.

Mallett, M. (1992). *Making Facts Matter. Reading Non-Fiction 5–11.* London: Paul Chapman.

Merchant, G. (2020). Reading with technology: The new normal. *Education 3–13*, 49(1), 96–106. https://doi.org/10.1080/03004279.2020.1824705

Ofcom (2023). *Children and Parents: Media Use and Attitudes* [online]. www.ofcom.org.uk/media-use-and-attitudes/media-habits-children/children-and-parents-media-use-and-attitudes-report-2023/

Office for National Statistics (ONS) (2019). *Exploring the UK's Digital Divide* [online]. file:///C:/Users/dskd/Desktop/Exploring%20the%20UK%20s%20digital%20divide.pdf

Picton, I. (2018). *Fake News and Critical Literacy: The Final Report of the Commission on Fake News and the Teaching of Critical Literacy in Schools.* London: National Literacy Trust.

Piggott, L., Gosschalk, K. & Webb. S. (2022). *Ofqual Public Sentiment 2021.* London: YouGov.

Prensky, M. (2001). Digital natives, digital immigrants part 1. *On the Horizon*, 9(5), 1–6.

Rosenblatt, L. (1995). *Literature as Exploration.* New York: Modern Language Association of America.

Rubin, V. L. (2017). Deception detection and rumor debunking for social media. In L. Sloan & A. Quan-Haase (Eds), *The SAGE Handbook of Social Media Research Methods* (pp. 342–364). London: Sage.

Smahel, D., Machackova, H., Mascherone, G., Dedkova, L., Staksrud, E., Olafsson, K., Livingstone, S. & Hasebrink, U. (2020). *EU Kinds Online 2020: Survey results from 19 Countries.* EU Kids Online.

Street, B. (1995). *Social Literacies: Critical Approaches to Literacy in Development, Ethnography and Education.* London: Routledge.

Tamborg, A. L., Herfort, J. D. & Fougt, S. (2018). Digital literacy – A qualitative systematic review. *Tidsskriftet Loering og Medier*, 11(19), 29.

Walsh, M. (2018). Multiliteracies, multimodality, new literacies and… what do these mean for literacy education? *Inclusive Principles and Practices in Literacy Education*, 11, 19–33.

Wohlwend, K. & Hall, T. (2017). Race and rag dolls: Critically engaging the embodiment of diversity in lalaloopsy transmedia. In G. Enriquez, E. Johnson, S. Kontovourki & C. A. Mallozzi (Eds), *Literacies, Learning and the Body: Putting Theory and Research into Pedagogical Practice* (pp.155–169). London: Routledge.

CHAPTER

9

Inclusive literacy classrooms

Sheila Sharpe and Moira Taplin

Books create belonging

(Evaristo, 2021)

Introduction

This chapter explores links between literacy and inclusiveness. Firstly, it considers the emphasis on literacy practices linked to the promotion of inclusion in society, tracing the historical politicisation of literacy provision in schools by successive UK governments. Secondly, consideration is given to the school and community projects that have arisen to ease social exclusion through developing literacy. The chapter explores the thinking behind the establishment of a variety of literacy practices within schools, families and communities designed to enhance literacy and therefore life chances. In the final section, consideration is given as to how diversity in literature can be used as a powerful force in allowing children to imagine, participate and belong.

Defining literacy

It is important to define what we mean by both literacy and inclusion. Using the UNESCO (2005, p27) definition, literacy is:

> the ability to identify, understand, interpret, create, communicate and compute, using printed and written materials associated with varying contexts [which] involve a continuum of learning in enabling individuals to achieve their goals, to develop their knowledge and potential, and to participate fully in their community and wider society.

We suggest that this functional definition of literacy is one that successive UK governments have used when making new policy directives concerning the teaching of reading and writing. Havelock (1976) argues that since human beings have used speech to communicate for much longer than writing systems, oracy should take precedence but speaking and listening does not appear to receive the same importance in government policy.

What does inclusion mean?

Personal perspectives of inclusion are shaped by politicians, teachers, parents, people with disabilities and one's own experiences (Glazzard, 2016). Inclusion itself is difficult to define. What is evident is that there are conflicting interpretations of inclusion giving rise to problematic

DOI: 10.4324/9781003381013-9

concerns of trying to define a concept that means different things to different people (Clough, 2000). Inclusion has links to a sense of belonging and participation in society, to valuing diversity, to notions of human rights and entitlements and to overcoming barriers to achievement (Topping and Maloney, 2005). When considering inclusion, Norwich (2010, p100) states 'its definition and use are seriously problematic', particularly when the term 'inclusive' is used to refer to inclusive schools or inclusive society. The concept of educational inclusion is set in a much wider context of social inclusion, and government policy discourses of literacy have become focused on improving reading standards in schools in order to give opportunities for enhancing life chances.

Inclusion of different literacy experiences and the impact of deficit models of literacy

Families and communities play a strong role in the advance of childhood and adult literacies which result in different kinds of literacies and literate practices. Schooled literacies may differ significantly to those experienced in the home and success in schooled literacies is greatly impacted by socio-economic factors and children's broader experiences. Governments very often apply deficit perspectives by using terms such as 'deprived' areas or 'disadvantaged' children, which may be seen as negative labels which can underline the divisions in society by suggesting that children who live in some regions may have negative attitudes and experiences towards literacy which impact their overall literacy performance. What is not acknowledged is that young children's literacy experiences are *different* but of equal worth. Ellis and Rowe (2020, p422) suggest: 'Equity in literacy learning requires educators to recognise these differences and to "bridge" them quickly and effectively by offering explicit encouragement, explanations, coaching and non-performative practise and opportunities for "school" ways of thinking and talking about texts.' Ellis and Rowe's perspective highlights the need for teachers to be sensitive and flexible towards children's literacy experiences, and to build on these.

What one reads and how one speaks are seen to hold different 'capital' in different strata of society (Nutbrown et al., 2017). There are different types of capital associated with literacy. Savage et al. (2013), in a class survey across Britain, concluded that a person's social capital is seen to be as important as their wealth. Social capital has been seen to be a desirable quality which 'some children have and others do not, rather than the knowledge and experience that *all* children and *all* families have' (Burnett et al., 2020, p115). The discursive intent, styles, skills and entitlement to voice an opinion that are often presumed in school literacy activities can unintentionally wrong-foot children from communities that do not habitually use or respond to texts in such ways at home (Lareau, 2011; Hiebert, 2017). In this way, the demands of school literacies may be seen to denigrate any home literacies that do not conform to the requirements of the school curriculum. It can be argued that government efforts to bridge the attainment gaps by introducing policies to raise standards, with the intention of giving greater opportunity, have conversely underlined the discrepancies between school literacies and the impact of socio-economic factors. Social exclusion is influenced by unemployment, poverty and poor housing, all embodied in the term 'social deprivation'. This label may in itself seriously limit motivation and enthusiasm for learning. Yet every child has a right to be educated to their potential (UNCRC, 1989) wherever they may live.

National Literacy Trust (2014) suggests: 'The UK's "literacy gap" undermines our economic competitiveness and sustainability. It creates obstacles to fairness across society. It is at the heart of economic and cultural inequalities and is creating obstacles to a fairer society.'

Successive governments, in highlighting such divisions in society, have attempted to alleviate the situation through inclusive education policies. However, progress has been slow with considerable variation across the country. Burnett et al. (2020, p113) state: 'an over simplistic analysis of children's perceived underachievement can lead to narrow, prescriptive approaches in language and literacy teaching that fail to provide the rich, meaningful experiences that could do much to foster children's linguistic and literacy repertoires'.

What follows is an overview of the significant government legislation and policy discourses which have attempted to address issues of social inclusion through literacy intervention.

Historic markers in literacy legislation and socio-economic legislation

The Conservative government under Margaret Thatcher introduced the first National Curriculum (NC) with the 1988 Education Reform Act (ERA) (DfES, 1988). A shift from local to central control gave the Secretary of State for Education overall control of education policy. The emphasis was on raising standards by establishing a National Curriculum (NC) framework for learning and assessing child performance with tests at the age of 7, 11,14 and 16. The results were published and formed local league tables. The ERA (1988) also introduced the concept of parental choice and local management of schools (LMS). The NC 1988 achieved a national standardisation of learning across the country which was previously in the domain of the Local Authorities. Checks were kept on the quality of schools with the formation of a common inspection framework and Ofsted Inspectors were created in 1992. The one-word Ofsted grades given to schools after inspection to denote implied progress are labels that do not readily reflect the real impact of schools on children's learning and emotional development.

The policy of improving national standards in schools is somewhat at odds with policies of inclusion and participation for *all*. The belief that the standardisation of learning through a National Curriculum and standardised testing would lead to a more cohesive and accessible approach to learning has not, in itself, led to more opportunity. The outcome was successful in producing a National Curriculum with suggested levels for age equivalent learning, but it did not produce a standardised population of school children. As Glazzard (2018, p186) suggests, 'Education continues to single out learners and categorise them by their inability to meet a set of norm related standards'.

There are difficulties in separating schooled literacies from wider socio-economic factors and children's broader experiences. Opportunities may be available but not always taken up due to other social factors such as poverty leading to poor living conditions, poor health and wellbeing for all the family. What is evident is the impact of social conditions on children's learning.

The Labour government's view (1997–2010) of educational inclusion was to put the responsibility firmly in the hands of the school and thereby teachers, to provide the desired quality of experience and participation for *all* children. The introduction of the new National Curriculum (DfEE, 1999) was not just intended to supply schools with ordered national schemes for learning and assessment. The new NC (1999) document also contained an inclusive statement; an entitlement giving effective learning opportunities for *all* children with three clear principles (DfEE, 1999, p30):

- Setting suitable learning challenges.
- Responding to children's diverse needs.
- Overcoming potential barriers to learning and assessment for individuals and groups of children.

There was the expectation that *all* schools had to provide an inclusive curriculum while maintaining an inclusive ethos in the school. Linked with the National Curriculum (DfEE,1999) was the National Literacy Strategy (NLS; DfEE, 1998). Both documents dictated how children were to be taught literacy. The National Curriculum (DfEE, 1999) contained clear, full statutory entitlements to learning for *all* children. The attainment targets for each subject were listed with guidance on how children's performance was to be assessed. It was the continuation of the move towards monitoring children and schools on their performativity that began with the previous government (Ball, 2003).

The Labour government (1997–2010) continued with accountability mechanisms designed to monitor both the performance of the children and thus the teachers and schools. Schools began to manage their public profiles in a 'highly marketised system in which improvement, levels of attainment and inspection ratings perform various forms of competitive advantage' (Burnett et al., 2020).

Concerns about standards in literacy

Evidence of slowing down of progress in reading between 2000–2003 was seen to be a failure of the standards agenda and consequently, the National Literacy Strategy (NLS), alongside the National Numeracy Strategy (NNS), was incorporated into the Primary National Strategy (PNS) in 2003. By 2006, the standard of literacy, and particularly the teaching of reading, was again put under scrutiny because the OECD Programme for International Student Assessment (OECD, 2008) indicated that the UK appeared to be going on a downward trajectory in the PISA tabulated results for reading performance. Since the PISA surveys encompass 30 countries worldwide, these findings could not be ignored.

A recent OECD (Organization for Economic Co-operation and Development) International Student Assessment (PISA) report (OECD, 2021) states data consistently shows that engagement in reading is a mediator of socio-economic status. However, there may be a variety of reasons why some groups in society do not become fully literate and, as a result, experience social exclusion.

Over the last 30 years, various governments have introduced policies that have tried to alleviate this situation, by simultaneously taking on the challenge of poverty and social exclusion in conjunction with the drive to raise standards of literacy. Large funding streams have been immersed in communities with social welfare issues to enable education and welfare to work together. Mostly, UK government policy has focused on schools and communities with a deficit perspective. There have been attempts to 'raise achievement', 'narrow the gap', 'close the disadvantage gap' or 'level up' in terms of their focus.

The document Removing Barriers to Achievement (DfES, 2004) was presented ostensibly, to address the issues of inclusion and the provision of children with the label of Special Educational Needs (SEN) in mainstream schools. Lloyd (2008, p225) argues that the underpinning of inclusive concepts in this document was based on an economic premise with 'a simplistic notion that inclusion itself had the potential to address issues of disadvantage and to remove barriers created by social deprivation'. It did establish that all children have a right to a good education and the opportunity to achieve their potential, but did not remove the 'inherent injustices' within the official policies of inclusion. What Lloyd (2008, p234) suggests is a demand on policy changes which recognises and values different forms of success.

One of the most important initiatives for children's services during this period was the linking together of education, health and social services in Every Child Matters: Change for Children (ECM) (DfES, 2003) – a landmark ten-year strategy plan which grew out of an appreciation that children's achievement at school is closely linked to their wellbeing and safety. The five main outcomes of ECM – being healthy, staying safe, enjoying and achieving, making a contribution, achieving economic wellbeing – were significant for both children's education and welfare and were embodied in the Children Act of 2004.

ECM (2003) brought integrated services making sure that the welfare of the child was paramount. A Children's Commissioner was appointed with a legal duty to protect the right of the child in accordance with the United Nations Convention on the Rights of the Child (UNCRC). Extended Schools and Sure Start Children's Centres were rolled out to support the early education of young children. There was a recognition that early education can counter the perceived disadvantages that some children experience. ECM policy essentially focused on the development of each child but there were also perceived economic gains within the globally competitive context because it is an important investment in human capital. The ECM policy lasted until 2010 when the Coalition government took over, but the principles of safeguarding children remain. Many schools still use the ECM principles as their aspirational values within their school mission statements.

In 2006, Jim Rose, was directed to conduct an Independent Review of the Teaching of Reading (Rose, 2006). The findings led to widespread changes in the application of the teaching of reading with a framework based on the Simple View of Reading (Rose, 2006), introducing the teaching of systematic synthetic phonics. Rose (2006) also argued that raising the profile of speaking and listening would enhance not just the teaching of phonics but also literacy development. There has been contrary discussion over the years of the best way to teach reading (Dombey, 2006; Wyse and Styles, 2007; Wyse and Bradbury, 2023). As Dombey (2006, p6) observed:

> The most successful schools and teachers focus both on phonics and the process of making sense of the text. Best practice brings these two key components together, in teaching that gives children a sense of the pleasures reading can bring, supports them in making personal sense of the texts they encounter and also shows how to lift the words off the page.

Since the Independent Review of the Teaching of Reading, the Conservative government has been unshaken in its support of systematic synthetic phonics teaching, becoming increasingly prescriptive in its DfE documentation of what should and should not be used to teach reading. Grundin (2018, p44) describes the government position as 'policy-based evidence, rather than evidence-based policy'. Concerns centre on the phonics screening, including 'birthdate effect ... articulation difficulties and differences in accent or dialect ... measurement error ... and "marking up"'(Grundin, 2018, p44). While a study commissioned by the Education Endowment Foundation found that phonics has a positive impact (five months' progress) and is therefore an important component in the teaching of early reading (EEF, 2021), other evidence has suggested (see Wyse and Bradbury, 2023) that systematic synthetic phonics teaching is not having the success that was forecast in 2006.

Concerns of child poverty and the impact on children's literacy learning

Linked to the creation of standards and targets in education was the recognition of child poverty and unequal opportunities. An Ofsted report in 2013 suggested 'right from the early years, there is a strong association between low family income and poor educational outcomes ... it is often called our "*long tail of underperformance*"'(Ofsted, 2013, p6). In 2002, a target was set to halve child poverty by 2010 and to eradicate it by 2020. Sadly, these targets have not been met. Between 2010 and 2015, 0.5 million more children fell into absolute poverty. The Institute of Fiscal Studies (IFS) estimated that the number of children in relative poverty would rise from 3.6 million in 2010 to 4.3 million by 2020. There is also a suggestion that there are an extra 1.7 million lost children living in poverty that are currently invisible in government statistical data. Andrews et al. (2017) considered that between 2007–2016, the education gap by the end of primary school narrowed by 2.8 months and the gap by age 5 narrowed by 1.2 months. But it was estimated that it would take around 50 years for the 'disadvantage gap' to close completely by the time primary children reach preparation for GCSE at 16.

There is an acknowledgement that children from poor homes are not reaching the same targets of learning as those from wealthier backgrounds. As a result, a deficit discourse has evolved surrounding children from working class and minority ethnic backgrounds. Social groupings or class may influence one's values, attitudes and beliefs and therefore one's aspirations. Money, parenting, family relationships, culture and community may also influence children's aspirations. This is not to say that poverty makes poor parenting, but it does greatly amplify and concentrate other risk factors (Goepel et al., 2015).

Ellis and Rowe (2020, p419) argue that the National Curriculum, with its focus on content driven learning, is 'irrelevant to many students' lives so it cannot deliver the emotional, social or intellectual inclusion and empowerment required for self-respect'. These perceived differences influence children's overt knowledge of school literacy but, crucially, they also position children to recognise and engage with school literacy in particular ways (Gregory et al., 2004; Barton and Hamilton, 2000; Heath, 2008; Smith, 2010) which may demotivate some social groups of children.

Politicians increasingly call upon education to correct the inequalities of class or background (Blair, 2006). Schools do have a vital role to play in encouraging and supporting the development of literacy and positive attitudes towards reading. It has been found that the impact of a school's influence on attainment can be up to three times greater for disadvantaged groups (Sutton Trust, 2011). Literacy in disadvantaged families can be complex, rich and varied. It is not reasonable to assume it to be deficient or inferior (Mol et al., 2008), but it is possible that disadvantaged families' literacy does not match school literacy as closely as does advantaged families' literacy (Hannon et al., 2006). Jurafsky and Reynolds (2019, p3), in a report of a language study in the USA, suggest that we live in a very polarised time, and further, maintain that by beginning to understand what 'different groups of people say and why, is the first step in determining how we can help bring people together.'

Language and literacy projects in schools with families and communities

Over the past three decades there have been a number of projects with families designed to get the whole family reading but as Auerbach (1995, p23) suggests, there are consequences in assuming that enhanced family literacy interactions will break the cycle of poverty or compensate for problems facing the educational system. He suggests that such interventions only reinforce the ideology that blames poor people for their own problems and leaves social inequities intact. Nevertheless, there are initiatives supporting families which have been seen to have a positive effect on reading.

Family literacy projects have, traditionally, focused primarily on print-based practices (Brooks and Hannon, 2013). Nutbrown et al. (2017) argue that family literacies are now stimulated by the range of digital literacies and technologies that have become part of the landscape of what it means to be literate in the 21st Century. This difference of the meaning of literacy has the propensity to 'drive a wedge between home and school literacy practices'. Marsh et al.'s (2017, p59) study indicates that a print-based approach is no longer sufficient, suggesting that family literacy programmes should address the way in which literacy is being transformed in a digital age if it is to be meaningful and relevant to families (see Merchant, this volume). Some projects request of parents a broader understanding of the school's approach to the teaching of reading. Hannon et al. (2006) describe this as 'instruction', with the opposite end of a reading continuum as 'facilitation', which is less planned, more opportunistic and embedded in real life contexts and applications.

PROMPTS FOR CRITICAL REFLECTION

Examine one or two examples of local and/or national policy for literacy (for example, DfE and/or school policy):

- How does the policy define literacy? What does it include and what does it suggest is valued/prioritised in literacy teaching? How does this sit with the Cox's five views of English, outlined in Chapter 1?
- How does it describe children's 'capabilities' in literacy? What terms or language are used to describe those who are less/more confident in literacy?
- What are the expectations of you as a teacher in supporting children's developing literacy skills?
- What is missing? Are there other aspects of literacy learning and pedagogy that you deem to be important that are not given priority in the policy?

The following section gives examples of how different literacy practices have been introduced into communities and schools with a view to encourage reading and develop language.

IDEAS FOR CLASSROOM PRACTICE

An example of a family reading project – Dolly Parton's Imagination Library

One of the most encouraging family reading projects now famous in the Rotherham area of South Yorkshire, England, is the Imagination Library, the brainchild of the USA country singer Dolly Parton. In an interview with BBC Radio 4 Extra (2024), Dolly explained that her motives were part altruistic and part self-interest. She came from a family of 12, none of whom had much formal schooling. Her father could neither read nor write. He was a farm labourer. Dolly said there were no books in her house. She felt a connection with children who did not have access to books and so the Imagination Library was born. First in the USA then Canada, Australia, the Republic of Ireland and the UK. It is a franchise scheme which Rotherham Borough Council has bought into. Rotherham Hospital gives new mothers a leaflet to ensure they are aware of the project. Every month, from birth to when the child is 5 years old, a book is posted directly to the child. The books are personalised and high quality, published by Penguin Random House, UK. The first book to be received is *The Tale of Peter Rabbit* by Beatrix Potter. A parent interviewed reported that her child looks forward to receiving something addressed just to her. The family could not afford to buy the books, so she was highly delighted for her child to receive the storybook through the letterbox every month.

IDEAS FOR CLASSROOM PRACTICE

Bookstart by Book Trust

'Bookstart' is a similar programme to the Imagination Library, run by the reading charity, Book Trust. It provides free books and resources to every baby born in England, Northern Ireland and Wales. Some resources are delivered in person by health visitors or are available in local libraries. The Trust gifts free books to children before school and at key ages. The aim is to help families read together and inspire children to develop a love of reading (Book Trust, 2021). It also aims to promote good reading habits in the early years of children who live within diverse communities.

The programme was devised to help children and parents interact through reading together. Coldwell et al. (2012, p75), in their evaluation of Bookstart, concluded that the main ways that the Bookstart programme was seen to impact on parents and carers were as follows: it increased families' access to books; it encouraged families to share books with their child at an earlier age; it increased adults' awareness of their child's enjoyment of books and provided a fun way for them to engage with their child.

Building participation and belonging in schools – creating positive experiences through reading

It is becoming increasingly recognised that reading is an affective experience. A variety of school approaches has been introduced to support children through reading to secure their sense of participation and belonging. Evaristo (2021, p153) believes that it is important for children to see themselves reflected in books as a validation of their own identity. Evaristo's experience as a child of colour in the UK in the 1960s did not afford such a pleasure. Children bring their own experiences to the texts that they read but books can also extend children's experiences and ideas, enabling them to see things as others may see them. It is through literature, be it print or on screen, that children are exploring and making sense of the world and their own emotions. When looking for reading material for children that is inclusive, it is important to move away from simplistic tokenism. There needs to be not only equal representation of the protected characteristics of the Equality Act (2010) but also the inclusion of a variety of genres within fiction and nonfiction (see Doxey and Doxey, this volume).

SPOTLIGHT ON RESEARCH
Ethnic representation within children's literature

The Centre for Literacy in Primary Education (CLPE) produces an annual survey of Ethnic Representation within Children's Literature and states from data collated since 2017 'not only has the gap between representation in literature and actual population been slow to close, but the proportion of representation of different demographic groups has also remained relatively static and very low' (CLPE, 2023, p6).

Although movement overall may be slow, there has been a significant increase in ethnic minority representation in children's books.

The key points documented by CLPE (2023) are:

- Annual reporting shows an increase in the number of children's books published featuring a minority ethnic character from 4% in 2017 to 20% in 2021.
- The percentage of books published with a main character from a racially minoritised background has risen year on year but remains extremely low at 9% in 2021.

Representation in fiction remains low and lags significantly behind increases in picture books and nonfiction. The data released by CLPE reports (2017–2022) continues to show a sustained and increased move by publishers towards the production of books that have a higher percentage of characters of colour in the main character role. The increase in this percentage over time suggests that considered editorial decisions are being made to ensure that characters of colour are given agency and voice. Comment was made in the report as to the importance of having a balance of literature available. While the prominence of narratives of struggle, strife or subjugation do have a place in the understanding of people's lives, there is also a necessity of having quality stories where difference is not the focus, but *incidental*. This balance gives children a well-rounded reading experience where they can see themselves and their experiences reflected in a meaningful way.

The range of books introduced to children is key to furthering their understandings of the world around them. Publishers are more aware of the concept of inclusive literature and there is more quality literature arriving on the market from publishers. There appears to be more open debate and acceptance of diversity and gender and the ways in which children from all races and cultures are represented. It is important to reflect not only the culture and ethnicity of the school but also of the wider world. Books can broaden children's outlooks and challenge stereotypical views.

IDEAS FOR CLASSROOM PRACTICE

Going back to the principles of inclusion of belonging, participation and achieving, it is important that children feel that their classroom environment reflects them and their experiences. Take the opportunity to review the range of literature with the children in your class. Classroom discussion about the books could begin by using one of the following suggestions:

Find a character in a story that interests you and say why. Response can be in the form of a drawing activity or teacher facilitating floor activity or P4C (Philosophy for Children) discussion. An incident or an illustration could be the artefact or provocation as focus for discussion.

Discuss how a character in a story may or may not feel a sense of belonging. Why do you think this is? What might happen within the story to change this?

Reading allows children to see things as others may see them. It allows a window on the world and lives of others who may see things very differently from themselves.

Being inclusive in choice of literature for children is not to overtly note difference, but to make sure that the representations within a usual story setting are incidental. For example, in the series 15 Things Not to do with (Granny or Baby or Puppy) series by Margaret McAllister – illustrated by Holly Sterling, Publisher Frances Lincoln Books (2016) – the books concentrate on the story content without focusing on the racial differences of the characters. It is important, too, that the non-white characters have a sense of agency within the story and are not just in the background.

Other examples of stories with inclusive insight are:

- *Julian Is a Mermaid* by Jessica Love (Walker Books, 2018). A story of a black boy, Julian, who has a wish to become a mermaid. His Nana helps him to fulfil that dream. A joyful story.

- *Pansy Boy* by Paul Harfleet (Barbican Press, 2024). Focuses on the topic of bullying in a distinctive way, allowing a child to feel proud of being different.
- *And Tango Makes Three* by Justin Richardson and Peter Parnell, illustrated by Henry Cole (Simon & Schuster, 2007). A true story of two male penguins, in Central Park Zoo, New York. They became inseparable friends, attempting to hatch a chick using a stone. The keeper found a spare egg and they successfully raised it into a young penguin named Tango. The front of the books says: 'All kinds of love can make a family'. A delightful story.

Recent projects in Animal Assisted Education (AAE)

More recently, there has been an interest in various projects in schools where forms of Animal Assisted Education (AAE), for example reading to dogs, chickens or pets, are believed to increase feelings of wellbeing in children and foster confidence in their reading. This work is in its infancy and marks a deeper interest in reading as an affective experience. It is suggested that reading to animals (an uncritical listener) reduces anxiety and improves positive associations with reading (Brelsford et al., 2017; Hall et al., 2016; Steel, 2022; Steel et al., 2021).

IDEAS FOR CLASSROOM PRACTICE
Reading to chickens

Taking up this idea about reading to a non-judgemental pet, a headteacher in West Yorkshire decided that he wanted the children in the school to have a desire to read, combined with a good emotional experience. The school was conscious of the fragile emotional nature of many of the children after a period of Covid lockdown, so chickens were introduced into the school. The children took turns to care for the hens, to collect eggs and to read to the chicks as they grew into hens. The intention was for the children to have an emotional investment in the chickens – from egg to chick to young hen.

If handled regularly, chicks grow into calm and friendly chickens that can be easily held and read to. The ongoing care and welfare of the chicks needed careful consideration prior to implementing the project. A comprehensive risk assessment for the children and staff was also required.

Certainly, there was a great deal of excitement about the new additions to the school but there is a case for closer monitoring required to judge the outcomes of reading to chickens.

Chapter summary

This chapter has illustrated how the development of literacy and inclusion are historically linked together with education policy designed to enhance life chances. This highlights the politicisation of literacy teaching by successive governments in an attempt to reduce social inequality by raising literacy standards. However, social exclusion is a challenging and complex area with multi-faceted problems.

This chapter summarises various strategies employed by schools and teachers in order to facilitate participation and belonging, including the selection of children's literature, to represent children and their ongoing lives and concerns.

References

Andrews, J., Robinson, D. & Hutchinson, J. (2017). Closing the gap? Trends in educational attainment and disadvantage. *Educational Policy Institute*. https://epi.org.uk/publications-and-research/closing-gap-trends-educational-attainment-disadvantage/

Auerbach, E. R. (1995). Which way for family literacy: intervention or empowerment? In L. M. Morrow (Ed.) *Family Literacy: Connections in Schools and Communities* (pp. 11–27). (Newark, DE: International Reading Association).

Ball, S. J. (2003). The teacher's soul and the terrors of performativity. *Journal of Education Policy*, 18(2), 215–228, DOI:10.1080/0268093022000043065.

Barton, D. & Hamilton, M. (2000). Literacy practices. In D. Barton, M. Hamilton & R. Ivanic (Eds), *Situated Literacies: Reading and Writing in Context* (pp. 183–194). London: Routledge.

BBC Radio 4 Extra (2024). *How Dolly Got Rotherham Reading*. www.bbc.co.uk/programmes/b012ql5c

Book Trust (2021). *Book Trust's Great Books Guide 2021*. www.booktrust-great-books-guide-2021-new.pdf

Blair, A. (2006). Tony Blair's speech. *The Guardian*. www.theguardian.com/politics/2006/sep/26/labourconference.labour3

Brelsford, V. L., Meints, K., Gee, N. R. & Pfeffer, K. (2017). Animal-assisted interventions in the classroom—A systematic review. *Int J Environ Res Public Health*,14(7), 669. doi:10.3390/ijerph14070669. PMID: 28640200; PMCID: PMC5551107.

Brooks, G. & Hannon, P. (2013). Research issues in family literacy. In J. Larson & J. Marsh (Eds), *The Sage Handbook of Early Childhood Literacy* (2nd Ed.; pp. 194–206). London: Sage.

Burnett, C., Merchant, G. & Neumann, M. (2020). Closing the gap? Overcoming limitations in sociomaterial accounts of early literacy. *Journal of Early Childhood Literacy*, 20(1), 111–113. https://doi.org/10.1177/1468798419896067

Clough, P. (2000). Routes to inclusion. In P. Clough & J. Corbett (Eds), *Theories of Inclusive Education. A Student's Guide* (pp. 3–30). London: Paul Chapman's Publishing.

CLPE (Centre for Literacy in Primary Education) (2023). *Reflecting Realties – Survey of Ethnic Representation within UK Children's Literature 2022*. London: CLPE.

Coldwell, M., Merchant, M., Clague, l., Stevens, A. & Willis, B. (2012). *Evaluation of Bookstart England: Survey of Operational and Strategic Stakeholders*. London: Book Trust.

DfEE (Department for Education and Employment) (1999). *The National Curriculum. Handbook for Primary Teachers in England*. London: HMSO. www.educationengland.org.uk/documents/pdfs/1999-nc-primary-handbook.pdf

DfES (Department for Education and Skills) (1988). *The Education Reform Act 1988*. London: HMSO.

DfES (Department for Education and Skills) (2003). *Every Child Matters: Change for Children*. London: DfES.

DfES (Department for Education and Skills) (2004). *Removing Barriers to Achievement: The Government's Strategy for SEN*. London: DfES.

Dombey, H. (2006). How should we teach children to read? *Books for Keeps*, 156, 6–7.

EEF (Education Endowment Foundation) (2021). *Teaching and Learning Toolkits – Phonics*. https://educationendowmentfoundation.org.uk/education-evidence/teaching-learning-toolkit/phonics

Evaristo, B. (2021). *Manifesto: On Never Giving Up*. London: Penguin Books.

Ellis, S. & Rowe, A. (2020). Literacy, social justice and inclusion: A large-scale design experiment to narrow the attainment gap linked to poverty. *Support for Learning*, 35(4), 418–439.

Glazzard, J. (2016). A critical interrogation of integration, special educational needs and inclusion. *International Journal of Learning, Teaching and Educational Research*, 15(12), 31–47.

Glazzard, J. (2018). The role of schools in supporting children and young people's mental health. *Education and Health*, 3 (3). ISSN 0265-1602

Goepel, J., Childerhouse, H. & Sharpe, S. (2015). *Inclusive Primary Teaching A Critical Approach to Equality and Special Educational Needs and Disability*. Northwich: Critical Publishing.

Gregory, E., Long, S. & Volk, D. (2004). *Many Pathways to Literacy: Young Children Learning with Siblings, Grandparents, Peers and Communities*. London: Taylor & Francis Group.

Grundin, H. U. (2018). Policy and evidence: A critical analysis of the Year 1 Phonics Screening Check in England. *Literacy*, 52(1), 39–46. https://doi.org/10.1111/lit.12124

Hall, S. S., Gee, N. R. & Mills, D. S. (2016). Children reading to dogs: A systematic review of the literature. *PLoS ONE*, 11(2): e0149759. doi:10.1371/journal.pone.0149759

Hannon, P., Morgan, A. & Nutbrown, C. (2006). Parents' experiences of a family literacy programme. *Journal of Early Childhood Research*, 4(1), 19–44. https://doi.org/10.1177/1476718X06059788

Harfleet, P. (2024). *Pansy Boy*. London: Barbican Press.

Havelock, E. (1976). *Origins of Western Literacy*. Toronto: Ontario Institute for Studies in Education.

Heath, S. B. (2008). The children of Trackton's children: Spoken and written language in social change. In R. Ruddell & N. Unrau (Eds), *Theoretical Models and Processes of Reading* (5th Ed.; pp. 187–209). Newark, DE: International Reading Association.

Hiebert, E. H. (2017). The texts of literacy instruction: Obstacles to or opportunities for educational equity? *Literacy Research: Theory, Method, and Practice*, 66(1), 117–134.

Jurafsky, D. & Reynolds, J. E. (2019). What is different about how Democrats and Republicans talk online? https://engineering.stanford.edu/news/what-different-about-how-democrats-and-republicans-talk-online

Lareau, A. (2011). *Unequal Childhoods: Class, Race, and Family Life* (2nd Ed.). Berkeley and Los Angeles, CA: University of California Press.

Lloyd, C. (2008). Removing barriers to achievement: A strategy for inclusion or exclusion? *International Journal of Inclusive Education*, 12(2), 221–236. DOI: 10.1080/13603110600871413

Love, J. (2018). *Julian Is a Mermaid*. London: Walker Books.

Marsh, J., Hannon, P., Lewis, M. & Ritchie, L. (2017). Young children's initiation into family literacy practices in the digital age. *Journal of Early Childhood Research*, 15(1), 47–60.

McAllister, M. & Sterling, H. (2017). *15 Things NOT to do with Granny*. London: Frances Lincoln Children's Books

Mol, S. E., Bus, A. G., de Jong, M. T. & Smeets, D. J. H. (2008). Added value of dialogic parent–child readings: A meta-analysis. *Early Education and Development*, 19(1), 7–26. doi:10.1080/10409280701838603.

National Literacy Trust (2014). *Vision for Literacy 2025*. London: National Literacy Trust. https://cdn.literacytrust.org.uk/media/documents/2016_01_01_free_other_-_Vision_for_Literacy_2025.pdf

Norwich, B. (2010). What implications do changes in practices and concepts have for the role of the SEN coordinator. In F. Hallett & G. Hallett, *Transforming the Role of the SENCO: Achieving the National Award for SEN Coordination* (pp. 37–50). Maidenhead, UK: Open University Press.

Nutbrown, C., Clough, P., Levy, R., Little, S., Bishop, J., Lamb, T. & Yamada-Rice, D. (2017). Families' roles in children's literacy in the UK throughout the 20th century. *Journal of Early Childhood Literacy*, 17(4), 551–569. https://doi.org/10.1177/1468798416645385

OECD (2008). PISA 2006 Volume 2 Data, PISA. Paris: OECD Publishing. https://doi.org/10.1787/9789264040151-en

OECD (2021). *21st-Century Readers: Developing Literacy Skills in a Digital World.* Paris: OECD Publishing.

Ofsted (2013). Unseen children: access and achievement 20 years on. *Evidence Report.* [online] www.gov.uk/government/publications/unseen-children-access-and-achievement-20-years-on

Richardson, J. & Parnell, P. (2007). *And Tango Makes Three, illustrated by Henry Cole.* Simon & Schuster.

Rose, J. (2006). *Independent Review of the Teaching of Early Reading.* DfES. https://dera.ioe.ac.uk/5551/2/report.pdf

Savage, M., Devine, F., Cunningham, N., Taylor, M., Li, Y., Hjellbrekke, J., Le Roux, B., Friedman, S. & Miles, A. (2013). A new model of social class? Findings from the BBC's Great British Class Survey Experiment. *Sociology*, 47(2), 219–250. https://doi.org/10.1177/0038038513481128

Smith, V. (2010). Comprehension as a social act: Texts, contexts and readers. In K. Hall, U. Goswami, C. Harrison, S. Ellis & J. Soler (Eds), *Interdisciplinary Perspectives on Learning to Read: Culture, Cognition and Pedagogy* (pp. 61–73). London: Routledge.

Steel, J. (2022). Children's wellbeing and reading engagement: The impact of reading to dogs in a Scottish Primary 1 classroom. *Education 3–13.* DOI: 10.1080/03004279.2022.2100442

Steel, J., Williams, J. M. & McGeown, S. (2021). Reading to dogs in schools: An exploratory study of teacher perspectives. *Educational Research*, 63(3), 279–301.

Sutton Trust (2011). *Improving the Impact of Teachers on Pupil Achievement in the UK – Interim Findings.* Sutton Trust.

Topping, K. & Maloney, S. (Eds.) (2005). *The RoutledgeFalmer Reader in Inclusive Education.* (Readers in education). RoutledgeFalmer. http://library.dundee.ac.uk/F/XR2KG2PDD1SLA4Y6PVCAVGEE4KEPCHDV8DC6ALDVEJ4DI78JBQ-14086?func=full-set-set&set_number=466457&set_entry=000001&format=999

UNCRC (United Nations Convention on the Rights of the Child) (1989). [online] www.unicef.org.uk/what-we-do/un-convention-child-rights/

UNESCO (2005). *Education for All: Literacy for Life Global Monitoring Report 2006.* Paris: UNESCO.

Walker, M., Sainsbury, M., Worth, J., Bamford, H. & Betts, H. (2015). *Phonics Screening Check Evaluation: Final Report.* Department for Education.

Wyse, D. & Styles, M. (2007). Synthetic phonics and the teaching of reading: The debate surrounding England's 'Rose Report'. *Literacy*, 41, 35–42. https://doi.org/10.1111/j.1467-9345.2007.00455.x

Wyse, D. & Bradbury, A. (2023). Teaching phonics and reading effectively: 'A balancing act' for teachers, policy makers and researchers. *Review of Education*, 11(3). https://bera-journals.onlinelibrary.wiley.com/doi/full/10.1002/rev3.3429

CHAPTER

10

Drawing on children's digital repertoires to enable playful digital literacies in the primary classroom

Jemma Monkhouse and Chris Bailey

Introduction

In this chapter, we explore several dimensions of digital play in classroom contexts that leverage children's existing digital repertoires. We present three illustrative examples of practice arising from our past experiences as teachers and researchers.

Firstly, we briefly explain our roles in relation to this work, to share our evolving viewpoints. Secondly, we establish the theoretical framework for the ideas and arguments outlined in this chapter. Thirdly, we guide the reader through three distinct projects that we participated in as teachers and/or researchers. Each project involves digital play situated within classrooms but drawing on skills and knowledge from elsewhere in the children's lives. This helped to blur the conventional understanding of a home/school divide existing in relation to digital literacies. Finally, we reflect on the insights gained from considering these three examples collectively, shedding light on children's literacy development in the realm of digital play and offering implications for practitioners and students alike.

Theoretical framework

The examples in this chapter are underpinned by three interrelated theoretical perspectives. Before narrating our practical examples, we will outline each of these perspectives in turn to explain how we are thinking about these instances of digital play. Here we address core ideas around:

- Digital literacies.
- Play/playfulness.
- Understandings of space.

While there is much work around the use of digital technologies in school contexts, it is the work specifically around digital *literacies* that provides the foundations for our thinking. Each of

DOI: 10.4324/9781003381013-10

the three case studies outlined later in this chapter mobilise an understanding of digital literacies, informed by work around new literacies, to frame our understandings both as teachers and researchers involved in these projects. There are multiple interpretations of what is meant by the term 'Digital Literacies' (e.g. Hobbs, 2010; Belshaw and Higgins, 2011) and these generally involve the creation and consumption of texts (in the broadest New Literacy Studies sense) using a device with a screen, while also taking account of the skills or competencies that are required by the individuals who interact with them.

Rather than drawing on any specific definition or framework, our own understandings of digital literacies are shaped more broadly by work around 'new literacies' (Lankshear and Knobel, 2011). Here, the 'new' is broadly synonymous with 'contemporary', while the 'literacies' involved are related to broad conceptions of reading and writing, rather than literacy used to mean 'competency'. New literacies therefore encompass the kind of digital literacy practices and events that are mediated by screen-based technologies (Pahl and Rowsell, 2005) and the kind of multimodal (Kress, 2009) texts that are generated using these screens. New literacies are also broadly positioned in relation to traditional literacies as being more collaborative, distributed and participatory than other more conventional types of literacy (Lankshear and Knobel, 2011), suggesting that it is not simply the individual's relationship with the device that is significant but that digital literacies often involve a network of other factors. This could, for instance, involve collaboration with other children on a shared project (a document, a multiplayer game, etc.), or the network might involve a child drawing on another cultural experience or artefact (such as a YouTube Video, or a song) to produce their own work via a process of remix.

Also important here are the concepts of multimodality and multiliteracies. Multimodal theory (Kress, 2009) suggests that communication and meaning making happen in a range of modes. While written text and speech are perhaps the main modes of communication that we associate with literacy, multimodality suggests that communication happens via modes in combination with each other, and with other modes including 'image, moving image, sound … gesture, gaze and posture' (Jewitt, 2013, p257). Multiliteracies (Cazden, 1996) draw on these understandings and suggest that literacies pedagogy should reflect and take account of the complex, culturally diverse nature of multimodal communication. In this way, texts are not only written but also spoken, visual, sonic and moving, as well as static and existing in physical and virtual space.

SPOTLIGHT ON RESEARCH
Angela Colvert and Fiona Maine explore an Alternative Reality Game

A. Colvert (2020). Presenting a New Hybrid Model of Ludic Authorship: Reconceptualising Digital Play as 'Three-Dimensional' Literacy Practice. *Cambridge Journal of Education*, 50(2), 145–165

F. Maine (2017). The Bothersome Crow People and the Silent Princess: Exploring the Orientations of Children as They Play a Digital Narrative Game. *Literacy*, 51(3), 138–146

Colvert's study is an example of work influenced by a New Literacy Studies conception of digital literacy. Here, the researcher explores the use of an Alternate Reality Game (ARG) in a primary school classroom, using a literacies lens. This work suggests that there are three key dimensions of literacy that relate to these experiences: operational, critical and cultural.

Maine's work uses similar theories to focus on the video game 'Monument Valley' as an interactive text that provides players with a digital narrative. This research, based on close observation of play, raises questions about whether we engage with narrative games by playing them, by reading them, or both.

Playfulness

Having expanded on the 'digital' aspect of 'digital play', it is important that we now address the concept of 'play' itself, given that this is also a term with multiple meanings for different readers. In this chapter we employ a broad understanding of play, drawing on the work of theorists who conceptualise play as having multiple dimensions. For Sutton-Smith (2001), for example, play can include 'exploration, practice, manipulation, mastery, experimentation, reading and listening, making music, painting, roughhousing and so on' (p134). Similarly, Hughes (2013) suggests that play is 'several different things' (p80). As such, Hughes' (2013) taxonomy of play positions the concept as multiple and complex, naming communication, drama, movement, exploration, fantasy, imagination and mastery amongst his 16 suggested observable play types. (To read more about the ways in which play and literacy can be understood, see Daniels and Hussain, this volume.)

The concept of play is also often conflated with the idea of playfulness. Here, the work of Caillois (2001) can be helpful. For Caillois (2001), play can be either ludic or paidic. Caillois (2001) suggests that 'ludus' is generally rule bound play, often involving practice and mastery; examples here include chess or football. 'Paidia', however, is akin to playfulness in that it is understood as much more spontaneous, improvisational or free-form in nature. In this chapter, our examples fall much more in line with this paidic, playful understanding of play, although the reader may also note some aspects of ludic play. Play, in the context of education, is often linked to what Sutton-Smith (2001) terms 'the rhetoric of progress' (p51), a perspective that draws on psychologically situated understandings of human development that position the value of play purely in terms of measurable cognitive or physical change. This can result in classrooms that more regularly feature examples of ludic play – maths games, spelling apps, etc – than of playfulness or paidic play, given that rule bound, ludic play can be accommodated more easily alongside the need for accountability and the restrictions imposed by modern day curriculum and policy. However, drawing more on socio-cultural understandings of play broadens the potential for the use of play in education, helping to make way for more open, paidic types of activity.

PROMPTS FOR CRITICAL REFLECTION

- How do you understand play and/or playfulness?
- How do you see the value of play in your own practice?
- How could you make more space for play in your setting?
- As a researcher, how might you examine the relationship between play and literacy?

Understanding space

Conventional understandings of space frame it in predominantly physical (or 'material') terms. In this sense, we understand a classroom 'space' as being made up of desks, a whiteboard, display boards, windows, walls, chairs, etc. These traditional ideas of space also reinforce set boundaries, by making clear delineations between what is or isn't school – anything that happens within the walls of the building is 'school', anything beyond is othered as external to school.

However, there are more complex, and potentially more useful, ways of understanding space. Spatial theorists such as Massey (2005) and Lefebvre (1991) help us to conceptualise space as consisting of much more than the physical. Massey (2005) describes space as a product of interconnections, which includes material and immaterial aspects. Here, the 'material' refers to objects and devices – the 'tangible' things that can be touched and held in classrooms, such as the chairs, the laptops, the books and the physical aspects we outlined earlier. The immaterial, however, refers to those aspects of space which are social, or cultural, or imagined – but also just as real. In a classroom context, this might be thoughts, ideas, emotions, cultural knowledge, etc. Understanding these things as contributing to classroom space means that thoughts, ideas, knowledge and even feelings that circulate in a classroom can shape the space. Lefebve (1991) also helps us to understand that space is socially produced, meaning that space is not as fixed as we might often consider it to be, and that it is shaped by the experiences of those who inhabit it.

This kind of understanding of space relates to this chapter's topic in two ways. Firstly, it helps us understand that children's lives are not lived in discrete, measurable spaces and that the divisions we often make – for example, between ideas of 'school' or 'home' experience – are not as fixed as we often assume. To move beyond the artificial separation of 'school' and 'out of school' as discrete sites of experience encourages us to explore how these spaces are connected by the lives lived in and between both. For example, both home and school exist in children's lives, and while the two settings are indeed different, there are also many ways in which home and school share objectives and outcomes – in relation to experience, care, learning, enjoyment, etc. As such, the boundaries between home and school are revealed to be porous, particularly in relation to the digital skills and knowledge that children build up in their lives. Understanding space as being more than physical also helps us to explore the idea of digital space, and the ways in which introducing digital space to schools changes the nature of classroom space.

Having outlined our theoretical assumptions, we will now share, via three case studies, the examples of practice – each demonstrating different ways in which children were encouraged to draw on their digital repertoires in a classroom context. In each case, ethical consent was gained for children to be part of the research component of each of these projects. Children who did not give consent were still welcome to take part in the projects but were not a focus of the research. In each of the projects, consideration was given to the power dynamics that come into play when acting as both a teacher and a researcher.

CASE STUDY FOCUS
Blogging Barnsborough

Barnsborough was the name of an onscreen 3D virtual world environment designed as a literacies opportunity for primary school children. On screen, Barnsborough resembled a small town with several different buildings and districts which children could explore as avatars. The town itself was 'mysteriously' devoid of human life, but featured several texts that hinted at what may have occurred to result in the town being vacated. Texts, both written and visual, hinted variously at signs of alien invasion, localised pandemic and nuclear disaster...

Both Chris and Jemma were involved in this research project exploring the use of this virtual world when we were working as teachers in two different primary schools. As part of the project, led by academics from Sheffield Hallam University, a group of children from Jemma's class visited a group of children from Chris's class to explore the game together while located in the same classroom space. Children played on laptops in pairs, entering and exploring the virtual world as avatars. They interacted with their peers from each of the two schools on and off screen, using both an onscreen chat function and speaking to those in the room around them.

Children were given the broad aim of exploring Barnsborough to investigate what might have happened. This involved them in a range of reading activities: selecting different reading pathways as they navigated the game; reading text and images (still and moving) as clues, as they discovered them around the world; piecing together evidence and drawing inferences; following and investigating lines of enquiry. As well as the reading aspects of the game constituting a kind of literacy, children were also engaged in various types of writing activity, including note taking (both handwritten and using iPads), contributing to online group chat and writing a blog post on a shared blog about their experiences in the game and what they thought had happened.

Children's play and playfulness was apparent throughout the project. There were elements of ludic (Caillois, 2001) play in the way children seemed to enter the world, search for clues and communicate. Although there was no set route to follow around the world or definitive answer to their mission, the children seemed to draw on gameplay experiences from their home lives to 'play the game' of Barnsborough, following an unwritten set of rules for the genre. However, these ludic elements did not restrict play. The freedom the children had to investigate the world and develop their theories around what had happened was more akin to paidic play (Caillois, 2001) in the way that they spontaneously journeyed around the world in their pursuit of evidence to answer their own questions. It was also multidimensional (Sutton-Smith, 2001; Hughes, 2013) as children explored, experimented and used their imaginations. This playfulness and creativity was apparent as children speculated about what had taken place, with tales of alien invasion or nuclear disaster abundant, as well as the more pragmatic suggestion that the world was actually a BBC film studio.

An important part of play when exploring the world was the suspension of disbelief children entered into, with all children seeming to collude to make the world 'real', referring to Barnsborough as a town or world but never as a game. Despite children pursuing different theories and ascribing meaning from clues to build individual theories, the existence of the world was never questioned and the sense of 'buying in' and working in role appeared to build a sense of mission and adventure and create a sense of reality and purpose.

The project involved a range of literacy practices. While many of these may be termed 'new' or contemporary literacies (for example, the use of a virtual world environment as a text, accessed via laptop; reading images and symbols; use of iPads to photograph, film and note take, communicating via online chat; writing on a blog), they were dispersed with what might be considered more traditional literacies (such as writing on paper; speaking with a peer). Indeed, some of the texts available in the virtual world, while digital, could still be viewed as traditional, e.g. 'Wanted' posters and signage in the virtual world. It was striking how children moved seamlessly between using these varied literacy practices. For example, when one child discovered some cups floating in the cafe in the virtual world, she quickly reached for an iPad to film the movement of the cups before reaching for pen and paper to add to her notes about her developing theory, while continuously glancing back at the laptop screen to check and observe the phenomena of the floating cups. She was not seeing the task as a 'digital' one but rather was selecting the best tool for the job moment by moment and deemed filming the best way to record movement but note taking on paper the most accessible way to record some ideas to use in her blog later. This serves to remind us of the interconnectedness of literacy practices as well as the value of purpose in setting literacy tasks in terms of the skills and tools it forces one to select. It also suggests her awareness of multimodality (Kress, 2009) and the affordances of different modes presented and available to her. The seamless way in which she moved between these modes implies their relevance and value to everyday literacy practices and may be representative of ways she might move between modes of in-school and out-of-school contexts. This calls for further consideration of how multimodality might be explored in school literacy contexts.

Children's exploration of Barnsborough warrants consideration in terms of what happens when open-ended tasks are set in classrooms. While it might be commonplace to prescribe to children set objectives, criteria, outputs and resources in literacy lessons, there is less opportunity to move between literacies and explore the affordances different media and resources have to offer when this approach is taken. While moving between literacies in this project, children used a range of different literacy skills. These included the reading skills of inference and deduction as they pieced together clues across the virtual world; for example, hypothesising, searching for evidence, note taking, descriptive writing, etc. This suggests that such open-ended opportunities can provide ample opportunity to meet literacy and National Curriculum aims without limiting what might be achieved within a particular lesson.

This example directly involves children drawing on their existing digital repertoires in a classroom context. The use of video gameplay would often be considered a cultural experience not usually located within school. However, by bringing it into the classroom, the children participating demonstrated a seamless ability to transpose skills and knowledge from different times and spaces. This included drawing on gameplay skills and expectations such as how to navigate a game with cries of 'I think we're meant to go down here', looking for things and expecting certain things to happen.

Observing these approaches from the children highlighted the parallels between the skills children drew on from their experiences and knowledge bought from outside of the classroom/confines of the subject being taught, and those taught in schools as part of the English curriculum, such as making predictions and inferences and navigating texts. This was also apparent in the knowledge they drew on from popular culture, such as aliens, zombies, Dr. Who and nuclear disaster. Such knowledge supported the richness, creativity and playfulness of theories and plots developed by the children as they explored Barnsborough. There was productiveness and relevance to the ways in which children drew on this knowledge from home experience and applied it to the literacy practices they are familiar with using in a school setting. This highlights the potential value of making space for children's existing knowledge, thereby facilitating children's use of their 'everyday' literacies.

SPOTLIGHT ON RESEARCH
Digital play and literacy

C. Bailey, C. Burnett, E. Gill, K. Daniels, J. Monkhouse, G. Merchant, J. Rayner & R. Taylor (2013). Zombie Apocalypse: Children's Problems Solving in a Virtual World, *English 4–11*, 48, 7–10

C. Burnett & G. Merchant (2014). Points of View: Reconceptualising Literacies Through an Exploration of Adult and Child Interactions in a Virtual World. *Journal of Research in Reading*, 37(1), 36–50

More expansive explorations of the previous example can be found in these two papers. The first article gives a more expansive description of the children's play in and around Barnsborough, demonstrating several of the creative and collaborative choices that the children made while playing in the classroom. The second paper uses the children's gameplay as a starting point for considering how we need to reconceptualise literacies to take account of digital play, while also noting the challenges faced by teachers in enabling this kind of work in the face of increasingly restrictive curricular expectations.

CASE STUDY FOCUS

The Street

'The Street' was a project that took place across three classes and two schools – Year 5 (age 9–10) classes in Derbyshire and a Year 3 class in Sheffield (age 7–8). It arose from discussions between the class teachers and researchers at Sheffield Hallam University (including Jemma and Chris) with an interest in how 21st Century literacies might be explored in primary school classrooms. These discussions were guided by Burnett et al.'s (2014) principles of 21st Century literacies and aimed to look at ways of meeting National Curriculum English and Computing aims in engaging and relevant ways by using multimodal and digital means of communication between the classes and schools. Particularly relevant here are the principles to 'Recognise and build on children's linguistic, social and cultural repertoires' and to 'Use Playful pedagogies'.

The idea of 'The Street' was an open-ended environment to allow children to communicate and collaborate across the schools. It began with a sound clip of the street (including a siren, wind, rain, footsteps, birds and tyres on a wet road) from which children imagined what it might be like. The Year 5 classes responded by writing descriptions which they shared with the Year 3s via a shared blog (using Kidsblog). The descriptions and sound clip were responded to by the Year 3s who drew pictures before developing their ideas into digital maps using the 'Explain Everything' app and then writing descriptions on the blog. From this point, what could have remained quite a separate activity between the two schools, other than the sharing on the blog, took off in terms of collaboration. The Year 5s in one school picked up on the idea of 'snatching birds out of the sky' in one of the Year 3 descriptions and the resultant activity of breaking news Tweets and filming of news reports explored the backstory of the alleged 'bird napper', who was named Tom O'Brien and became The Street's first character.

It is interesting to consider how this plot was developed between the two schools, with ideas being built upon almost in a ping-pong fashion via the shared blog and both schools taking genuine ownership and investing in the character. It is as if working on an online space removed the geographical barrier between the two schools and the barrier one might expect when working with strangers. Although such a response to others' ideas could potentially have happened within the walls of one classroom, it was as if working in the boundless online space multiplied the impact of working with and building on each other's ideas, giving them a sense of authority and credence. Drawing on the thinking of Massey (2005) and Lefebvre (1991), the space created for shared thinking and creation of The Street could be thought of as the product of social interconnections afforded by the blog and responding to each other's texts. The impetus working in this shared space provided for building on each other's ideas continued throughout the project, with children composing multiple texts including Haiku poems and estate agent brochures. While the project made use of shared space between classrooms and schools, it is also worth considering the potential such an approach holds for creating shared spaces between school and out-of-school spaces, and the opportunities this might open for engaging in literacy practices.

The multimodal and digital form of texts created is worthy of discussion too. The use of sound as a stimulus to set the scene for multiple modes of communication from the project's inception, and the response to this through drawing, creating digital maps and blogging, invited the children to play with and pursue multiple modes from the outset. The invitation to explore different modes seemed to impact in various ways. Choices over the directions the project took and the texts they would pursue were very much child led. This led to greater exploration of what might be considered home or contemporary literacies, such as Tweets and television broadcasts. Children brought their home experiences to these literacies, and these experiences seemed to lead to the creation of texts that the teachers identified as being different from what they might expect the same children to produce in typical English lessons. The valuing of contemporary literacies not only brought about different potential for the types of texts, but also the way the texts were constructed. Children seemed to draw on more sophisticated language, as if the audience they were writing for demanded it. They also seemed less concerned about issues of transcription and used iPads and software to support these elements, seemingly being much happier to commit words to the page and then return later to edit and improve. The approach also seemed to offer a platform to children who may have been considered reluctant by their teachers when working with more traditional school literacies. It was as if the privileging of contemporary literacies benefitted these children and enabled them to draw on their repertoires effectively and creatively. The use of audience afforded by sharing texts on the blog (and other platforms such as Twitter) seemed integral to this as children were focused on the need to communicate effectively and selected modes accordingly. As the New London Group (Cazden, 1996) suggests, the types of literacies and modes of communication explored reflected the complex and culturally diverse nature of communication and enabled children to draw on the full range of modes of communication available to them. As well as an awareness of a wider audience, the Year 3s appeared particularly aware of having Year 5 children within their audience. This seemed to spur them on with wanting to be accurate in their use of grammar and punctuation, and ambitious in their use of vocabulary. It also led to some children including more mature themes in their writing than they usually would, as if the Year 5 audience demanded it. While the aim of the project was not to cover specified National Curriculum objectives, it should be noted that participating in these literacies resulted in many curriculum objectives being met and for some children to a level that exceeded teacher expectations.

The use of the digital and the multimodal in this *Case study focus* seemed to invite a level of playfulness. The open-ended invitation to create based on a sound clip acted as a springboard for this playfulness, akin to Caillois's (2001) understanding of paidic play being spontaneous, improvisational and free form in nature. This was apparent in the playful ways in which characters such as Tom O'Brien the 'bird snatcher' were created; the playful use of language in descriptions, poetry and other texts; and the playful use of drama as children took on various roles for their television broadcasts. Each of these separate episodes in themselves could be described as playful but the spontaneous and often unpredictable ways in which they emerged in real time and were led by the children could also be described as playful, as if children from the different schools and classes were taking turns as they played the game across the gameboard of the blog. Another interesting example of playfulness from the project comes from the level of investment in the fiction some of the Year 3 children entered into. This became apparent to the teacher of those children one afternoon as a group of children asked about The Street, 'Is it real?', apparently dismayed after hearing rumours on the playground that the teacher had been 'caught' finding images for The Street online and that it might have been made up all along. This level of investment is suggestive of the level of playfulness children are willing to enter into and what this offers to the exploration of texts. A more detailed exploration of the previous example can be found in Monkhouse et al. (2017).

CASE STUDY FOCUS
Building a virtual community

Chris first set up a Minecraft Club for a group of children aged 10 and 11 years old as a primary school teacher, at the request of a child in his class. Unsure of how to incorporate Minecraft into his classroom, but eager to make connections between school and children's wider cultural interests, he initially ran a weekly lunchtime club, using an adapted version of the world building videogame Minecraft. Minecraft was a game which many of the children already played and talked about, and it was interesting to see those who might be considered experts in the game teaching others who were less experienced how to play. In the club, located in their classroom, children played the game using laptop computers remotely connected to a server running the game world on a laptop. A very open objective was set for the club – for the children to create a 'virtual community'.

The children interpreted this invitation in multiple ways, and engaged in a range of playful behaviours during the club both on and off screen. They clearly loved playing the game, and the playful, paidic (Caillois, 2001) atmosphere generated seemed to afford a kind of socialising opportunity that wasn't usually available to children coming to the end of their primary school experience. The open and exploratory nature of the club, afforded by the onscreen sandbox videogame and the very broad remit for play, felt like a refreshing change from the more directed, objective driven nature of the rest of the school day. Children were working together, organising themselves, making plans and, largely, enjoying themselves while collaborating with a broadly shared purpose. The club wasn't entirely unproblematic, and there was some conflict and upset at times. However, the children generally worked through these issues independently, self-organising to work out ways to avoid these instances which punctuated their play. The children voluntarily took part in the club, and this level of engagement and enjoyment encouraged Chris to think of ways in which he could extend this experience into the more 'formal' space of our subject driven curriculum. This led to the children producing creative writing based on their experiences in the game, and exploring a 'destroyed' world as part of a topic relating to environmental disasters.

Having run the club for a year at lunchtime, Chris left his role as a teacher and undertook a PhD examining another iteration of Minecraft Club, in the same school but with a different group of children, once per week in an after-school club. Here, the children collaborated on a weekly basis to create a space that they named 'Banterbury'. The use of the term 'banter' in the name of their community directly echoed the friendly, bantering nature of the children's interactions. Research around this subsequent club showed that the children often engaged in a kind of play that was termed 'emergent'.

As well as building on screen, in the game, children also played and interacted in and around the physical environment. This involved a diverse range of literacy practices including: collaborative singing (particularly memorable was the adaptation of the song 'Feed the World' to fit the words 'Free the Sheep'); self-directed reading and writing; and even, on one occasion, a very sensitive and collaborative role play – on and off screen – of a funeral about the death of an in-game horse. As such, this case study shows the diverse ways in which children again drew on existing digital repertoires in their game, but in ways which were collaborative, spontaneous and coexisted effortlessly with other dimensions of their wider cultural experiences albeit in the classroom context.

The *Spotlight on research* that follows provides further information on Chris's research and publications.

SPOTLIGHT ON RESEARCH

Free the sheep and neurodivergent literacies

C. Bailey (2016). Free the Sheep: Improvised Song and Performance In and Around a Minecraft Community. *Literacy*, 50(2), 62–71

C. Bailey (2021). *Screen Play Experiences in Education: Visual Methods in Research Representation.* Palgrave Macmillan

C. Bailey (2023). Neurodivergent Literacies': Exploring Autistic Adults' 'Ruling Passions' and Embracing Neurodiversity Through Classroom Literacies. *Literacy*, 57(2), 120–131

The following work expands on the ideas presented in this example. The first chapter focuses on one 'episode' of gameplay from the club, examining the significance of children's spontaneous and playful singing that was prompted by an in-game event. The second text is a book that explores the club from multiple perspectives, while also exemplifying how the kind of multimodal literacies engaged in by the children can also make their way into other contexts. To do this, the book uses comic strips to expand on theory and to represent aspects of the club. The third paper focuses on the ways in which children's own interests, digital and otherwise, can play an important part in creating inclusive spaces in schools. It emphasises this with a particular focus on neurodivergent children, providing recommendations for how teachers can promote 'neurodivergent literacies' in their classrooms by including wider cultural experiences, like Minecraft, in their practice.

In this chapter, we have explored several dimensions of digital play in classroom contexts that leverage children's existing digital repertoires. In the *Prompts for critical reflection* that follow we invite you to consider ways of integrating children's digital repertoires into your own practice and research.

PROMPTS FOR CRITICAL REFLECTION

- What experiences of literacies do children you work with seem to draw on as they transition between in school and out of school spaces?
- What opportunities are there for you to further enable children to draw on their out of school experiences of literacies when in the classroom?
- How do you draw on children's digital repertoires within your classroom literacy practice?
- How might further space be made for acknowledging and drawing on digital literacies in your English pedagogy?
- In what ways might you embrace playful pedagogies in your teaching of English? What opportunities might this open up?

Chapter summary

The three *Case study focuses* presented here show how it is possible to integrate digital experiences alongside traditional learning. Drawing on children's existing digital repertoires in the classroom not only reflects the evolving nature of literacy but also acknowledges the diverse experiences and skills children bring with them. By embracing both physical and digital learning environments, educators can create more inclusive and dynamic spaces that resonate with children's everyday lives.

Broadening our conception of literacy to include digital literacies is essential. Traditional curricula often emphasize rigid structures that can limit the exploration and utilisation of digital tools. However, recognising digital literacy as a critical component of education allows for a more holistic approach, addressing the multi-faceted ways in which children engage with and interpret the world. Overcoming the challenges posed by a rigid curriculum requires innovative strategies that integrate digital tools and methodologies, ensuring that education remains relevant and engaging for today's learners.

Children's ability to navigate a range of literacies in each of the examples presented here highlights their expertise in drawing on multiple sources and seamlessly transitioning between them. This fluidity is a testament to their adaptability and proficiency in using various forms of communication and information. Encouraging children to harness this expertise not only enriches their learning experiences but also fosters a deeper understanding of how different literacies intersect and complement each other. Educational experiences that embrace a playful approach can unlock a wide range of literacies, fostering creativity and collaboration. Playfulness in learning encourages experimentation, emergence and the exploration of new ideas, making the educational process more engaging and effective. By creating an environment where play and learning coexist, educators can support children in developing a robust and versatile literacy toolkit, preparing them for the complex and interconnected world they will navigate as they grow.

References

Bailey, C. (2016). Free the sheep: Improvised song and performance in and around a Minecraft community. *Literacy*, 50(2), 62–71.

Bailey, C. (2021). *Screen Play Experiences in Education: Visual Methods in Research Representation*. London: Palgrave Macmillan.

Bailey, C. (2023). Neurodivergent literacies': Exploring autistic adults' 'ruling passions' and embracing neurodiversity through classroom literacies. *Literacy*, 57(2), 120–131.

Bailey, C., Burnett, C., Gill, E., Daniels, K., Monkhouse, J., Merchant, G., Rayner, J. & Taylor, R. (2013). Zombie apocalypse: Children's problems solving in a virtual world. *English 4–11*, 48, 7–10.

Belshaw, D. & Higgins, S. (2011). *Digital Literacy, Digital Natives, and the Continuum of Ambiguity*. Retrieved from Dougbelshaw.com.

Burnett, C. & Merchant, G. (2014). Points of view: Reconceptualising literacies through an exploration of adult and child interactions in a virtual world. *Journal of Research in Reading*, 37(1), 36–50.

Burnett, C., Davies, J., Merchant, G. & Rowsell, J. (2014). New meaning-making practices: A charter for literacy education. In J. Rowsell & K. Pahl (Eds), *New Literacies Around the Globe* (pp. 154–166). New York: Routledge.

Caillois, R. (2001). *Man, Play, and Games*. Champaign, IL: University of Illinois Press.

Cazden, C. (1996). A pedagogy of multiliteracies: Designing social futures. *Harvard Educational Review*, 66(1), 60.

Colvert, A. (2020). Presenting a new hybrid model of ludic authorship: Reconceptualising digital play as 'three-dimensional' literacy practice. *Cambridge Journal of Education*, 50(2), 145–165.

Hobbs, R. (2010). *Digital and Media Literacy: A Plan of Action. A White Paper on the Digital and Media Literacy Recommendations of the Knight Commission on the Information Needs of Communities in a Democracy*. Washington: Aspen Institute.

Hughes, B. (2013). *Evolutionary Playwork and Reflective Analytic Practice*. London: Routledge.

Jewitt, C. (2013). Multimodal methods for researching digital technologies. In S. Price, C. Jewitt, & B. Brown (Eds), *The SAGE Handbook of Digital Technology Research* (pp. 250–265). London: Sage Publications.

Kress, G. (2009). *Multimodality: A Social Semiotic Approach to Contemporary Communication*. London: Routledge.

Lankshear, C. & Knobel, M. (2011). *New Literacies: Everyday Practices and Social Learning* (3rd Ed.). Maidenhead: Open University Press.

Lefebvre, H. (1991). *The Production of Space*. Oxford: Blackwell.

Maine, F. (2017). The bothersome crow people and the silent princess: Exploring the orientations of children as they play a digital narrative game. *Literacy*, 51(3), 138–146.

Massey, D. B. (2005). *For Space*. London: Sage.

Monkhouse, J., Baker, W., Daly, A., Power, D., Bailey, C., Burnett, C., Daniels, K. & Merchant, G. (2017). The word on the street: A cross-school collaboration. *English 4–11*, 59, 17–20.

Pahl, K. & Rowsell, J. (2005). *Literacy and Education: Understanding the New Literacy Studies in the Classroom*. London: Paul Chapman.

Sutton-Smith, B. (2001). *The Ambiguity of Play*. London: Harvard University Press.

CHAPTER

11

Drama

Movement and meaning making

Jemma Monkhouse and Laurel Smith

Introduction

In this chapter we explore drama as a diverse literacy practice and consider its wide-ranging potential in terms of supporting meaning making and personal and social development. We begin by presenting some key conceptualisations that position different perspectives on drama in education. We then share two examples from our own practice and research as teachers and facilitators of drama: one drawing on Jemma's doctoral research and another from Laurel's classroom practice. Both examples draw on extra-curricular clubs exploring plays by Shakespeare with children in Key Stage 2. Finally, we discuss themes emerging from these examples along with some implications for practice.

PROMPTS FOR CRITICAL REFLECTION
Reflecting on your own conceptualisations of drama

- What do you think of when you hear the word drama? How does that change if you think about it from the perspective of a teacher?
- What forms of communication do you associate with drama? How is this aided by use of the body? Use of the voice? Movement?
- How do you see it in relation to literacy or English? Do you see it as sitting within the subject of English or do you see it as a subject in its own right?
- What value do you see in drama in your role as a teacher? Do you see it as a tool to support learning or do you think of a performance to be rehearsed and shared?
- What do you see as the potential benefits of using drama? Do these relate to English specifically, areas of the curriculum more broadly, or to aspects of personal and social development?

Considering drama within the English subject domain

Now you have reflected on your own ideas about what drama is, we will introduce the purpose of this chapter within a book about diverse literacies. Drama is positioned within the subject of English in the National Curriculum rather than as a subject in its own right. Within this

DOI: 10.4324/9781003381013-11

chapter we will consider what some of the potential benefits of drama are, both within English and more broadly, and in so doing consider its affordances as a diverse literacy practice.

The perceived importance of drama to the subject of English was clear in key government reports prior to the first National Curriculum being published in 1989. John Dixon's *Growth through English* (1967) reported on the discussion of teachers from England, America and Canada at the Dartmouth Conference in 1966. This advocated a 'personal growth' model of English and spoke of the role of drama within this. These views were echoed in the Bullock Report – A Language for Life (DES, 1975) and the Cox Report – English for Ages 5–16 (DES, 1989), both of which were influential in the development of the first National Curriculum.

Further iterations of the National Curriculum in England have continued to highlight multiple ways in which drama forms a part of the English curriculum. Broadly, this includes its potential for language development and how this might feed into oral and written communication. More specifically, it also requires learners to develop their comprehension of plays (and other texts), to perform them with understanding and to apply this understanding to the writing and performing of their own compositions. McGuinn (2014) has summarised the many affordances of drama to the teaching of English:

> The attractions for English practitioners of the drama-as-process approach are many: democratic access – particularly for those who find written forms of literacy difficult – to a wide range of empowering language registers and structures; learning alongside the teacher through discovery rather than learning through transmission from the dais; exploration of one's personal and social identity within a safe fictional context; breaking down of the academic barriers that can place canonical literature beyond popular reach; the acknowledgement that sound, movement and gesture are important components of literacy.
>
> (McGuinn, 2014, p72)

The value of drama within the English subject domain is therefore seen as wider ranging, with benefits relating to the key strands of reading, writing and oracy as well as affordances in terms of how learning in English may take place.

Further conceptualisations of drama in education

Debates surrounding the value of drama in education have extended beyond its positioning within the National Curriculum. Over the past century, advocates have argued strongly for a range of reasons for its purpose in education. Here we will outline some key perspectives that have emerged, drawing on the work of influential practitioners in the field.

Process versus product drama

Thinking around drama in education has often been conceptualised as drama as process or drama as product (McGuinn, 2014; Neelands, 1992; Neelands and Goode, 2015). Process drama conceptualises drama as a vehicle for learning (whether that be personal development, learning related to English or learning across the curriculum), whereas product (or performance) drama views drama as theatre and as an art form to be taught in its own right. As Neelands argued, drama in education practice is not always so clear cut and 'increasingly, good drama practice at all levels is characterised by a more holistic approach that seeks to capture the strengths of both the process and the product traditions' (Neelands, 2008, p5). Bowell and Heap (2012, p3) argued that while drama is a process that enables 'development of cognitive, emotional, social, cultural and creative understanding and skills', all drama work in an educational context is underpinned by elements of theatre and performance. They used a helix (Figure 11.1)

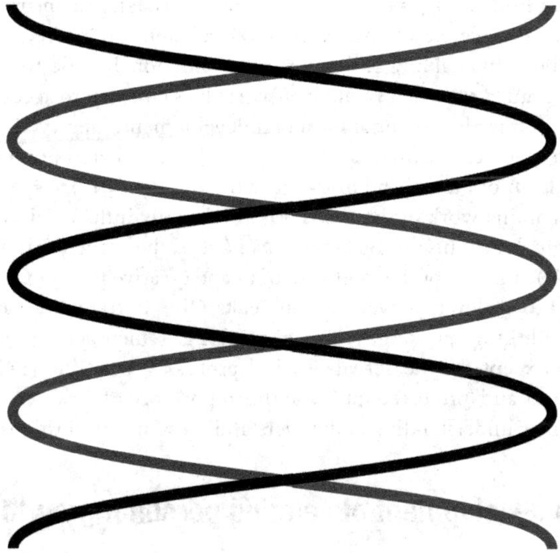

Figure 11.1 The Drama Learning Helix
Source: Bowell and Heap, 2012, p4

to explore the relationship between drama form and content and how this leads to learning about drama or learning through drama. This demonstrates how the two strands of learning are always present, as drama has to have content and also requires performance skills to engage in, but that the focus of each may come into sharper focus at different times.

Throughout this chapter we will outline some of the perceived ways in which drama can support learning both as a process and a product.

Drama's role in supporting learning through play

Although their work dates back prior to the 20th Century, the work of philosophers Rousseau and Froebel in the 18th and 19th Centuries is worthy of mention as their work has been used retrospectively in discussion about drama in education (Bolton, 1985; McGuinn, 2014). Their thinking influenced a move in education towards more child-centred approaches which acknowledged the importance of children learning through play. This highlighted the active role children play in learning (contrary to opposing empty-vessel models of learning) and how children are actively engaged in constructing meaning from their experiences, therefore highlighting the significance of children's play to learning. They also challenged the idea of unequal power relationships between the child and the teacher, suggesting a relationship of learning together rather than the child necessarily having to learn from the teacher. Rousseau and Froebel also placed importance on children learning through the senses and by engaging with the physical world and argued that such experiences and play would lead to understanding of not only the immediate but also the abstract. From a drama practitioner's perspective, these philosophies support the role drama can play in providing such experiences and opportunities for children to learn through play and such potential for creating relationships in which the child is not reliant and subservient to the teacher (McGuinn, 2014).

These foundations from Rousseau and Froebel are reflected in the work of Piaget and Vygotsky (McGuinn, 2014), who regarded children as active constructors of meaning from the earliest age. They were each interested in the relationship between drama and play and the affordance of drama in enabling children to enter a fictional world from which they can make meaning. They argued that such symbolic play enables children to access higher order thinking skills as well as having the potential for moral development. Dewey also advocated the contribution play can make to learning, arguing that if it is facilitated properly it can contribute to learning in the form of mental and moral growth (Dewey, 2012).

Peter Slade's drama work in the 1950s was also heavily influenced by a belief in the value of learning through play. In his seminal text, *Child Drama*, he argued that play is 'inborn and vital' (Slade, 1954, p41) and 'one of the most strenuous and creative forms of work' (p42). He believed play was central to children's developing understanding of the world, arguing that 'Play is the child's way of thinking, proving, relaxing, working, remembering, daring, testing, creating and absorbing. Except for the actual physical processes, it is life' (p42). Slade distinguished between 'personal' and 'projected' play and the importance of flow between the two of them to develop both inner understanding and understanding of material things.

Drama's role in development of self and personal growth

Many key drama practitioners have argued for the role and value of drama from a social and emotional development perspective, including the seminal work of Heathcote, Bolton, and Neelands. Dorothy Heathcote's work in this field was highly influential (O'Neill, 2015). Her work valued the importance of providing learners with experiences from which they can reflect and build their understanding. She noted that this had the potential to develop critical thinking, reflection, responsibility, collaboration and communication and described the purpose of drama as being about 'developing the skills of being a person in a community' (O'Neill, 2015, p44). Neelands (1992) recognised drama's value in exploring and representing human experience, arguing that by providing simulated experiences drama can help children to develop an understanding of themselves and others. He therefore saw drama as a useful tool for exploring children's spiritual, moral, social and cultural development, as well as citizenship and Personal, Social and Health Education. Bolton (1998; Bolton and Warwick, 1983) also recognised drama's potential for children to experience emotions and argues that through this process a child's view of the world may be changed.

Drama's role as a vehicle for learning across the curriculum

Another way of seeing drama's role as a process is the view of drama as a vehicle for learning across the curriculum. Process drama techniques such as hot seating, freeze frames, thought tracking and writing in role can all be used to explore the content of a range of curriculum areas. A key technique developed by Heathcote was that of 'teacher in role'. This enables the teacher to lead the direction of the drama, and similar to Vygotsky's theory on the Zone of Proximal Development, enables the teacher to work in role to extend what the child is able to achieve in the drama. The potential for learning across the curriculum afforded by drama is so great that Heathcote and Bolton claimed they 'cannot think of a subject that cannot or should not be tackled through drama' (Heathcote and Bolton, 1995, p84).

While process drama methods offer a wide range of potential for learning across a range of curriculum subjects, for the purposes of this chapter we draw you back to the case potential drama offers to English as a vehicle for learning. This includes providing access to and rehearsal of registers of language; development of vocabulary; opportunities for presenting orally and in writing; writing of texts for specific purposes; reading for research; and developing rich comprehension of texts, to name but a few. In the *Spotlight on research* that follows, we consider some of the potential learning process drama supports in relation to working with challenging texts.

SPOTLIGHT ON RESEARCH

Drama's affordances in exploring challenging texts

A number of research studies have looked specifically at how process drama can be utilised to support children's meaning making when working with challenging texts, such as the works of Shakespeare.

B. Edmiston and A. McKibben (2011). Shakespeare, Rehearsal Approaches, and Dramatic Inquiry: Literacy Education for Life. *English in Education*, 45(1), 86–101

Edmiston and McKibben's (2011) study looked at the use of dramatic enquiry to explore Shakespeare's *King Lear* with 10–12-year-old children. This indicated the power of rehearsal-based approaches in enabling children to make meaning about complex texts that would normally be considered too difficult for that age. They also made claims as to drama's potential for individuals to project themselves into situations that would otherwise remain inaccessible, thus creating possibilities to learn from the situations, relationships and themes contained within the text and to consider the moral and philosophic significance of Shakespeare's plays.

D. Kidd (2011). The mantle of Macbeth. *English in Education*, 45(1), 72–85

Similarly, the results of Kidd's (2011) study into using 'Mantle of the Expert' to explore Shakespeare's *Macbeth* with underachieving GCSE students, also suggested drama's power to increase understanding of a text and relate it to students' own life experiences. It also showed a positive impact on students' speaking and listening skills. Kidd noted the impact the project had on the students' confidence to rise to challenges and their perception of their own ability, as well as the absorption and commitment to tasks the project created and the participants' increased ability to work collaboratively.

Drama's role as a subject in its own right

Having explored views of drama in relation to process and its affordances in supporting a wide range of learning, we return to the sense of drama as a subject in its own right: what could be considered as drama as product. The case for this has been put forward strongly by David Hornbrook (Hornbrook, 1985; Hornbrook, 1986; Hornbrook, 1998a; Hornbrook, 1998b), who argued that what is lost with the popular ideas around learning *through* drama is the sense of drama and theatre as an art form. While he acknowledged that learning through drama has value, he called for 'an appropriate balance between a knowledge of drama and the mastery of its practices' (Hornbrook, 1998b, p9). Hornbrook's view of drama places it within the arts and establishes it as a subject with its own body of knowledge, including conventions and techniques that can be taught.

Examples from practice

As the mapping out of the role of drama in education demonstrates, the potential benefits are multi-faceted and wide ranging. However, from our experience in our current roles working in Initial Teacher Education, when introducing the idea of tackling Shakespeare with primary aged children it is usually met with a mixture of disbelief and utter horror! Initial discussions with student teachers at the beginning of our drama workshops suggest that the negative views they hold of using Shakespeare in a primary setting are often deeply rooted in their own experiences of studying Shakespeare in their secondary education. It seems that the need to dissect, analyse and offer insight on Shakespeare's plays leaves little room for engaging in the rich ways in which he plays with language and makes fundamental connections with the very stuff of what it means to be human. Interestingly, the majority of these student teachers leave the workshop with a different perspective and much more energised and engaged than when we started!

Our own experiences of working with young children to explore Shakespeare's plays through a combination of process and product drama were both inspirational and illuminating.

In the sections that follow, we will apply thinking about affordances of drama to examples from our own practice through two case studies that examine the ways in which we have each used drama to explore Shakespearean texts with children in Key Stage 2. The first case study, from Jemma, provides a spotlight on her research and focuses on the affordances of drama through consideration of an individual child The second, from Laurel, provides a spotlight on classroom practice and builds on key aspects of Jemma's research to consider affordances in relation to the collective group. We hope that these case studies will offer some inspiration, first and foremost, but also reassurance that performing Shakespeare's greatest works with primary school children is not only feasible, but utterly magical!

SPOTLIGHT ON RESEARCH
Jemma' research: Drama and movement supporting meaning making

My case study draws on data generated from an after-school drama club I ran with 21 Year 6 children as part of my doctoral research. The club ran for ten weeks and used drama techniques to explore Shakespeare's *Macbeth*. The aims of the club centred around process drama, as I was interested in how drama supported meaning making in relation to a text as well as its impact on personal, emotional and social development. However, it is worth noting that as the club progressed, a product drama element emerged as participants expressed a desire to perform scenes from the play for an audience. Throughout the ten weeks the club ran, participants explored the text, characters and plot of *Macbeth* using a range of drama techniques. They also played a range of drama games that served as warm-ups for each session of the club and fed into the drama skills needed when working with particular scenes from the text of *Macbeth*. Data was generated through recording each session using Go Pro cameras (one attached to me filming from the point of view of facilitator and another filming a more general overview from the back of the room); interviews with participants; reflective notes from me as a researcher; and collection of artefacts, e.g. participants' entries in their personal Actor's Notebooks and artefacts created collaboratively such as through role on the wall activities.

For the purposes of this chapter, I will focus on process drama elements. In particular, I will explore how physical elements of the drama process seemed to impact on meaning making for a specific participant in the club. When using the term 'physical' I am referring to both physical movement of the body and physical interaction with objects. Such physical elements are arguably significant aspects of drama practice, opening up affordances in the way that the body represents and communicates, quite often in motion. I also include in my consideration of movement what I would term oral movement or vocalisations, in that the production of sound and speech (further affordances of drama) are produced through bodily movement.

I will outline three examples relating to a single participant in the club and explore how the physical aspects of the practice of drama seem integral to how she makes meaning.

Example 1: Involuntary and spontaneous movement supporting ongoing meaning making

The first example focuses on a sequence typical of a participant in the club in which their physical movement appears integral to their continuous meaning making. The sequence is presented here to exemplify such a sequence of meaning making. It covers a period of time when I was explaining and giving instructions to the club and the participant featured seemingly uses movement of her body and voice to support how she makes meaning throughout that sequence.

The participant is sat cross-legged on the classroom carpet and is listening to my instructions as a facilitator of a drama workshop. The participant asks, 'What's a tableaux?' in response to me using the word in my instructions. The question is spoken seemingly without conscious thought as soon as the word 'tableaux' has left my mouth. It could be thought of as an involuntary oral movement.

The participant starts the sequence sat in a neutral cross-legged position, with her arms relaxed over her legs and her head and gaze angled towards me as she listens. I start to explain, 'I am going to tell you a certain type of person I want you to be and you are going to use your body to show me you're that type of person.' As I speak she straightens up her posture as if becoming a character. She flicks her hair and reangles her head as if in role as that character. She then adjusts crossing over of legs and arms as if taking on the role of a sophisticated lady. She turns her head and pinches her lips in this imagined role while continuing to listen to my instructions. I continue, 'You don't need to use your voice. You just need to use your bodies and your face.' As I give this instruction the participant's body moves continuously, reflecting the instructions. I add, 'You might want to try out some different things'. The participant's body moves continuously in response.

The movements in this sequence do not appear pre-planned but almost emerge unconsciously in response to what is being spoken about or occurring at that time. The immediacy of the participant calling out 'What's a tableau?' when I first say the word suggests an automaticity of the oral movement rather than planning to ask it, suggesting the question is an automatic and involuntary part of her meaning making process when hearing the instructions. As the instructions continue, she moves physically throughout as if her processing of the instructions takes place through her whole body.

Example 2: Physical representation supporting understanding of character and plot

As well as the seemingly involuntary physical movement that can be observed in the first example, more deliberate physical movements seem a key feature of the participant's dramatic representations and therefore meaning making about characters and plot. When rehearsing and performing a scene where she plays the character of Macbeth, she holds her arms and shoulders out throughout this time in what appears to be her representation of a male stance. This embodiment of Macbeth suggests her need to take on a character physically to become them rather than relying simply on the language of the play.

Another example of this can be found in her portrayal of the ghost of Banquo:

The participant moves hauntingly as Banquo's ghost, eyes fixed on Macbeth. As she swings her hair about in response to Macbeth crying, 'Never shake thy gory locks at me', the 'gory locks' settle on her face, where she lets them remain while she continues in role. She later exits the scene and when she returns she has rearranged and positioned her hair deliberately across her face: the decision to do so seemingly integral to her representation of the character.

The use of every aspect of her physical being, from body stance to positioning and movement of hair, emphasises the important role physical representation is playing in her understanding of character and plot. Such use of her physical being seems integral to her interpretation and portrayal of the characters she plays.

Example 3: Interaction with physical objects enhancing meaning making

Interaction with physical objects, including costumes and props, also seems integral to the meaning making process. This appears to enable an extension to the participant's own physicality. Examples include asking for a crown when playing an apparition, linking to the wording of the text 'THIRD APPARITION: a child crowned, with a tree in his hand'.

In later weeks when the focus of the club switched towards preparing for a performance, the use of physical objects appeared to become increasingly important for the participant, as described in the vignette that follows. On the day of the performance, she arrived with a collection of props and costumes (by her own volition) for the roles she would play. A lot of thinking had clearly gone into the selection and making of these costumes and props, thus supporting her meaning making in becoming the characters she would play. During rehearsal time prior to the performance, she spent most of her time engaged in business with her costumes and props, both trying on and exploring her movement in them and making additional items she felt were needed. This included the making of a brush that she decided she would need to play the role of the gentlewoman. This period of intense activity could be described as her becoming those characters in preparation for the performance. The physicality and movements she made reflected the costumes she had created for the character, as if the costume was the character and those were the movements someone wearing that outfit would make. It is as if the costume and props became the interpretation of each character.

There is an ongoing exploration of costumes. First the participant stands in a bloodied and ripped t-shirt she has worked on at home to wear in her role as an apparition. She bends her knees and pushes her torso forward as if to emphasise the prominence of the costume in being that character. Costume changes are ongoing in this exploration. In one minute the participant is exploring a red cape to add to her apparition costume but in the next is exploring an apron she has brought from home to form a costume for another role she will play, the gentlewoman. Momentum builds in her exploration of the gentlewoman costume as she declares, 'I need a brush'. She locates a tube and then starts digging about in the paper tray. She works on the floor with a range of craft materials to make the brush, appearing very focused and independent in this activity. Before long her crafting becomes a sweeping brush. Once it is complete she stands and tests out her sweeping action.

Thinking across the three examples

Throughout the three examples shared here, physical movement and interaction seems integral to the participant's meaning making. Her movement (both physical and vocal) seems at times involuntary and automatic (such as the continual movement of her body in response to listening to me as the facilitator of the drama workshop) and at other times more deliberate and planned (for example, her interactions with costumes and props). Across these examples it appears as though processing and thinking is taking place across her whole body. Thinking and understanding could be seen as a cognitive process, taking place within the brain, but in the examples presented here, this thinking appears visible throughout her body. It is as if the processing and assimilation of information and thinking through interaction with others and with material items (text, props, physical space) takes place throughout her entire body. This includes a need for understanding to be felt (physically and viscerally as well as mentally) and to be tested and experimented with (practically through the body and not just hypothetically through the imagination). This is not to suggest that thought and mental cognition becomes redundant, but rather the body and mind act as one in the processing and development of meaning and understanding. It is useful to draw on the thinking of Perry and Medina (2011) here, whose work explores the notion of embodiment in performative pedagogies:

> Embodiment in performative pedagogical practices ... describes teaching and learning in acknowledgement of our bodies as whole experiential beings in motion, both inscribed and inscribing subjectivities ... the experiential body is both a representation of self (a 'text') as well as a mode of creation in progress (a 'tool'). Embodiment is a state that is contingent upon the environment and the context of the body.(Perry and Medina, 2011, p63)

This sense of the body as both a 'text' and a 'tool' helps us to see the ways in which the participant's body is integral to their meaning making as an experiential being. The body acting as a tool that supports the process of creating meaning, and as a text that becomes a product of that meaning making. Perry (2015) also draws on the work of Ellsworth (2005) to consider participants in drama as what Ellsworth terms 'body/mind/brain' and 'a learning self in motion' (Perry, 2015, p15). This idea of the body, mind and brain working as one and in motion to create meaning appears apparent in the three examples presented.

The examples presented also reflect some of the conceptualisation highlighted earlier in this chapter in terms of drama's affordance as a form of learning through play (Bolton, 1985; McGuinn, 2014; Dewey, 2012; Slade, 1954). Across the examples there is a sense of the participant as an active constructor of meaning, drawing on senses and engaging with the physical world through her own movement and interaction with props to deepen understanding. Slade's (1954, p42) assertion that 'play is the child's way of thinking, proving, relaxing, working, remembering, daring, testing, creating and absorbing' seems particularly pertinent here. Movement appears to accompany and be integral to thought processes and to aid absorption of information and understanding. Similarly, her interactions and movements with props, costumes and her own body appear to be forms of testing and creation as she becomes the characters she seeks to create.

In the next section, we move to Laurel's work with children, focusing on performing Shakespeare's work.

Laurel: co-constructing meaning through drama and movement

The three case studies that follow are from my reflections on classroom practice and my experience of running an extra-curricular drama club for children in Key Stage 2, to prepare and then perform a Shakespeare play as part of the UK-wide Shakespeare Schools Festival. The festival aims to increase access and exposure to Shakespeare's works across the primary and secondary age ranges, with the focus being placed on performance – or product – as a way to develop children's enjoyment of Shakespeare and their understanding of the significant themes within his plays, which are as relevant today as they were in the 16th Century. During the festival, children from across the UK perform Shakespeare's plays in local theatres, having worked with their teacher-director over a period of approximately four months to develop the production of their chosen play.

As a teacher-director, I worked with children on two productions – Hamlet and Macbeth – and so this presents a contrasting approach to Jemma's example. In this case study, the children and I were engaging primarily in product drama, with the performance of the play being the end point to which we were all working. However, in this example we used process drama approaches and techniques in developing the performance, demonstrating how an understanding of process drama, for both teachers and children, is essential when engaging in product drama with the aim of producing a performance for an authentic audience. This approach reflects Neelands (2008) assertion that within practice, drama is often a more holistic approach, with product and process interwoven and coming to the fore at different points.

For the purposes of this chapter, I reflect on the affordances of process into product drama for co-constructing meaning through drama and movement. This focus relates particularly to the ways in which engaging collectively and collaboratively in meaning making can support children's personal growth and self-development. It builds on the examples within Jemma's case study, where the focus is on individual meaning making through physical movement (including voice), to consider collaborative and collective meaning making. That the product drama approach (and the process drama used in developing a performance) is fundamentally rooted in spoken language is important: as Bearne and Reedy (2018, p13) assert, spoken language is the bedrock of 'personal, social, cultural, cognitive, creative and imaginative development'. Thus, the opportunity to co-construct meaning and engage with language outside the normal constraints, expectations and anxieties that existed within the classroom for a number of these children was significant. There remained a structure for our collaborative learning and there was the clear end goal and destination of the performance; but the space we created was different and one which was negotiated and co-constructed.

CASE STUDY FOCUS

Example 1: Working collaboratively to communicate meaning through collective physical movement within the performance space

Tableaux and freeze frame were two ways in which the children explored the themes and key moments of the plays through collective physical movement. These two techniques allowed children to work together to present still images of a scene in the play, including characters and the setting, and to represent characters and objects through body-shapes and postures. Thinking about objects as representations of themes within the play was extremely helpful in supporting children to develop their understanding of the text, but these 'tableaux' – or still images – also then became key parts of the final performance. For example, collectively using body-shapes to create a cauldron, forest, crown and dagger helped children to understand themes (crown/power, dagger/murder) and key scenes (cauldron/witches on the heath, forest/the murder of Banquo) within *Macbeth*, and then became ways to share and communicate these with the audience as part of the production.

At the start of the after-school sessions, the two groups struggled to work collaboratively when creating a tableau or freeze frame and generally children's use of their bodies and postures was rather limited. However, the success with which they were able to use these techniques improved both as they came to know the play better, and as their own awareness and confidence in their own physicality developed. It is important to note that we cannot expect children to come to a drama session with an innate sense of how to use physical movement within the performance space – this, like learning to read and write, needs to be taught and then practised. These rehearsal-based approaches – using techniques such as tableaux and freeze frame – helped children to explore and deepen their understanding of a challenging text (Edmiston and McKibben, 2011) and also develop their awareness of how physical movement can communicate meaning. This aspect also demonstrates the wider affordances of drama within English, as it can be a crucial way in which to help children develop their inference skills when reading: authors frequently convey meaning through nuanced choices about how characters move, walk, turn, even sit within a space; and so as children develop their understanding of this through drama and performance, they will hopefully become more aware of this when reading.

With a relatively small cast for each play and limited use of props, we had to find a way to present a range of different settings and complex narrative arcs in a simple way. Key to communicating meaning to the audience was the children working collaboratively and drawing on the process drama used to develop understanding of the text. In each of the plays, I identified key scenes to develop as ensemble pieces, where children worked together as a group to physically represent a setting. For example, children used the tableaux they had created during the process drama activities to represent the king's chamber and the forest in *Macbeth* where the crucial murders take place. When Hamlet is banished to England and narrowly escapes being murdered, children used a series of freeze frames to present key parts of the action being described by the narrator, with central characters moving between each freeze frame as the narrative unfolded. In each of these examples, children had to develop their ability to work as a group to both present a coherent still image to the audience and to move around each other and across the stage during transitions from one scene, or setting, to another.

However, some of the most powerful moments in the two plays came when the cast worked together as one 'character' or body of characters. In *Macbeth*, virtually the entire cast became a homogenous group of witches to create a distinct and unsettling atmosphere for the scenes when Macbeth encounters them. The children worked individually and then as a group to develop a specific and slow series of body movements to take them on a winding route from the very back of the stage to the front, then moving and freezing as one group as key lines of the text were delivered. Later in the play, they devised a procession to follow Lady Macbeth, mimicking her movements as she walks through the castle at night trying to scrub the imagined blood from her hands. In Hamlet, as Ophelia buries her father and begins her descent into madness, children worked as a group to create a repeated series of movements which conveyed her sadness, grief and mourning. Then, in the final scene of the play, they developed a slow-motion sword fight to echo and amplify Hamlet's fatal duel with Ophelia's brother.

In each of these truly collaborative moments in the play, children worked together as a group to powerfully convey atmosphere, feelings, emotion and meaning for the audience. These examples reflect Bolton and Warwick's (1983) assertion that drama offers a unique opportunity for children to explore and experience emotions. The collaborative nature of these scenes further emphasised this, as the groups had to develop a shared understanding of the emotions they wanted to convey to and create within the audience. It was clear as the rehearsals progressed and developed, and then in the performance itself, that they had understood and embodied the significance of these moments within the narrative arc. Everyone within the group was aware of how they individually contributed to sharing that meaning with the audience.

Furthermore, during the process of developing these collaborative scenes, the children had to guide and manage their interactions within the group; take turns when sharing, explaining and challenging ideas; listen actively and respond appropriately to each other. This took time and space for them to be able to experiment with ideas, and to make collective decisions to reject some ideas and retain and build on others. Engaging in the development of these scenes, then, offered particular affordances for the development of collaborative and communicative skills as noted by O'Neill (2015). It was through the process, but with a clear focus on the product, that the children developed their ability to work with others as part of a coherent cast.

CASE STUDY FOCUS

Example 2: Co-constructing dialogue and movement to develop characterisation

One of the most challenging aspects of performance for the children was understanding how their physical movement within the performance space related to the other actors. Practicing dialogues between characters often began with the children standing rigidly at opposite sides of the stage with the dialogue just going backwards and forwards between them. Alternatively, they would stand very close together in the centre of the stage, again with very little movement. Tackling this issue required children to understand how dialogue and movement worked together to convey meaning in the text by showing characters' emotions, thoughts and feelings. To help children understand this, we first practised key parts of dialogue using just movement and no words: in the dialogue each character would move closer to or further away from the other character(s) for each line of speech. This helped them to focus on the meaning of the text, consider how their body language could show the emotions and feelings of the character at that point, and how their character related to the other characters on the stage.

Consider, for example, the dialogues between Macbeth and Lady Macbeth as they formulate their plan to murder the king. Here, tensions and emotions are running high, but this cannot simply be conveyed through words: it is through the physical movements of the actors within the performance space and in relation to each other which give these moments in the play deep significance. It is important to note that this process is also giving agency to the children within the performance: What meanings do they feel are being conveyed at this particular point? How do they believe the character is feeling about events and in relation to the other characters in the scene? This focus on the performance of the text supported children to make links between what the characters say and how they say it, embodying meaning through the performance. It was also a central part of how, as product drama came to the fore, the children were able to develop their understanding of drama as a subject in its own right; the mastery of its practices which Hornbrook (1998b) highlights in advocating for drama to be given its own status.

CASE STUDY FOCUS

Example 3: Collective use of the voice to co-construct meaning

Undoubtedly, children developed their confidence in speaking, and their ability to listen and respond, throughout the process of working towards a performance of the play. As discussed earlier, specific drama activities helped to develop their understanding of the text and the relationships between the characters, all of which supported them in delivering their lines with confidence, liveliness and flair. However, just as some of the most powerful physical moments in the play were collaborative, we worked a number of moments into each of the plays when the cast collectively used their voices to co-construct, and communicate, meaning. As a group, the witches collectively delivered key lines of the script: in whispers, hisses and echoes, building to shouts, screams and cackles! It may at first seem like a relatively straightforward thing to do, but this kind of collective delivery of the script requires children to develop a nuanced understanding of pace, tonal variation and clarity of pronunciation. Without these key aspects, it becomes a confusing mess of words and sounds, and as the children's awareness of the audience developed, so did their understanding of how to use their voices collectively to co-construct meaning within the play.

Table 11.1 Example of choral and echo ensemble dialogue

			Pairs 1, 2 and 3 start the scene in freeze frame
PAIR 1	OPHELIA	Good, my lord. I have remembrances of yours that I have longed to redeliver. I pray you receive them.	*Pair 1 unfreeze the frame*
	HAMLET	No, not I. I never gave you aught.	
	OPHELIA	My honoured lord, you know right well you did.	*Pair 1 into freeze frame*
PAIR 2	OPHELIA	My honoured lord, you know right well you did. *[repeated line]*	*Pair 2 unfreeze the frame*
	HAMLET	I did love you once.	
	OPHELIA	Indeed, my lord, you made me believe so.	*Pair 2 into freeze frame*
PAIR 3	OPHELIA	Indeed, my lord, you made me believe so. *[repeated line]*	*Pair 2 unfreeze the frame*
	HAMLET	You should not have believed me. I loved you not.	
	OPHELIA	I was the more deceived	*Pair 2 into freeze frame*
ALL PAIRS	HAMLET	Get thee to a nunnery.	*All pairs unfreeze*
ALL PAIRS	OPHELIA	Oh, help him, you sweet heavens.	

Within *Hamlet* we developed the use of a choral and echo ensemble piece for Hamlet and Ophelia's central dialogue within the narrative (see Table 11.1). For this, there were several couples of 'Hamlet and Ophelia' in different places on the stage. Key lines within the dialogue were delivered as a chorus – i.e. all the Ophelias or Hamlets speaking together. In addition, the dialogue moved from one couple to the next, with the last line being repeated at the beginning of the next couple's section. Again, this more complex ensemble approach required the children to listen extremely carefully to each actor on the stage. They were responding not only to their partner within their part of the dialogue, but also to the other couples on the stage.

In each of these examples, the children moved beyond a focus on their own lines to an understanding of how the collective group worked together to convey meaning. The need to listen actively in these scenes inevitably benefitted children's delivery and performance of dialogue in the rest of the play, and it was clear to see as the rehearsals progressed that their understanding of their own character became situated in the interactive nature of the dialogue.

Implications for teachers and practitioners

Having introduced a range of perspectives on what drama in English education might do and having presented two examples from our own practice, we now turn to what our chapter suggests might be important for teachers and practitioners. We will focus this on the key themes we have sought to draw out so far.

We began by considering how drama has been conceptualised as process and product and the potential for these elements to entwine depending on the focus of drama work, as suggested by Bowell and Heap (2012). In the examples we present, the relationship between process and product was fluid as participants continually engaged with learning on multiple levels while at times holding a clear focus on working towards a performance. We would suggest that regardless of the planned focus of any drama work, the relationship between process and product will always emerge. The potential for what can be gained from the practice of drama will be maximised if practitioners work with this understanding in mind and make space for the affordances that both these approaches offer.

A feature of the approaches to drama used in the examples within this chapter is the positioning that drama gives children as active meaning makers with agency in the process. This can be seen in the way that children learned through their own explorations and creations and engaged in negotiating meaning individually and collectively through their interactions – with each other, the text, material items and the space itself. Through these interactions, children actively construct meaning, drawing on senses and engaging with the physical world. Through this they deepen understanding. This highlights the benefits of positioning children as active meaning makers and utilising drama as a playful pedagogy, as we set out in the positioning of drama as play earlier in the chapter (Bolton, 1985; McGuinn, 2014; Dewey, 2012; Slade, 1954). Furthermore, it is worth highlighting that our roles within the examples presented here were not as teachers as transmitters of knowledge. While we certainly guided and facilitated children's explorations and play, we sought as far as possible to create more equal relationships within the workshops.

In considering the value of drama in supporting active meaning making and learning through play, it is important to consider what drama practice specifically has to offer. Throughout the examples presented, it is clear that the affordance of drama drawing on the whole experiencing body to facilitate and make meaning is integral to its value. This can be seen in the way both spontaneous and planned movement appear to support exploration and meaning making in both examples shared. We would argue that such opportunity for movement and valuing the role of the physical in meaning making opens up opportunity for children to explore and discover in ways that they might not within more static literacy pedagogies. While experiencing through physical movement and interaction is not something that is exclusive to drama practice, drama does draw heavily on such affordances. It is therefore important to consider how these elements of drama practice can be utilised to support children's meaning making.

It is also important to recognise the affordances of drama for children's personal growth and development. As we discussed earlier in the chapter, these opportunities are presented through the need to explore and express emotions when performing and playing in drama, and the fact that the content of drama is fundamentally about human experience (Bolton, 1998; Bolton and Warwick, 1983; Neelands, 1992). In both case studies, children engaged deeply with characters within the texts, through their exploration of characterisation and narrative arc. Through the process of working in collaboration with others – both their peers and adult facilitators – they developed their ability to communicate through spoken language using their voices to work and learn collectively (O'Neill, 2015). This, we would argue, highlights the potential drama offers to both support children's speaking and listening skills within English, and for the holistic development of the whole child, through social, emotional and personal aspects.

Finally, the nature of the texts one chooses to explore through drama is also worthy of consideration. Within the two case studies in the chapter, we, and the children we worked with, explored plays by Shakespeare. These texts might be considered, by some, to be too complex for the age of the children we worked with. However, we have demonstrated how drama pedagogies can be utilised to support children's engagement with and understanding of such challenging language and texts, as was also explored by Kidd (2011) and Edmiston and McKibben (2011). We would argue that such pedagogy extends beyond Shakespeare and can be used with any challenging texts. This might include texts which would not traditionally be seen as challenging texts but are complex for the children which you are working with, in terms of language, ideas or themes. Drama is a way of deepening comprehension of texts which may otherwise be potentially out of reach for the age and linguistic development of the children you are teaching.

PROMPTS FOR CRITICAL REFLECTION

Considering how your understanding of drama as a diverse literacy practice has developed as a result of reading this chapter:

- Look back at your reflections from the beginning of this chapter and consider how your thinking about drama has changed.
- What is your understanding of process and product drama?
- What do you now see as the affordances and value of drama?
- What implications for practice will you take forward from this chapter?

Chapter summary

In this chapter we have explored drama as a diverse literacy practice and considered its wide-ranging potential in terms of supporting meaning making and personal and social development. We hope the two case studies have offered insight and inspiration for how drama can be used to explore challenging texts as part of your own practice, and that the implications for practice we have discussed offer you further thoughts to support you in working with this pedagogy. As we draw the chapter to a close, we invite you to reflect on some final thoughts from Boal (2008), who has inspired our own thinking about the purpose of drama in education:

> I was a teacher of theatre. Now I understand that there is no such thing. Those, like myself, who are teachers - and students - of theatre, in reality we are students and teachers of human beings ... When we study Shakespeare we must be conscious that we are not studying the history of the theatre, but learning about the history of humanity. We are discovering ourselves. Above all: we are discovering that we can change ourselves, and change the world.
>
> (Boal 2008, pix)

References

Bearne, E. & Reedy, D. (2018). *Teaching Primary English: Subject Knowledge and Classroom Practice.* Abingdon: Routledge.

Boal, A. (2008). *Theatre of the Oppressed. New ed.*, London: Pluto Press.

Bolton, G. (1985). Changes in thinking about drama in education. *Theory into Practice*, 24(3), 151–157.

Bolton, G. (1998). *Acting in Classroom Drama: A Critical Analysis.* Chester: Trentham Books.

Bowell, P. & Heap, B. (2012). *Planning Process Drama: Enriching Teaching and Learning* (2nd Ed.). London: Routledge.

Bolton, G. & Warwick, D. (1983). *Drama in Education: Learning Medium or Arts Process?* London: Longman.

DES (Department of Education and Science) (1975). *A Language for Life (The Bullock Report).* London: HMSO.

DES (Department of Education and Science) (1989). *English for Ages 5–16 (The Cox Report).* London: HMSO.

Dewey, J. (2012). *Democracy and Education*. New York: Start Publishing LLC.

Dixon, J. (1967). *Growth through English: A Report Based on the Dartmouth Seminar 1966*. Oxford: Oxford University Press.

Edmiston, B. & McKibben, A. (2011). Shakespeare, rehearsal approaches, and dramatic inquiry: Literacy education for life. *English in Education*, 45(1), 86–101.

Ellsworth, E. (2005). *Places of Learning: Media Architecture Pedagogy*. New York: Routledge Falmer.

Heathcote, D. & Bolton, G (1995). *Drama for Learning: Dorothy Heathcote's Mantle of the Expert Approach to Education*. Portsmouth, NH: Heinemann.

Hornbrook, D. (1985). Drama, education, and the politics of change: Part one. *New Theatre Quarterly*, 1(4), 346–358.

Hornbrook, D. (1986). Drama, education, and the politics of change: Part two. *New Theatre Quarterly*, 2(5), 16–25.

Hornbrook, D. (1998a). *Education and Dramatic Art* (2nd Ed.). London: Routledge.

Hornbrook, D. (1998b). *On the Subject of Drama*. London: Routledge.

Kidd, D. (2011). The mantle of Macbeth. *English in Education*, 45(1), 72–85.

McGuinn, N. (2014). *The English Teacher's Drama Handbook: From Theory to Practice*. Oxon: Routledge.

Neelands, J. (1992). *Learning Through Imagined Experience: The Role of Drama in the National Curriculum*. London: Hodder & Stoughton.

Neelands, J. (2008). *Drama: The Subject that Dare not Speak its Name*. London: Hodder and Stoughton

Neelands, J. & Goode, T. (2015). *Structuring Drama Work* (3rd Ed.) Cambridge: Cambridge University Press.

O'Neill, C. (Ed.) (2015). *Dorothy Heathcote on Education and Drama: Essential Writings*. Oxon: Routledge.

Perry, M. (2015). Devising in the Rhizome: The "sensational" body in research in applied arts. In M. Perry & C. Medina (Eds), *Methodologies of Embodiment Inscribing Bodies in Qualitative Research (Routledge Advances in Research Methods; 15)* (pp. 14–27). New York; London: Routledge.

Perry, M. & Medina, C. (2011). Embodiment and performance in pedagogy research: Investigating the possibility of the body in curriculum experience. *JCT (Online)*, 27(3), 62.

Slade, P. (1954). *Child Drama*. London: University of London Press.

CHAPTER

12

Changing literacy and changing literacy education

Guy Merchant

Introduction

The defining moments of the early 21st Century work together to paint a picture of uncertainty and human fragility. Faith in the march of progress, the triumph of science and the dream of world peace have stalled as we have been forced to count the cost of political conflict, environmental crisis, economic turbulence and a global pandemic. The fact that we are more closely connected than ever before, that we recognise the extent of our interdependence, has so far failed to contribute to harmonious co-existence or an equitable settlement. Whilst we may be better connected, we are as divided as ever. And yet the communicative resources at our disposal are now more sophisticated than at any point in the history of humanity – perhaps they still hold the promise of developing more intelligent responses to the challenges we now face.

In less than a lifetime, the labour of the typist, the craft of penmanship and the leisurely pace of the postal service have been swept aside by new technologies of writing. A revolution that began with the development of the humble transistor has morphed into the large-scale production of micro-engineered chips, each containing millions of the tiny transistors that make smartphones, tablets and laptops work so reliably and efficiently. With sufficient manual dexterity, we can communicate directly with others so easily that it seems as if the gap between pressing send and receiving a reply is shrinking by the day. Such ingenuity, itself the product of complex collaboration and co-ordination, is surely an indication of possibilities we have yet to imagine. Human communication has undoubtedly changed, and the pace of that change is unremitting.

The history of written communication is a story of changing ways of making and displaying texts, and of storing, sharing and distributing them (see Merchant, 2024). It is, and always has been, a story of technological innovation. And the technologies themselves, as well as those who own and distribute them, wield a new kind of power, so that it seems to me to be crucially important to understand the processes involved in making digital texts, how they work and what they make possible, as well as how they bestow privilege on some and exert control over others. This is particularly true now, because of the rapidity with which digital technology has revolutionised communication.

I want to suggest that considerations of literacy, and of literacy education, need to begin here, because these new forms of writing are shaping the world we live in and, as I have suggested, they also have the power to shape our future, too. Looking back to our own introduction to literacy, or to an imagined golden age in which spelling, grammar and handwriting seemed like sufficient foundation for learning about written language, is just not good enough.

DOI: 10.4324/9781003381013-12

In what follows, I outline some of the key features of contemporary writing, the technologies that drive it and some of the issues that this raises. I begin by looking at the ways in which technological innovation has reshaped the appearance of writing, leading to a shift in the contours of human communication and how such deep-routed change influences how we interact. This exploration provides the basis for considering what literacy is, and what it has become, establishing a foundation for considering what our priorities in the education of the young, and the not so young, might be.

A new technology for writing

The unifying feature of practically everything that could be described as new in writing is the digital technology that makes it possible. What we might properly call digital writing depends on the visual configuration of electronic data, stored as bytes of information and displayed on a screen or monitor. The phenomenal rise of screen-based digital writing has taken place over the last 30 to 40 years, and in many different domains of practice there has been a gradual shift from page to screen. Screens are ubiquitous, varying in size – from the 35-mm square of the smallest smartwatch, to the latest generation of giant monitors – some of these being over a metre wide. And, of course, digital text is also displayed on large billboard-sized video screens. But for most practical and everyday purposes, screen sizes fall within a narrower range, the size of tablet and laptop screens, as well as larger desktop monitors.

Let's pause at this point to acknowledge the fact that the process of displaying something that is stored as bytes of digital information introduces a new and significant dimension into the writing process. A hidden coding language intervenes between the physical act of pressing keys and the material display of text. In older writing technologies, the link between what you might call the mark making principle and the display principle was direct. Cuneiform script on a clay tablet is simply the result of the impression of a stylus; the characters on a silk scroll are the visible trace of brush strokes – and the same goes for pen and paper. In these examples, the logic of mark making is that of *formation* – letters or characters are directly formed by the movement of the hand. On a keyboard the logic of mark making is that of *selection* – letters or characters are chosen from those presented; the movement of the hand or fingers is essentially the same for each character, the only alteration being the characters they target. There is a crucial difference between hand-formed script and the use of a keyboard – a difference that emerges with the mechanization of writing, the development of the typewriter (see Lyons, 2021) and the spread of the telegraph (see Gleick, 2011).

But there's another difference, too. In digital writing, as I've already mentioned, a hidden process intervenes. The pressure on the keyboard or touchscreen turns those symbols into bytes, and renders those bytes as a visual display – all in the blink of an eye. Without getting bogged down in too much technical detail, we can say that those bytes are a stream of electrical signals, described in terms of a binary code and combined together as letters, characters and emojis in Unicode. Unicode is a way of coding language, a sort of meta-language in which each Unicode character is a few bytes of information. Although the English language dominated the earliest kinds of digital writing, now all the most commonly used scripts and symbols are rendered in Unicode. There are currently over 15000 items in Unicode – roughly 160 modern and historical script systems. The significance of Unicode should not be underestimated, since it is the process through which all these languages and symbols can be displayed on any computer. Of course, Unicode is normally hidden from us, it is part of what happens in that imperceptible gap between a keystroke and the appearance of a letter on the screen.

Although the interruption or gap that is inserted between mark making and display may seem like a trivial matter, or even unnecessarily technical detail, it is the key to understanding some very particular features of digital writing. Firstly, display is separated from storage, and this means that the same text can be read on the screens of different devices and it also means that many different texts can be read on one single device. This introduces an element of flexibility unknown to earlier writing technologies. It also makes it possible to create smooth connections between texts, in ways that form the basis of hyperlinking and tagging. Secondly, the fact that the text itself is digital means that it can be sent in compressed form to someone else who can, under most circumstances, read it back in full. This opens the way for new forms of distribution – distribution in which the original textual 'object' is simply shared. Contrast this with the idea of transporting a single manuscript book, weighing around 30 kg, by horseback, over the muddy terrain and unmade roads of Medieval Europe and you might get a glimpse of why some people talk about a digital revolution.

The separation of display from storage and the resultant gains in speed, portability and distribution are highly significant and provide the foundations for changing writing practices. Distribution is dependent on digital information moving between the writer and the reader through a portable storage device, like a memory stick, or over the internet. When digital writing combines with internet connectivity, new possibilities arise. But of course, connectivity and the devices involved in the digital writing process are not freely available. It is here that we meet the politics of literacy head on – not everybody, even in the most affluent countries of the world, has full access to the new tools of communication. Availability and access are economically determined and, in some locations, the necessary infrastructure is still underdeveloped. But building on this understanding of storage and distribution we can at least see that the digital mediation of writing is at its most transformative when it combines with connectivity. At this point, instant and interactive communication – online chat and text message exchange – becomes possible.

Text exchanges are now so common place, and often so banal, that we can easily overlook their significance. In writing means it has always been possible to reply to something that has been previously written, digital technology has now speeded up this process so that it is something equivalent to a conversational exchange. And because it is so common place, it's easy to forget that texting hasn't been around that long. Although emails were in use in the early 1970s, discussion boards some ten years later, and IRCs (internet relay chats) in the early 1980s, text messaging, first developed in 1992, has changed what we can do with writing, and it has certainly transformed everyday communication practices. Even though writing has always allowed us to communicate across time and space, this has usually depended on the movement, distribution or discovery of a physical object – the text – and its safe delivery into the hands of the reader. When the speed of distribution is reduced to the speed of an internet connection, writing and responding have a sense of immediacy, suggesting a sort of remote co-presence, even if this 'ideal state' is only sporadically achieved. Immediacy, even an imagined immediacy, is a mixed blessing. It can be advantageous, for instance in co-ordinating our arrangements, or problematic if it implies that we must be tethered to our mobile devices *all the time* and alert to any incoming message – the condition sometimes referred to as hyperavailability.

Before moving on, there is another no less radical effect of the gap that code introduces, that additional stage between mark making and display. It relates to the fungibility of strings of Unicode, or what the writer perceives as blocks of text. Words, sentences, paragraphs and larger chunks of text can be moved around at will – copied, cut, pasted and deleted, moved into another template altogether, used, re-used, indented, justified and so on. The result being that the average user of a word-processing package has considerable control over the design of writing. For example, I can lift those words, 'the average user has considerable control over the design of writing', out of the thing-that-looks-like-a-page on my screen and publish it on my personal blog, paste it into X or just send it to a colleague to comment on by email. This would take a few seconds and could be achieved with a few keystrokes. The written message itself would look different, because of the different design principles or template of each text type. In my blog, I could put it alongside an image, categorise it as a post on writing and technology, and on X I could add a hashtag or insert a hyperlink to a journal article. Perhaps I might insert a few emojis to signal tentativeness in the email. In each text type there are limitations to what

I can do in terms of design, but the point is that I can easily change the look of what I write and in doing this create a new text – or at least a new iteration of an existing text. This is the versatility of Unicode, since although it represents a letter symbol, the user controls the size, shape, font and style in which it appears on screen.

What else is changing?

It is helpful to think of writing as having two technologies. The first is a technology of marking and displaying, always dependent upon the tools, materials and techniques of inscription, as well as the preparation and availability of writing spaces. The second is a technology of meaning making, concerned with the ways in which we use writing to organise, direct, control and entertain ourselves and each other. The first is realised in the impressions of a stylus on a wax tablet, or the keyboard strokes that result in letters on the screen – the technology of mark making. The second is the motorway sign, or the development of an argument such as the one that I hope you are following – the technology of meaning making. Both technologies are in flux, and interact with each other. A WhatsApp thread requires digital tools and writing spaces, but it also thrives on the distributed co-presence that enlivens conversational interchange (see Merchant, 2024).

In the case of WhatsApp we can see how contemporary configurations of technology have enacted deep level changes in how writing gets done and how it relates to other modes of communication. These could be described as changes in the topology of communication. Rapid, interactive and sometimes unpunctuated exchanges can seem more like talk than writing. Even before they started appearing on our screens in speech bubbles, such exchanges were being described as chat. This suggests that, in some domains of use, writing is moving closer to speech. As if to underline this, WhatsApp, by allowing users to include voice-notes, makes it easy to include a spoken turn in an otherwise written conversation, or of course, to switch entirely to a back and forth audio exchange. This softens the distinction between speech and writing. Other technologies are working to redefine the boundaries between different forms of communication, too. For example, speech-to-writing transcription is now so much more accurate than before that it has become relatively easy to dictate an email, or to read an answerphone message. Using an Echo Dot, I can say 'Alexa, add pumpkin seeds to my shopping list' and, when I access my app in the supermarket, there it is – pumpkin seeds, on a written list! Advances in automatic transcription really do seem to suggest a major change in what does writing and what writing can do.

Although speech-to-writing software may be useful in composing lists and short messages, the more extended forms associated with 'thinking with writing' may be harder to achieve in this way. Extended pieces of writing – such as texts that develop an argument, explore multiple threads, or develop a complex narrative – seem to need the written form, to hold information, to take over the cognitive load or to store what would otherwise be too hard to hold in mind. Put quite simply, extended writing allows time for deliberation, to develop more precision in meaning and this is because it is freed from the immediacy of real-time interaction. And so it seems that a blurring of the divide between speech and writing is most likely to become prevalent in the case of shorter utterances and interactive exchanges – and we can see that this is already happening in the world of texting.

If there is a shift in the relationship between speech and writing, there are also important changes in the relationship between word and image, too. As many commentators have pointed out, following the innovative work of Kress (2003), there is nothing new in combining words and images. From Tifinagh inscriptions on Berber rock art to illustrations on Medieval manuscripts, image and writing have long been close companions. Technological development has, however, made it far easier to bring the two into close proximity and dialogue with one another, and they can easily share the same graphic space. The only thing that prevents me from slipping in a relevant illustration here is the tedious routine of copyright clearance that protects the ownership of many relevant visual images.

Again, social media and messaging apps illustrate the intimate relationship between word and image. In both, there is a seamless interplay. Many message exchanges incorporate smartphone stills and gifs. Earlier developments – particularly in printing and photography – feed into this. In the 20th Century, advertisers were for the first time able to display billboard-sized images of photographic quality, magazines like the *National Geographic* prided themselves on high-quality photojournalism and there was a rapid spread of colour printing, popular photography and cinema. All these histories are drawn upon in the multi-media context of online communication. In much of everyday life, writing takes its place alongside other modes of communication – particularly image – to the extent that a new sensibility in appreciating the visual seems to have emerged. Because of its prominence in contemporary culture, it is arguably the case that we now read the visual in more subtle ways than before, and our continual exposure to multimodal texts in some ways normalises more complex readings across modes. This topic is, of course, both extensive and important, receiving detailed coverage in some important key texts[1].

It has also been suggested that new developments in communication, and particularly online interaction, bring reading and writing closer together. This claim may be harder to gauge, partly because they are already so closely woven together and have always co-existed. It's pretty difficult to write anything at all without reading it back, and although it is certainly possible to be able to read without being able to write, it is difficult – perhaps impossible – to conceive of writing without reading. The rise of interactive writing is an obvious example of a more rapid movement between reading and writing. Although we *can* be passive on a social media site like X, it's far more common to be both a reader and a writer in such environments. Consider also the very act of searching, whether it's done to gather information, to follow a thread or whatever – it usually involves typing in keywords, phrases or titles in order to find what we want to read in the first place. There is also a more fundamental way in which reading and writing are interwoven in the rise of predictive text, and the appearance of stock phrases in email applications. These change writing into something more like making a menu choice working by what I referred to earlier on as the logic of selection. We have to read back, or in the case of predictive text *check* the spelling, in order to compose and send an appropriate message.

This takes us into the realm of machine-generated text, a more recent shift in the history of writing. Most of us are now familiar with automated messages. Perhaps the most commonly used is the 'out of office' email, which is something akin to the written equivalent of an answerphone prompt. Increasingly, though, we are likely to encounter automated responses, and with the increased sophistication of chatbots and AI, it may be a challenge to work out whether we are communicating with a person or a machine. It's completely feasible that we will encounter this more as systems increase in sophistication, and as more and more routine operations, enquiries and communications will get delegated to machines. As an experiment I asked the AI chatbot, ChatGPT[2], the question that animates my recent book: Why does writing matter? In under 30 seconds the chatbot replied with the following:

> Writing matters because it is an effective way to communicate ideas, thoughts, and emotions. It can be used to document and preserve history, share knowledge, express opinions, and influence others. It also serves as a powerful tool for self-expression and reflection, allowing us to explore our own thoughts and feelings. Writing also allows us to create art, literature, and other forms of creative expression.

It could easily have been the opening to my book. It said the kind of things I was saying and in a style not altogether dissimilar to my own. This really does seem like a seismic shift in the history of writing. The use of machines to reproduce writing has been around for a long time, but a machine that can compose something that is indistinguishable from human writing is truly revolutionary. We are only just beginning to wrestle with the implications and possibilities of 'machine writing'.

I want to conclude this section by addressing a possible misconception. In what has gone before, I have repeatedly used social media and text messaging as illustrations of some fundamental changes in how we do writing and what writing does. These might be seen as rather lightweight or banal examples of writing, but it's important to underline their significance in a couple of ways. Firstly, as should be quite clear, these are examples only. They could be thought of as instances in which technical innovation and development and human creativity are at their most striking. More conventional examples of written language are changing, too. But partly because they are tied to more formal processes and conventions, the changes may be less apparent. Academic writing is a case in point. Card indexes for cataloguing references, the postal submission of manuscripts and the importance of the hard copy have given way to referencing software, online submission and platforms for publishing and accessing texts. The outputs may look deceptively similar to those of a previous era, but their production and distribution are radically different. And when you add in hyperlinking and video content, they become different kinds of texts altogether. The same is true for other areas of activity, too – the digital aspect of practices such as the collaborative preparation of reports and presentations is now taken for granted. Complaints about having to 'be on email all the time' aren't just a product of remote working, but an indication of a more fundamental shift in how social and economic transactions are conducted. The second point is really a point of principle. If we are to truly understand the nature of writing as human communication then we have to put aside any idea that there are certain kinds of writing that are somehow superior or proper, and others that hardly count. A scribbled shopping list has as much claim to be considered as writing as the complete works of Shakespeare. They clearly have different purposes, different kinds of value, different social and cultural significance – but they are nonetheless both examples of writing in use.

Literacy, reading and writing

I usually sign for deliveries with my forefinger now. I get news bulletins on my phone, keep up with family and friends on WhatsApp. I tax my car and register to vote online, and occasionally – just occasionally – I use a pen or pencil to take a note or scribble on something I'm reading. That's just the way things are in the connected world, in affluent societies that have the internet, the infrastructure, the devices and all the rest. In these contexts literacy *is* digital, the older combination of those words has ceased to make much sense (digital literacy always was a bit of a mouthful, anyway). In fact the idea of 'the digital' forces a separation between the page and the screen that is no longer helpful (Burnett and Merchant, 2020). It may be better to just think about reading and writing, how we do it and how we can encourage children and young people to use it.

In a recent conversation with a local primary school teacher, we stumbled onto the topic of writing. 'It's about the only place I write by hand' he said, drawing an arc in the air with a claw-like hand, thumb on fingertip. 'Come to think of it, it must be the only job where you do that, now.' And why is that the case? It's because of expectations and accountability, because of the curriculum. In our curriculum (DfE, 2014), young children are supposed to 'sit correctly at a table, holding a pencil comfortably and correctly.' There's plenty of correctness, there's an emphasis on standard English, and a lot of spelling, grammar and punctuation. But there isn't very much about children expressing themselves in different media and, strange as it may seem, there's no mention of keyboards. In fact the only technology for writing that gets a mention is the pencil. Is *this* the kind of writing we're familiar with in our everyday world?

What we sometimes rather loosely refer to as the everyday world is the sum total of ordinary day-to-day activity – and that's quite a lot. Everyday literacy includes the ways we use writing to label, organise, navigate and retrieve things, the ways in which we enact formal and informal relations and social interactions, as well as the ways in which we share information and misinformation, develop arguments and create imaginary worlds. Thinking about everyday literacy might help us to imagine kinds of reading and writing that could reach out of the walled garden of the classroom, kinds of reading and writing that not only connect with children but also connect them to the world they live in. Reading and writing should be relevant to children now, as well as to the uncertain future that awaits them. Perhaps we should give up worrying about what's digital and what's not and ask instead: Is the reading and writing we promote in the classroom fit for purpose?

I opened this chapter with some rather sweeping comments about the times we live in, suggesting that developments in human communication could bring us closer together in addressing some of the challenges and uncertainties we now face. Even if this is not a persuasive argument, there is plenty of evidence that the written world has become a place of controversy and concern. Perhaps it was ever thus, but new forms of aggressive nationalism, misleading conspiracy theories and hate speech are perpetuated in online communication – predominantly in writing. Fake news, bad science and partisan journalism are part of the ecology of social media. And undesirable social behaviour has taken on new forms, as the frequency of reports about stalking and grooming, trolling and gaslighting suggest. This has led some commentators to argue for a more rigorous and more focused kind of critical literacy (see for example Luke et al., 2018).

My own view is that there are limitations baked into many critical perspectives, and that sometimes these lead to unnecessary polarisation, to an unhelpful reification of the targets of critique and sometimes even to the emergence of new orthodoxies. Although outrage, disgust or moral condemnation are perfectly legitimate responses, a more generative approach may be to identify what matters and the agentic possibilities that are available to us (Bennet, 2010). In schools and classrooms this would involve a celebration of community, an attentiveness to children's interests and an exploration of the possibilities of what might be created together. This sort of orientation would necessarily involve writing and communication and the newer tools that are available. It is an orientation that has underpinned my own work, and my collaborations with both teachers and colleagues over a number of years.

Educational principles

In 2018, my colleague Cathy Burnett and I developed a framework for 21st Century literacy that built on earlier collaborative work (in Burnett et al., 2014). In this we were keen to show how everyday literacy life can be part of classroom life – with all its liveliness and unpredictability. We wanted to show how reading and writing could enrich and extend the sense of being together that makes classrooms what they are; but also how reading and writing can build on and extend children's interest and experience (Burnett and Merchant, 2018). Our book *New Media in the Classroom* (Burnett and Merchant, 2018) spells these out in detail, illustrating them with practical examples. The principles are as follows:

Acknowledge the changing nature of meaning making

More and more official transactions now take place online. Everyday interactions are often entangled with mobile technology, and as a consequence how we make, negotiate and exchange meaning is rapidly changing. Now that written words can speak to us and voice recognition can write for us with predictive text suggesting plausible word choices, old certainties about what literacy looks like and how it gets done have to change. This change is bound to enter the classroom in some way or another.

Recognise and build on children's linguistic, social and cultural repertoires

Many children have experience of moving fluidly across devices, using different modes and media, and seamlessly combining them in digital and non-digital interaction. This fluidity reflects their linguistic, social and cultural repertoire, their diverse experiences and out of school lives. Recognising this repertoire, and the choices it generates, may entail allowing and encouraging students to draw in open- ended ways across this developing repertoire: to combine and re-mix varied textual and linguistic practices in contexts that matter to them.

Acknowledge diverse modes and media

An explicit recognition of multiple modes and media can enable students to explore, develop and convey meanings in ways that might otherwise be overlooked. Opportunities to create using multiple modes helps learners to explore ideas and possibilities in more nuanced ways, and digital media certainly make this easier.

Recognise the affective, embodied and material dimensions of meaning making

The meanings we make are always inflected by what we feel, what has just happened and who we are with, as well as how we are positioned by the people and things around us. The immediate environment, materials, personal and shared histories all play an important part in what students do with digital media.

Encourage improvisation and experimentation

Creative engagement is often unplanned and emergent in nature. Many out of school engagements with digital technology have this quality. Facilitating this sort of experimentation is based on an understanding of how meaning is made in the moment which may, or may not, result in a finished product. This forms an important counterpoint to the designed and output-driven character of current educational provision.

Use playful pedagogies

Schools have a role to play in providing risk-free environments in which students may follow passions, experiment, explore, gain feedback and consider alternatives. This involves adopting playful pedagogies and allowing work to take new or unexpected directions.

Create opportunities to work with the provisionality of digital media

Digital texts are often provisional, allowing them to be easily added to, re-worked and re-mixed. Working with provisionality can generate rich opportunities for students to reach new audiences, to give and receive feedback and to re-mix what others have done in ways that are both critical and creative.

Provide contexts that facilitate criticality

Providing contexts in which children and young people can critically consider the practices in which they engage, and how they position themselves and are positioned by others in various social networks, is important. Opportunities to re-work texts and to reflect alternative experiences may be particularly supportive.

Promote collaboration around and through texts in negotiating meaning

Learning about new media is not just about doing things with technology, it's also about doing things with others. While encouraging such collaborations, we need to be alert to the complex ways in which such interactions are managed and support children to take up such opportunities with confidence. (From Burnett and Merchant, 2020.)

For me these still work as principles to stand by. But to conclude, I want to return to the topic of technology, because this has been what has animated this chapter. In order to provoke more discussion about contemporary learning practices, I want to ask some straightforward questions about where technology fits in.

1. How can we ensure equal access?

Research and anecdotal accounts that surfaced during lockdown repeatedly underlined the fact that some children do not have reliable technology at home, they may not have a stable internet connection and cannot always find a suitable place to work (IFS, 2020). This laid bare some fundamental issues about equity. If access aligns with other patterns of disadvantage then technology will simply magnify inequality. Some things are beyond the influence of educators, but schools can at least help children to get their hands on technology that works and they can provide regular and meaningful experiences of reading and writing on digital devices.

2. How can we achieve balance?

Moral panic over the negative effect of too much screen time has resulted in an unfortunate over-simplification of what's really at stake. In project work with colleagues we have reported on how children used tablet computers in innovative and creative ways in participatory theatre work, both in and outside the classroom (Burnett et al., 2020), how very young children move around and play together as they share interactive story apps (Merchant, 2015) and how virtual world play can be dynamically embedded in classroom life (Burnett and Merchant, 2014). It is important for children to use a variety of different forms of media for different purposes. No one should be arguing that typing a story is preferable to writing one by hand, or that a printed book is better than a story app – but they need to co-exist in classrooms just as they do in the real world.

3. What do we offer online?

Because it's time-consuming and expensive to produce online resources, remote learning has become a competitive environment for commercial developers. Commonly used resources like Reading Eggs and Numbots may have a role to play, but they are not particularly effective in helping children to explore the rich possibilities of digital communication. Perhaps over-dependence on such resources accounts for why many parents reported on the challenges of motivation and engagement in children's remote learning during lockdown (Ofsted, 2021). But some children responded well to submitting word processed documents, and even if waving at each other on a video call was no substitute for the playground, it at least offered some experience of what was happening in the adult world. Now all that's behind us, I wonder how we could build online provision that's varied, more effective and offers some continuity with learning at school?

4. What sorts of communication do we encourage?

Many children are familiar with exchanging messages in family WhatsApp groups, talking about the videos they watch on YouTube, making short movies on portable devices and much else, too. Important as handwriting and book reading may be, children experience communication in all its breadth and they bring these experiences with them into the classroom

(Merchant, 2021). Part of what teachers do is to acknowledge, extend and develop the communication repertoire of the children they teach. Schools that tap into children's everyday experiences are in a better position to enrich communication, to foster intelligent and critical engagement than those that do not.

5. How do we foster critical awareness?

Worries about safety online, fake news and digital surveillance are unlikely to disappear overnight. Teachers and children need to face these issues together. Creating opportunities for children to think about what they share online, where they share it and who with is a useful starting point (Burnett and Merchant, 2018). And although children can be astute in distinguishing between what is true and what is misleading, they do need practice, working together to critically evaluate sources of information – after all this is the bedrock of critical reading and knowledgeable writing. Digital surveillance, and particularly the ways in which platforms track and trade data about users, is a harder practice to critique because these activities tend to be hidden from users – but they can still be important topics for discussion.

6. How can we promote a sense of playfulness?

The success of Minecraft, sport simulations and other games are testimony to the popularity of new forms of digital collaboration in children's lives. Sometimes referred to as digital play, Marsh et al. (2016) show how children move fluidly between digital and non-digital spaces as they engage in playful meaning making. The same sense of enjoyment, experimentation and improvisation can be harnessed in school contexts. Drawing on children's enthusiasm for digital literacy can contribute to this sense of being together, playing together and learning together.

Looking at primary schools with a sense of appreciation can help us to recognise the vibrancy of childhood culture. This is a culture that does not distinguish between digital and non-digital worlds, but it is one in which communication is part and parcel of everyday life – and technology plays an important part in all this. The challenge for primary school teachers today is how to ensure that everyday literacy practices are used wisely in the classroom. This, as I have argued in this chapter, is important in creating a sense of relevance, as well as in preparing children for an uncertain future.

Notes

1. The whole field of multimodality is now well developed, for example in a foundational text by Kress (2010).
2. ChatGTP is an AI-based chatbot capable of generating written text through a free and easily accessible web interface. Accessed at https://openai.com/blog/chatgpt/

References

Bennett, J. (2010). *Vibrant Matter: A Political Ecology of Things*. Durham, NC: Duke University Press.

Burnett, C., Davies, J., Merchant, G. & Rowsell, J. (Eds.). (2014). *New Literacies Around the Globe: Policy and Pedagogy*. London: Routledge.

Burnett, C. & Merchant, G. (2020). *Undoing the Digital: Sociomaterialism and Literacy Education*. London: Routledge.

Burnett, C. & Merchant, G. (2018). *New Media in the Classroom: Rethinking Primary Literacy*. London: Sage.

Burnett, C. & Merchant, G. (2014). Points of view: Reconceptualising literacies through an exploration of adult and child interactions in a virtual world. *Journal of Research in Reading*, 37(1), 36–50.

Burnett, C., Parry, B., Merchant, G. & Storey, V. (2020). Treading softly in the enchanted forest: Exploring the integration of iPads in a participatory theatre education programme. *Pedagogies: An International Journal*, 15(3), 203–220.

DfE (2014). *National Curriculum*. Available at www.gov.uk/government/collections/national-curriculum

Gleick, J. (2011). *The Information: A History, A Theory, A Flood*. London: Fourth Estate.

IFS (2020). *Family Time Use and Home Learning During the COVID-19 Lockdown*. https://mk0nuffieldfounpg9ee.kinstacdn.com/wp-content/uploads/2020/04/R178-Family-time-use-and-home-learning-during-the-COVID-19-lockdown-1.pdf

Kress, G. (2003). *Literacy in the New Media Age*. London: Routledge.

Kress, G. (2010). *Multimodality: A Social Semiotic Approach to Contemporary Communication*. London and New York: Routledge.

Luke, A., Sefton-Green, J., Graham, P., Kellner, D. & Ladwig, J. (2018). Digital ethics, political economy, and the curriculum: This changes everything. In K. Mills, A. Stornaiuolo, A. Smith & J. Pandya (Eds), *Handbook of Writing, Literacies and Education in Digital Cultures* (pp. 251–262). London: Routledge.

Lyons, M. (2021). *The Typewriter Century: A Cultural History of Writing Practices*. Toronto: University of Toronto Press.

Marsh, J., Plowman, L., Yamada-Rice, D., Bishop, J. & Scott, F. (2016). Digital play: A new classification. *Early Years*, 36(3), 242–253.

Merchant, G. (2024). *Why Writing Still Matters: Written Communication in Changing Times*. Cambridge: Cambridge University Press.

Merchant, G. (2021). Reading with technology: The new normal. *Education 3–13*, 49(1), 96–106.

Merchant, G. (2015). Keep taking the tablets: iPads, story apps and early literacy. *Australian Journal of Language and Literacy*, 38(1), 3–11.

Ofsted (2021). *Remote Education Research*. www.gov.uk/government/publications/remote-education-research/remote-education-research#pedagogy–keeping-it-simple

Index

Note: Page locators in **bold** refer to tables and page locators in *italic* refer to figures.

9781032462974